Making Immigrants in Modern Argentina

MAKING IMMIGRANTS
IN MODERN ARGENTINA

Julia Albarracín

UNIVERSITY OF NOTRE DAME PRESS

NOTRE DAME, INDIANA

University of Notre Dame Press
Notre Dame, Indiana 46556
undpress.nd.edu

Published in the United States of America

Library of Congress Cataloging-in-Publication Data

Names: Albarracín, Julia, author.
Title: Making immigrants in modern Argentina / Julia Albarracín.
Description: Notre Dame, Indiana : University of Notre Dame Press, 2020. |
  Includes bibliographical references and index.
Identifiers: LCCN 2020007567 (print) | LCCN 2020007568 (ebook) | ISBN
  9780268107611 (hardback) | ISBN 9780268107642 (adobe pdf) | ISBN
  9780268107635 (epub)
Subjects: LCSH: Argentina—Emigration and immigration—Government policy.
Classification: LCC JV7442 . A47 2020 (print) | LCC JV7442 (ebook) | DDC
  325.82—dc23
LC record available at https://lccn.loc.gov/2020007567
LC ebook record available at https://lccn.loc.gov/2020007568

To my family, old and new.

CONTENTS

FIGURES

TABLES

ACKNOWLEDGMENTS

This book has had a long gestation, and I have accumulated many personal, intellectual, and financial debts along the way. My parents supported me unconditionally during the writing of my dissertation after they moved to Gainesville, Florida. My dad made me take two daily walks in Florida's brutal summer weather and helped keep my brain oxygenated. And my siblings, Dolores and Carlitos, were always there for me.

More recently, Ben and the boys gave me the love and strength to engage in a round of updates and revisions. My in-laws, Diana and Tom, and friends in Macomb and at WIU made my life fuller and easier. Last, but not at least, Mac and Niko slept by my side and feet during my long hours of writing and reminded me of the perks of my beloved profession.

I'm also indebted to my brilliant committee members: Philip Williams, who taught me that social justice and academic endeavors are great companions; and Peggy Kohn and Aida Hozic, who pushed me to write more boldly.

Finally, I am indebted to the many institutions that financed my research, including the Tinker Foundation; the O. Ruth McQuown Scholarship and McLaughlin Dissertation Fellowship from the University of Florida's College of Liberal Arts and Sciences; and the National Science Foundation Americas Program.

ONE

Introduction

Argentina as a Case Study and
Theoretical Framework

Some 232 million people lived outside their countries of origin in 2013 (Leal, Rodríguez, and Freeman 2016, 1). Most advanced democracies face the dilemmas of immigration control as economic pressures push for openness to migration, and political, legal, and security concerns push for greater control (Hollifield, Martin, and Orrenius 2014). Further, these democracies are converging in their solutions as their governments grapple with common problems (Freeman 2006). These advanced democracies, however, are not alone. Argentina, as well as other, less advanced immigration-receiving countries, also struggles to control unwanted immigration and must answer several related questions: how many immigrants to admit, from where, and with what status (Hollifield, Martin, and Orrenius 2014)? This book explores how Argentina has answered these questions in the last two centuries.

In nations of immigrants such as the United States, Canada, and Australia, immigration is part of the founding myths. Argentina is a nation of immigrants, but not "just any immigrants" (Zolberg 2006, 1). Right after independence, Argentina designed a national project for which it sought to select European immigrants, especially from Northern Europe (Albarracín 2004). Argentina claimed to seek Western Europeans to build an economically viable, "civilized" society. In practice, though, it proved open to a great many more local, Latin Americans, as well as Jewish and Middle Eastern immigrants. Even though Argentina became widely open to immigrants from Latin American countries after 2003, their reception remains ambiguous. Today, Argentines are quick to blame them for crime, drug violence, and increasing the number of people living in shantytowns. Further, in 2017 the Mauricio Macri administration, maybe emulating President Trump's immigration policies, rolled back some of the rights awarded to immigrants by law in 2003 through an executive order (decree). What factors led Argentina to establish different immigration policies over the years? How are Latin American immigrants received in Argentina today? These questions are also explored in this book.

It is also important to understand the nature of the Argentine State and its immigration decision-making process. This study argues that immigration policies enacted by the Executive and the Legislative branches can be qualitatively different and affected by different factors. Between 1876 and 2003, the Argentine Congress was unable to pass comprehensive immigration reform. Moreover, after the 1983 reestablishment of democracy, it still took Congress twenty years to replace the restrictive immigration law passed during the last military dictatorship (1976–1983). Why was the Argentine Congress unable to pass comprehensive immigration legislation for 125 years? What were the policy preferences of Argentine legislators? Would the congressional policies have been more permissive than those enacted by executive decrees if passed? This study answers these questions.

This book makes an important contribution to the literature that studies immigration policies as a dependent variable in the world, including Argentina, and argues that immigration policies respond to a number of economic, cultural, and international factors. Importantly, state decision-making processes, whether enacted by the Executive (centralized) or the Legislative (decentralized), determine the influence of these factors. In addition, the weight of the factors affecting immigration policy is not the same for executive and legislative decisions. For instance, the Executive, with a few exceptions, responds quickly to changes in economic conditions or crises such as wars, is more concerned with legitimacy, and seems to select certain groups of immigrants over others. In turn, in recent times, Congress has responded to long-term factors such as regional integration.

During the consolidation of Argentina as a nation, the ethnic preference for European immigrants advocated by the Constitution prevailed (i.e., cultural factors), even when it was Congress that enacted immigration policies. Later, when immigration from other Latin American countries became a necessity for the incipient industrialization process (i.e., economic factors), Latin American immigrants were tolerated and played a role similar to that of Mexican laborers in the United States: they were not considered ideal citizens, but this was not important because Latin American immigrants usually returned to their home countries (Villar 1984). Instead of enacting rules that facilitated immigration from Latin American countries, during democratic periods the Executive started a tradition of post-facto, ad-hoc regularization for these immigrants, as in 1949. Thus, during times of economic expansion, the Argentine Executive proved relatively open to Latin American immigration.

Economic downturns, however, provided opportunities (economic factors) for redrawing the boundaries of the imagined community. If these downturns coincided with a centralization of power in the Executive, immigration restrictions for Latin American immigrants were enacted and the ethnic preferences for European immigrants remained intact (cultural factors). Argentine legislators became accustomed to this decision-making centralization, and it took twenty years after the reestablishment of democracy for Congress to finally pass comprehensive immigration reform. For instance, this study shows that, in the 2000s, Argentine legislators expected the Executive power to make decisions regarding immigration even though the Argentine Constitution assigns this function to Congress. Once Argentine democracy reached a certain level of maturity, and in the midst of the most severe economic downturn Argentina had ever faced, Congress was able to agree on a new, comprehensive immigration policy that, for the first time in history, gave priority to immigrants from Latin American countries, thus consolidating the Southern Common Market (international factors).

This research also contributes to the literature on democratization. Argentina has been cited as the paradigm of delegative democracy, a type of democracy in which presidents rule as they see fit (O'Donnell 1994). This research shows that sometimes it is not that presidents override congresses, but instead that congresses withdraw from their responsibility to enact policies, especially in the early years after redemocratization. It also shows that congresses can fulfill important roles beyond enacting legislation and supervise executive action. Finally, it highlights the important roles that specialized standing committees play in (new) democracies, allowing the development of complex policies that can only be devised by specialized legislators.

This study also contributes to the literature on the state. Following Bob Jessop (1990), it shows that the state is a complex, sometimes contradictory actor, and that its diverse competing institutions can answer to different societal interests and respond differently to the need for creating and perpetuating state legitimacy. In this regard, this research shows that, in democracies with centralized decision-making processes and practices, special interests can more easily penetrate state structures. For instance, in the 1990s, in a context of rising unemployment, the Argentine Executive quickly "responded" to union demands and restricted immigration from Latin American countries. However, the Argentine Executive was also concerned with gaining legitimacy and hiding the growing failure of its neoliberal economic plan, and thus it restricted immigration instead of addressing the incapacity of its economic plan to create jobs (Calavita 1980).

This work also speaks to the literature on nationalism. It shows that immigrants provide a differential signifier through which the nation both defines itself as an imagined community and draws the juridical boundaries of the legal community (Behdad 1997; 2005; Brubaker 1992; Higham 1955; Hing 2004). It further shows that the boundaries of the imagined community can change over time. For instance, in times of crisis these boundaries can be redrawn to exclude certain immigrants. Sometimes these new boundaries are crystalized as new immigration policies that prioritize certain groups of immigrants as desired members of the imagined community.

Finally, this book adds to the academic work concerned with the portrayal and representation of immigrants (Albarracín 2005; Bauder 2008; Beyer and Matthes 2015; Blinder 2015; Branton and Dunaway 2008; Demo 2004; Erjavec 2001; Gotsbachner 2001; Mehan 1997; Santa Ana 1999; 2016). It shows that newspapers can have an important role in the constitution and reconstitution of the imagined community (Anderson 1991). It also tests a number of hypotheses concerning the content of immigration headlines, stories, and editorials (Van Dijk 1994) and concludes that the type and frequency of themes and topics depends on the kind of immigration covered, the social/economic context at the time of publication, and the ideological position of the newspaper/author under consideration.

CASE SELECTION

Foner, Rumbaut, and Gold have emphasized the need to produce more comparative immigration work that goes beyond the North Atlantic countries (2000). By virtue of its experience, Argentina is a key immigration-receiving country for comparison. Between 1830 and 1950, 8.2 million European immigrants arrived in Argentina, a total exceeded only by the United States during this period. Yet, with rare exceptions (Novick 1997; Oteiza and Aruj 1997), almost no literature focuses on understanding immigration and the extensive number of policy shifts questioned here. In 2010 Argentina had 1,805,957 immigrants, 81 percent of whom came from other countries in the Americas (INDEC 2010). Further, in the twentieth century, the country attracted 80 percent of the intra–South American migration (Albarracín 2004). Argentina has also paralleled the industrialized countries in that immigration originates increasingly from non-European countries, mainly South America.

The intellectuals who were influential during the consolidation of Argentina as a modern nation believed that European immigration was needed to replace the small, vagrant, racially mixed Argentine population and thus become a modern, "civilized" nation, a legacy that marked the history of Argentina forever (Albarracín 2004; Shumway 1991). Thus, the Argentine Constitution of 1853 gave equal rights to all inhabitants but nonetheless enacted preferences for European immigration (Devoto and Benencia 2003). Several countries around the world similarly enacted ethnic preferences for certain types of immigrants, including the United States (Calavita 1994), Australia (Jupp 2002), and South Africa (Peberdy 2009). With the purpose of recruiting European immigrants, Argentina's congress established immigration-recruiting offices in Europe and offered subsidized transportation and land. By the late nineteenth century, Argentina paralleled advanced countries in its wealth (Rock 1987). At the turn of the

century, as in the United States (Calavita 1998), ideas about who constituted an ideal citizen changed (Moya 1998). The elites felt threatened because immigrants were joining unions and organizing strikes (Albarracín
2004). Thus, the government enacted important deportation provisions
to prevent the arrival and settlement of potential troublemakers.

The Great Depression put an end to the era of mass migration and liberal immigration policies (Novick 1992). Several nations restricted immigration to preserve jobs for natives during this period, including Canada
(Boyd and Vickers 2000) and the United States (Calavita 1998). In addition,
countries around the world, including the United States, were indifferent
to the plight of Jewish people trying to flee the territories occupied by the
Nazis (Laqueur 2004). Similarly, Argentina enacted several immigration
restrictions to preserve jobs for Argentines and to prevent significant numbers of Jewish refugees from entering the country. Interestingly, it was the
Executive and not Congress that enacted all of these restrictions. Immigration from bordering countries (namely Brazil, Chile, Paraguay, and Uruguay) also increased during the 1930s. However, the government, paralleling the treatment of Mexican immigrants in the United States, allowed
these immigrants to apply only for temporary visas and merely tolerated
their presence, first in the regional agricultural economies and later in the
industrial sector developed during the Peronist era. After 1949 immigrants
from Latin American countries were able to regularize their immigration
status through sporadic amnesties enacted by executive decree.

One feature that makes Argentina different from the North Atlantic
countries of immigration is the succession of military governments that
characterized the twentieth century. The immigration policies of the military governments that followed the fall of Juan Perón in 1955 had several features in common (Albarracín 2004). These governments passed a
number of immigration rules and regulations, all establishing a preference for European immigration and strictly regulating immigration from
neighboring countries. More specifically, they enacted strict requirements
for the admission of neighboring immigrants, together with broad deportation provisions and fines to repress immigration offenses. In addition,
anti-communist ideologies shaped immigration policies that discouraged
and/or scrutinized immigration from communist countries during the
Cold War era.

Finally, the democratic governments after 1955 had contradictory immigration policies (Albarracín 2005). Not unlike Italy, Spain, Portugal, and Greece (Peixoto et al. 2012), and as mentioned earlier, Argentina passed periodic amnesties to regularize the immigration status of immigrants from neighboring countries. However, it failed to pass immigration rules that would address the situation of these immigrants on a more permanent basis. Between 1983 and 2004, Argentine governments continued to hold a double standard: strict immigration rules for immigrants from Latin America and more open ones for immigrants from Europe. To achieve the latter, several administrations signed agreements or passed special rules to favor the immigration of European citizens.

In December 2002, the presidents of the Southern Common Market (Mercosur) countries and associates (at the time Argentina, Bolivia, Brazil, Chile, Paraguay, and Uruguay) announced that they would allow free movement of people within Mercosur borders. (Mercosur is a free trade bloc established by Argentina, Brazil, Uruguay, and Paraguay in 1991 and expanded to include associate members [Mercosur n.d.].) A year later, the Argentine Congress passed a new immigration bill that facilitated migration from these countries. The benefits of this legislation were later extended to include immigrants from Colombia, Ecuador, Peru, Suriname, and Venezuela. Since this decision, the immigrant population in Argentina has become more diverse. To be sure, the major immigrant groups in Argentina are still Paraguayans, Bolivians, Chileans, and Uruguayans. However, almost 10 percent of the immigrant population that lives in Argentina today comes from other countries in the Americas (INDEC 2010).

More recently, the administration of President Mauricio Macri rolled back some of the rights awarded to immigrants by the law. After demonizing immigration from Latin American countries for seven straight years, purportedly for populating shantytowns and increasing crime rates, especially drug trafficking offenses, Macri passed an executive order (Decree 70/2017) creating an expedited removal process a la Trump and authorizing deportations for people accused of (not indicted or sentenced for) committing certain crimes. This decree was upheld in the courts and became law in Argentina. What factors led to this extreme decision? This and other questions are explored in this book.

SCOPE AND METHODS

This book explains over two centuries (1800–2017) of Argentine immigration policy decisions. It is based on a broad selection of research and methods, including historical analyses (covering 160 years); analysis of immigration legislation; economic data; media coverage of immigration (from the 1980s to 2010); interviews with key policy makers and congresspersons (N=37); public opinion data; and analysis of congressional documents (N=200 plus). I argue that empirical works that do not consider the complex nature of immigrants and immigration policies are doomed to have limited explanatory power. This book contemplates how economic, cultural, and international factors intersect state decision-making processes in shaping immigration policies.

To clarify the focus of this study, some notes are in order. First, immigration policies encompass the regulation of outward and inward movement across state borders, and also the rules governing the acquisition, maintenance, loss, or voluntary relinquishment of "membership" in all its aspects: political, social, economic, and cultural (Zolberg 1999, 81). Therefore, immigration policy has two dimensions and encompasses what are called immigrant policy and immigration control policy (Lee 1999; Meyers 2000; Zolberg 2000). Immigrant policy deals with the situation and rights of immigrants once they settle in a country. This study focuses on immigration control policy, which is concerned with the rules and procedures that govern the selection and admission of foreign citizens. Refugee and asylum policies are not included in this study.

A NOTE ON RACE AND RACISM IN ARGENTINA

I came to the United States from my native Argentina to get my Ph.D. at the University of Florida in 1999. As soon as I arrived, I realized Argentines had a reputation for being arrogant and racist. Other Latin American students complained to me that Argentines were always quick to state, "Argentina is not like the rest of Latin America; in Argentina we are all of European descent." Although this statement is part truth and part myth, Argentines, especially those from Buenos Aires, imagine themselves as "white." But what does *white* mean in the context of Argentina?

I had been "white" in Argentina all my life and was surprised that in the United States, even before I opened my mouth, I was perceived as non-white. Now I know that, if we use the United States' old one-drop rule to establish race and ethnicity, I'm not white. My recent genetic ancestry report indicates that I'm 89 percent European, 8 percent Native American and East Asian, 1 percent North African, and 1 percent South Asian. But the definition of whiteness in Argentina tolerates many drops of blood from different parts of the world, including the Middle East (especially Syria and Lebanon), the former Ottoman Empire, North Africa (especially indirectly through the immigration of Southern Spaniards), and native Argentine blood. Persons of Jewish ancestry are also considered white but are nonetheless discriminated against. Thus, it is important to keep in mind that the definition of whiteness in Argentina, as everywhere else, is socially constructed and context specific. Further, racism also intersects classism, so if I had been born in a shantytown and not in a college-educated household, I could have been considered nonwhite.

Who do Argentines discriminate against? Mostly, other Latin Americans who come from poorer, less white countries such as Bolivia, Peru, and Paraguay, to mention just a few. Or internal migrants from the provinces, who are more likely to have indigenous blood and who, when they moved to Buenos Aires in the 1940s due to industrialization, were called "little black heads." Is it racism or classism? I believe it's a combination of both. For starters, the term *black heads* is racially loaded. But it's also true that Argentines don't treat an immigrant from Bolivia working in construction and the cultural attaché of the Bolivian Embassy in Buenos Aires in the same way. In the last few decades, as is true of the United States and other countries, many manifestations of racism are of the so-called new racism (Barker 1981). Immigrants are accused of being more poorly educated, accepting low-paying jobs, competing for jobs with Argentines, increasing crime, and, more recently, contributing to gangs and drug violence. Therefore, Argentine racism is context specific and intersects with classism.

IMMIGRATION POLICY: THEORETICAL FRAMEWORK

International migration is inherently a political process that arises from the organization of the world into categories of mutually exclusive sovereign states, commonly called the Westphalian system (Zolberg 1999).[1] Some authors believe that restrictive immigration policies prevail worldwide because they constitute a sine qua non condition for the maintenance of the international state system (Petras 1980; Wallerstein 1974; Zolberg 2000). Modern states decide on the admission or rejection of new members (Joppke 1998). In most cases, decisions on the acceptance of foreign citizens are highly discretionary and defined in relation to specified categories of persons established on the basis of a wide array of criteria, including socioeconomic and cultural attributes (skills, education, wealth, religion, nationality, and race) as well as moral or political disposition (judged likely or unlikely to commit crimes, or to support or oppose a regime). To understand the factors shaping state decision making regarding immigration policy, it is helpful to consider the different spheres of social interaction that a person's admission to a country involves. According to Aristide Zolberg (1999), immigrants of any kind are first and foremost workers and, secondly, a cultural and political presence. Immigrants are also subjects of nation-states and as such can be affected by the relationship between sending and receiving countries.

This study draws primarily on the growing body of literature on immigration policy as a dependent variable and attempts to account for the reasons underlying policy decisions. This study classifies the different approaches proposed in the immigration literature to account for immigration policy—economic, national identity or cultural, and international relations—and assesses the explanatory value of these theories in general and for Argentina in particular. In addition, this book draws on the literature termed *state centered*, which attempts to understand the role of the state in general and in immigration policy.

ECONOMIC APPROACHES

This label encompasses Marxist and interest group approaches to the study of immigration policy. The Marxist approach (Beard and Beard 1944; Bovenkerk, Miles, and Verbunt 1990; Castles and Kosack 1973; Gorz 1970; Marshall-Goldschvartz 1973; Marx 1976; Portes and Walton 1981) argues that economic factors and a class-based political process shape immigration. According to Marxist theory, immigration is the result of the submission of the worker to the organization of the means of production dictated by capital and the uneven development among sectors, regions, and countries. Capitalists import migrant workers to exert a downward pressure on wages. Thus, migrants constitute an industrial reserve army of labor (Petras 1980; Portes and Walton 1981).

The reproduction of all forms of social organization depends, first, on production of the means of human existence and, second, on the maintenance of a mechanism to regulate scarcity in relation to socially defined human needs (that is, distribution) (Bovenkerk, Miles, and Verbunt 1990). Relationships of production and distribution are therefore essential in all modes of production and in all social formations. Certain characteristics are used to typify individuals and sort them into groups. In this process of classification, some individuals are included and allocated scarce resources while other individuals are excluded. The complex processes of class formation and reproduction in the capitalist mode of production are based on these processes of inclusion and exclusion. There are also other, nonmaterial dimensions by which individuals are excluded. Sexual difference and gendered division of labor is one possibility. Phenotypical characteristics, often referred to as race, are also widely signified to exclude or include certain groups of people from access to wage labor positions, depending on circumstances. This racialization of the process of class formation gives rise to a racialized labor market.

Alejandro Portes and John Walton (1981, 20) consider the "circulation of labor as it affects the social relationships of production and promotes internal divisions within the working class." These authors propose to view migration as a process that unfolds over time, generating interaction among a variety of actors. International migration also reveals how economic concentration and inequality are perpetuated by the initiative of the dominant groups and their victims. The function of migrant labor is to increase the supply of cheap labor. This cheapness is also partly assured by fostering conditions that make migrants particularly vulnerable. For this reason, illegal immigration is widely tolerated.

Marxist theory provides several insightful observations about immigration. First, most authors agree that the economic effect of immigration is to exert a downward pressure on salaries. Second, and consequently, it is also widely accepted in the literature that the flow of immigrants favors capitalists and is feared by the resident working class. Marxism also helps understand, and correctly predicts, the short-term correlation between economic cycles and immigration policies. Marxism has been particularly helpful in explaining illegal immigration and guest worker programs (Albarracín 2004). In the case of Argentina, it accounts for immigration policies for Latin American immigrants, which tended to respond to economic cycles. It also helps to understand situations in which labor unions requested immigration restrictions.

Several authors use an interest group approach and assume that groups compete in society to exert their influence on the state (Facchini, Mayda, and Mishra 2011; Freeman 1995; 2006; Hollifield 1992a; Joppke 1999; Zolberg 1991). The pluralist or interest group view of immigration policy making is that a variety of groups and individuals compete, bargain, and mutually adjust incrementally, pursuing policy goals that they believe are in their self-interest. According to Keith Fitzgerald, the state is, in this view, a "conflict resolving system" and a "common benefit organization" (1996, 37), and the pluralist system of policy making conceives of political problems as involving primarily the allocation of goods. The state is not autonomous but is a reactive allocation device;[2] individual behavior, usually economically or culturally motivated, is the major explanatory variable, and the relative power of groups decides which ones have the most influence.

Gary P. Freeman provides valuable insights for the study of immigration policy from an interest group perspective. His analysis focuses on the role of distinct modes of interaction between elites and the public in shaping immigration policy. Freeman asserts that the political dynamics of immigration in liberal democracies "exhibits strong similarities that are, contrary to the scholarly consensus, broadly expansionist and inclusive" (1995, 881). His starting point is a model in which state actors who make policy are vote maximizers responsive to pressures from the public. The public, in turn, is composed of utility maximizers, assumed to have complete information about the consequences of policy alternatives.

Freeman argues that the public's mode of organization varies as a function of how the costs and benefits resulting from policies are distributed. In the case of immigration, benefits are concentrated and costs tend to be diffuse. The main beneficiaries of immigration are employers (who obtain economic benefits) and ethnic groups (who support the admission of their co-ethnics). The costs include increased competition for jobs among some groups of the resident population and increased demand for certain services. The general public, in turn, tends to be misled about the long-term costs and benefits of immigration, tending to see the former and ignore the latter.

The consequence of the distribution of costs analyzed by Freeman is the production of "client" politics. Small, well-organized groups, intensely interested in a policy, develop close working relationships with the officials responsible for it. This process, however, takes place outside of public view and with little outside interference. Consequently, policy makers are more responsive to their advocating clients than to the general public (opposed or ambivalent).[3] How and why the public comes to hold such views, however, is not specified (Zolberg 1999). As a result, Freeman (1995) argues, immigration policies tend to be more liberal than public opinion and annual intakes are larger than what is politically optimal. Interest group theory, for instance, can account for U. S. family reunification policy and some aspects of labor market management policy (Fitzgerald 1996).

A serious limitation of the interest group approach is that, though the distribution of costs and benefits of particular policies does shape political dynamics, the model says little about how policy issues arise not in a political vacuum but rather in a field structured by previous historical experiences and ongoing practices (Statham and Geddes 2006; Zolberg 1999). Another limitation is that the state is not the neutral arbitrator that this model claims. Rather, the state is an actor that has at least some autonomy from society. Still another limitation is that interest group theory tends to downplay the weight of identity and culture in immigration policy. Rogers Brubaker (1995) argues that an immigration policy analysis must make room for a cultural-political story that is not logically independent from political economy. Domestic closure against noncitizens does not always rest on material reasons alone. It is also based on an understanding of modern states as bounded nation-states that treat members and nonmembers differently.

NATIONAL IDENTITY AND NATION BUILDING

The scholarship on national identity and nation building makes room for cultural and identity factors and implies that ideas of nation shape immigration policy (Behdad 1997; 2005; Brubaker 1992; Higham 1955; Hing 2004). The national identity approach encompasses a group of theories that argue the unique history of each country, its conceptions of citizenship and nationality and the debates derived from them, and broader social conflicts shaping immigration policy (Meyers 2000). Ideas of nation and how the boundaries of the "imagined community" are drawn tell us about who is welcome and who is not in the polity (Anderson 1991). Thus, the figure of "alien" provides a differential signifier through which the nation both defines itself as an imagined community and draws the juridical boundaries of the legal community (Behdad 1997). This cultural engineering of nations is generally done by dominant elites through the state (Laitin 1986).

The national identity approach, when combined with materialist perspectives, provides a more compelling explanation of immigration policies. John Higham, in *Strangers in the Land* (1955), analyzes the history of American anti-immigrant spirit and shows how it evolved its own distinct patterns. He defines nativism as "intense opposition to an internal minority on the ground of its foreign connections" (4). Higham identifies America's three nativist responses as anti-Catholicism, racism, and antiradicalism. His study traces the history, causes, and impact of all three reactions. Interestingly, he believes that prejudice and nativism do not necessarily go hand in hand. He explains that nativism does not come from external forces or from new people, but from internal problems that seem to threaten the well-being of a nation.

Higham thus shows that when the United States was in an optimistic mood and the economy was strong, prejudice against foreigners may have arisen but nativism did not. In these situations, there was no fear that America's greatness would be somehow undermined. When the United States went through periods of economic depression or external threats, nativist anxiety arose. Nativism, however, did not remain unchallenged. The continuous need for cheap labor, the liberal ideals, and the confidence of a country about being able to assimilate foreigners worked against it.

According to Higham (1955), history moves in cycles and each outbreak of nativism leaves its mark.

Faced with mounting public pressure to control immigration and the material impossibility of regulating the forces of the global economy, politicians in many countries have turned increasingly to symbolic policy instruments to create the appearance of control (Albarracín 2004; Andreas 2000; Calavita 2010; Hollifield, Martin, and Orrenius 2014). It is wrong to assume that there was ever a time when states could perfectly control their borders (Andreas 2000). Restrictions on immigration may not be effective, but they can still serve important political purposes, giving the impression that state officials take care of problems associated by public opinion with immigration, such as unemployment, health risks, and crime (Andreas 1999). Immigration policies have strong symbolic meanings: they reinforce territorial identities, symbolize and project an image of a state project, and relegitimize the boundaries of the imagined community (Andreas 1999).

Bill O. Hing (2004) frames the history of U. S. immigration policy as an ongoing debate between two moral visions of America. Both visions understand the United States as a nation of immigrants, but they differ in their views of the groups of immigrants who have the potential to become Americans. One vision has embraced the idea of welcoming immigrants from different parts of the world with different backgrounds and languages. Anyone from a different part of the world can become American, according to this vision. The other vision, however, is Eurocentric and sees the true American as white, Anglo-Saxon, English-speaking, and Christian. Thus, American conceptions of national identity are intertwined with U. S. immigration policies.

Ali Behdad's *A Forgetful Nation* (2005) starts by questioning how the Ellis Island Museum's exhibits eclipse the violent history that characterizes the peopling of America and the actualities of the nation's immigration policies, which continue to regulate, discipline, and exclude certain aliens to this day. Further, historical amnesia about immigration is, according to the author, paramount in the founding of the United States as a nation. For this author, "Immigrant America" was always a myth rather than a fact. The myth projected a collective idea of how Americans wanted to represent themselves to the rest of the world. This myth reproduced what Americans wanted to believe about themselves, and what Americans wanted to believe required ignoring historical facts that contradicted such beliefs.

To be an immigrant implies by definition a certain attachment to another country, consequently marked as "un-American" (Behdad 2005, 122). The figure of the alien provides a differential Other whose perpetual presence is necessary in order to manufacture a homogeneous national identity. America's Other, however, changes over time, for every historical period demands a new representation that is shaped by different cultural conditions, economic needs, political exigencies, and social conflicts. These anti-alien sentiments become codified in the law. The project of imagining a homogeneous nation is never complete. It requires the continual presence of the immigrant as the Other through whom citizenship and cultural belonging are rearticulated.

The conceptions of national identity that lie behind immigration policies are disclosed through discourses. Media offer a fertile ground for analyzing the conceptions of wanted and unwanted immigration. Several works have analyzed media discourse in relation to immigration (Albarracín 2005; Bauder 2008; Bertoni 2001; Beyer and Matthes 2015; Blinder 2015; Branton and Dunaway 2008; Demo 2004; Devoto 2001; 2002; Devoto and Benencia 2003; Erjavec 2001; Gotsbachner 2001; Grimson 1999; Mehan 1997; Oteiza and Aruj 1997; Santa Ana 1999; 2016; Senkman 1985; 1992). Language is not simply a way of representing objects. Language is an active political force composed of "practices that systematically form the objects of which they speak" (Foucault 1972, 49). Thus, through discursive practices, objects are produced and reproduced.

Additionally, a connection exists between the media and nation building. Benedict Anderson (1991) posits that nations are imagined because, although fellow citizens do not know each other face-to-face, an image of their communion lives in each one's mind. Newspapers are a "one-day best seller" that have a crucial role in the construction of the imagined community that allows an extraordinary mass ceremony to take place (35). The ceremony consists in the almost simultaneous consumption of the newspaper every morning or evening. Although this ceremony is performed in privacy, each communicant is well aware that the ceremony thus performed is being replicated simultaneously by thousands (or millions) of others.

Otto Santa Ana (1999) analyzes the metaphors and metonyms used to characterize immigrants by supporters and opponents of California's Proposition 187 with the intent to persuade the electorate to vote according to each position. Proposition 187, an anti-immigrant referendum, was intended to deprive immigrants of a range of public benefits in California. Santa Ana concludes that the dominating metaphors used to portray immigrants were racist and helped to construct racism in society by portraying immigrants as undesirable, inferior beings.

According to Santa Ana, metaphors are ways of using the conceptual structures of the familiar to make sense of a target domain. Metaphors in public discourses permit the creation of common ground by appealing to shared cultural frames. An example of a metaphor used to describe illegal immigrants in the U.S. public discourse is that of animals: for instance, "agents must quit the chase" (1999, 200). Metonyms are part-to-whole relationships in which the immigrants stand as a part to the nation as a whole. These metonyms are linked as parts of two metaphors that are normally used to characterize the nation. First, in the metaphor of the nation as a body, immigrants can appear as a burden on the body or a disease afflicting the body. The second metaphor commonly used is the nation as a house. In this metaphor, immigrants can be characterized as dirt to be swept out. Many metaphors regarding immigrants express a threat to the nation in different ways.

Hugh Mehan (1997) developed a different study also dealing with the debates around Proposition 187.[4] He analyzes the discourses that fabricated immigrants as the enemy and contends that the state, in an alliance with business and other elite interests, encourages citizens to treat the immigrant and other excluded members of society as the enemy. He believes that an understanding of the discursive practices of prejudice and discrimination helps us understand the structures of inequality in a society, and that the modes of representation are not only descriptive but also constitutive of the group being represented. The *illegal alien* designation, for instance, invokes the representation of people who are outside of society. It conjures images of foreign, repulsive, threatening, even extraterrestrial beings.

The *illegal alien* denomination is reinforced by the SOS metaphor implied in the title of the proposition, "Save Our State" (Mehan 1997, 258). According to Mehan, it is not uncommon for immigrants to be represented as the enemy. In these situations, undocumented workers are blamed for the economic and social problems facing the people of a certain region or country. In many cases, such discourses serve to distract public opinion from the activities of the government. Additionally, the use of indexical expressions such as *we* and *here* helps to create a shared sense of community, whereas the use of indexical words such as *them* can be instrumental to exclude or insult (259). Mehan observed that these expressions were used to alert the public to the dangers that the society as a whole would face from undocumented immigrants.

The national identity approach contributes to our understanding of immigration policies in several ways. First, it explores the traditions and cultural idioms that "frame and shape judgments of what is politically imperative" (Meyers 2000, 1255). State policies are not constructed in a vacuum, but are influenced by a society's history and traditional ways of thinking. Authors writing within this tradition help shed light on how the boundaries between members and nonmembers are drawn in the national community and how these boundaries shape immigration policy. Some authors also investigate how these processes of inclusion and exclusion are accentuated in periods when national unity seems to be at stake.

Other studies reviewed in this section illustrate an often-disregarded aspect of state action: its discursive practices. Through discourses, the state contributes to shaping the imagined national community and defining the boundaries between members and nonmembers. A way of representing a group does not simply reflect its characteristics. Each mode of representation has the capacity for constituting the groups being represented (Foucault 1972). Overall, immigration policies are not always effective and fail most of the time to stop nonmembers from entering the community (Hollifield, Martin, and Orrenius 2014). Nevertheless, they carry important symbolic meanings and allow the state to appear as the caretaker of the native population when restricting immigration in the name of preserving jobs for natives, stopping crime, and preventing other social ills.

INTERNATIONAL RELATIONS APPROACHES: LIBERALISM AND ITS STRANDS

International relations theories can also help our understanding of immigration policies by complementing the domestic politics approaches reviewed above. Liberalism holds an optimistic view of the international system and maintains that international economic interdependence, transnational interactions, international institutions, and the spread of democracy can jointly lead to cooperation and peace among states. Liberalism assumes that nonstate actors, such as international organizations and multinational corporations, are important in international relations. This approach also contends that economic and social issues are as important as military ones. Some strands within liberalism have less influence in immigration policy, but others, notably neoliberal institutionalism and globalization theory, shed light on immigration policy making (Meyers 2000).

Neoliberal institutionalism argues that supranational organizations and international regimes help overcome dilemmas of common interest and common aversions and facilitate collaboration and coordination between countries (Meyers 2000). More recently, experimentalist governance is said to represent a form of adaptive, open-ended, participatory, and information-rich cooperation in world politics in which the local and the transnational interact through the localized elaboration and adaption of transnationally agreed-upon general norms, subject to periodic revision in light of knowledge that is locally generated (de Búrca, Keohane, and Sabel 2012). The concept of experimentalist governance illustrates one set of ways in which complex interdependence has become institutionalized in order to cope with problems of uncertainty in which continued discord is widely perceived as costly to all participants.

Several authors (DeLaet 2000; FitzGerald and Cook-Martín 2014; Hollifield 1992b; Hollifield, Martin, and Orrenius 2014; Keohane 1985; Krasner 1983; Zolberg 1991) examine the applicability of neoliberal institutionalism to immigration. They conclude that international regimes usually have had little impact on immigration policies. The authors writing within this perspective believe that receiving countries do not need to cooperate internationally due to the high political costs of immigration, the difficulty of distributing its benefits, and the almost unlimited supply of labor (Hollifield 1992b). This is reversed, however, in cases where special integration agreements among countries exist. This insight can shed light on immigration policies within regional processes of integration like the European Union and Mercosur. Still, even within the European Union, international cooperation on migration issues faces many obstacles (Jurje and Lavanex 2014).

James F. Hollifield, Philip L. Martin, and Pia M. Orrenius (2014) argue that there is a convergence between advanced industrialized countries on issues such as the policy instruments chosen to control immigration, the policy instruments chosen to integrate immigrants, and attitudes toward immigration. The second main argument of their book, of less interest for this study, is that there is a growing gap between national immigration policy goals and outcomes. Policies converge for different reasons, including parallel path development, emulation, regional integration, and global events. Because of the world's transformation due to globalization, designing and implementing effective immigration control policies has become difficult.

David FitzGerald and David Cook-Martín (2014) explore the democratic origins of American racist immigration policies. The authors argue that the rise of an international rights regime, as codified in the Universal Declaration of Human Rights, helped to set the racist societies of the United States, Canada, and Australia on a different, more tolerant path. The United States was compelled by international forces to confront its racist heritage (Hollifield 2015). The final repeal of the racist National Origins Quota Act of 1924 came in 1965, soon after the passage of the Civil Rights Act of 1964. Thus, the "fate of immigrants in the USA cannot be separated from the political struggles over race and the fate of African Americans" (Hollifield 2015, 1313).

Writing within globalization theory, Saskia Sassen argues that globalization is challenging the stability and territoriality of the state, as well as its capacity to control its economic and welfare policies (1996a; 1996b; 2005). Overall, economic globalization is causing a loss of sovereignty on the part of the state. Sassen (1996a) believes that the nature of nation-states, based on territoriality, may have been transformed. She argues that a combination of pressures—including the emergence of de facto regimes on human rights and the circulation of capital, as well as ethnic lobbies, EU institutions, and unintended consequences of immigration policies, among others—has restricted the sovereignty of the state and reduced its autonomy where immigration policy is concerned.

Sassen analyzes both citizenship and immigration control policy. With respect to the latter, she points out the difficulty of maintaining a double standard: a liberal one for trade and goods and a restrictive one for immi-

grants. Sassen argues that states must reconcile the conflicting requirements of border-free economies and border controls to keep immigrants
out (1996b). She highlights the limited influence of globalization on immigration policy as, generally, international systems of labor circulation
have been uncoupled from any notion of migration. In general, Sassen
states, there is a consensus in the international community with regard to
the sovereign right of the state to control its borders (1996b).

Neoliberal institutionalism has gained applicability in immigration
policy with the removal of obstacles to the free movement of people within
the European Union and the increased cooperation among its member
states with regard to immigration policy. It can also help us understand
the impact of the Southern Common Market on Argentine immigration
policies. Globalization theory, in turn, contributes more to our understanding of the causes of international migration than to explaining immigration policies. Its more compelling examples of how globalization influences immigration policy (such as the European Union's enabling the free
movement of people and the impact of human rights on refugee policy)
partly overlap with neoliberal institutionalism. However, the literature's
inattention to the fundamentally political nature of immigration has ob-
scured the critical effects of national policies within both the migratory
and globalization process (Walsh 2008).

STATE-CENTERED APPROACHES

Theorists of the "bringing the state back in" approach conceptualize the
state as an actor in its own right, capable of defining and pursuing its
own goals (Calavita 2010; Fitzgerald 1996; Simmons and Keohane 1992;
Skocpol, Evans, and Rueschemeyer 1985; Tichenor 2002). Within this
trend, the pure institutionalist approach argues that political institutions
can be autonomous: they can form public policy according to the interests of the state and remain unaffected by interest groups. The state is not,
however, a monolithic entity (Boswell 2007). Rather, political systems are
complex and contradictory in themselves (Castles 2004a; 2004b). New institutionalism highlights the interdependence of relatively autonomous
social and political institutions and the importance of symbolic action for

understanding politics (March and Olsen 1983). It also stresses the decisive role of shared values and beliefs in shaping behavior (Boswell 2007).

Reginald Whitaker, in *Double Standard* (1987), traces immigration and refugee policy in Canada from 1945 onward. He views the state as nearly autonomous. The title of the book refers to the different standards dominating the Canadian Ministry of the Interior for the admission of foreigners. These standards varied from extreme vigilance over the admission of immigrants with sympathies toward postwar communist regimes to temporizing attitudes toward those with Nazi or fascist sympathies. Whitaker describes how "the policies and practices of immigration security have been deliberately concealed from the Canadian public, the press, members of Parliament, and even bureaucrats" (4). In cooperation with the United States, Canada diligently screened left-wing visitors and barred union leaders or others suspected of being sympathetic to communist interests.

Whitaker succeeds in demonstrating that the domination of the Royal Canadian Mounted Police over the immigration department led to administrative restrictions upon citizens and applicants who had been affiliated with the communists (Whitaker 1987). Canadian discriminatory practices only abated when public opinion in the 1970s demanded explanations for the ideological accusations used to discriminate against foreign citizens. Although the 1976 Immigration Act distanced itself from the overt security domination characteristic of the previous policy, it still reserved wide discretionary powers for the Executive to decide over admissions. Whitaker observes that by the time he was writing the book, in 1987, double standards were still visible in Canadian immigration policy. As an example of this, he explains that two-thirds of the refugees admitted through Canada's category of "Designated Class" had come from communist regimes.

Keith Fitzgerald's *The Face of the Nation* (1996) develops a theory of improvisational institutionalism intended to account for American immigration policy. The author argues that most empirical theories that guide research ignore the role of the state in the policy process and consequently yield a distorted and incomplete understanding of immigration policy. His work is founded on the division of immigration policy into three segments dealing with front-door immigration (permanent residency), back-door immigration (unsanctioned migrant laborers across the U. S. border with Mexico), and refugee policy. Fitzgerald argues that these segments display different policy dynamics, and that each of them can be accounted for by one of the major contending theories of policy making.

The development of these three segments is integral to the transformation of immigration policy from being decentralized and dominated by state and local governments to a federally determined national policy. Fitzgerald explains that each segment has an identifiable policy network that includes a distinct set of actors who use a particular rhetoric to advance their goals. This study also contends that each policy network has remained uninvolved with the other networks, although each group's efforts may affect the interests of the other two. The existence of three distinct policy networks pursuing diverse objectives leads to the conclusion that immigration policy is disjointed and contradictory.

Fitzgerald (1996) argues that once the state became institutionalized as an actor in immigration policy in the 1920s, it pursued its own interests both by developing a specific policy segment to serve its distinctive needs (refugee policy) and by influencing the design of front-door and back-door policies to ensure compatibility with its interests. The author concludes that improvisational institutionalism explains how the state has become the dominant actor in immigration policy and shows that state interests link all three segments and bring coherence to an otherwise contradictory policy. Therefore, the study succeeds in showing that the state—or specific sectors within it—has a policy role that is independent of societal actors.

Kitty Calavita (1980; 1998; 2010) has also argued that the state has a certain degree of autonomy when deciding on immigration policy. The author borrows from the state-centered scholars who insist that the state has its interests and periodically enjoys autonomy. Her interpretation of U. S. immigration policy making and the contradictions driving it draws on a dialectical-structural model of law and state, as outlined by William Chambliss (1979). This dialectical model posits that the political economy of a capitalist democracy contains contradictions, and that the law often represents the state's attempt to grapple with or reconcile the conflicts derived from those contradictions. The state's different resolutions of these conflicts often lead to further conflicts.

The main contradictions driving immigration policy are clearly developed in Calavita's contribution to a volume on global immigration issues.

In this study, she identifies a number of tensions or "paired oppositions" that characterize immigration policy (1998, 92). First, there is an opposition between employers' and workers' interests on the issue of immigration, making a national economic interest difficult to identify. Second, the structure and composition of labor force needs are economic in nature, but they have profound political implications. Finally, the liberal principles on which liberal democracies are grounded are sometimes at odds with the policy functions necessary to control immigration. The state resolves these contradictions through the enactment of immigration policies, sometimes creating new tensions in the process.

Calavita sees the state as fragmented across institutional lines. It faces contradictions not only from outside but also from within its own structure. As she puts it, "The picture that emerges from my research is of structural contradictions penetrating the institutions and bureaucracies of the state in different ways, posing different dilemmas, and eliciting different responses depending on the location of those institutions in the state apparatus" (2010, 9). Calavita follows Theda Skocpol, Peter Evans, and Dietrich Rueschemeyer (1985) in arguing for the need to investigate the internal complexities of state structures and, at the same time, avoid treating the state agencies as disconnected collections of competing agencies.

In *Inside the State* (2010), Calavita explains the activities of the former U. S. Immigration and Naturalization Service (INS) vis-à-vis the Bracero program and related immigration policies. In addition to recognizing that the state has interests, the author argues for the need to consider that individuals within agencies shape agency behavior. In contrast to other immigration specialists who argue that the INS has been the handmaiden of agricultural interests, Calavita explains the INS bureaucratic behavior as a function of its own bureaucratic interests. She argues that the INS was capable of substantially independent action, often taking the lead in policy formation and aggressively persuading growers to cooperate. The author also notes that the INS occasionally ignored the demands of growers when those demands jeopardized the agency's priorities.

Putting the state at the center of immigration policy analysis gives these authors an advantage. The picture they create, reviewed above, highlights the intricacy of the immigration policy decision-making process.

Unlike interest group theories, statist approaches leave room for politics and culture. In this regard, Calavita's development of the contradictions or "paired oppositions" involved in immigration policy is a good starting point for analyzing the state's involvement in immigration policy. Understanding that immigrants constitute not only economic agents but also a political and cultural presence, capable of shaping or altering the identity of a nation, is crucial for understanding immigration policy.

Recent statist research on immigration policy provides detailed accounts of the processes leading to major legislation. However, this research has not been transformed into a systematic theoretical analysis of both the external pressures impinging on the state and the internal dynamics of the legislative and administrative bodies. Theorizing about the role of the state has proven a problematic task in political science. Exaggerating the split between the state and society-state approaches runs the risk of reifying the state as an omnipotent, independent entity (Jessop 1990; 2007; Migdal 1997; 2001; Mitchell 1991). This work argues that a relational understanding of the multiple connections between state and society, which make them almost indistinguishable from each other, can enrich a state perspective (Barfield 2010; Jessop 1990; 2007; Laitin 1986; Migdal 1988; Mitchell 1991; Scott 1998).

The first challenge is to provide a theory that is both as rich and as systematic as possible. Second, an approach to studying the role of the state also needs to address its double nature: structural and discursive (Jessop 1990). Modern states are paradoxical. For one thing, the growth in the power and number of state institutions make them more independent from society. For another, many subsystems of power penetrate society. This engenders a paradox in which modern societies reveal both a growing independence and a growing interdependence among their parts. For this reason, it is not enough to look at state structures. It is also necessary to analyze state projects, political practices, and discourses through which the state's interests are articulated. In addition, the state is not a monolithic actor and it is important to distinguish executive and legislative policy making. This study argues that in countries with strong executive powers, such as Argentina, societal interests can more quickly penetrate executive power. This power is also more susceptible to economic swings and more concerned with maintaining legitimacy.

ORGANIZATION OF THE BOOK

Chapter 2 of this book presents Argentine immigration policies in historical and comparative perspectives, analyzing the factors shaping immigration decisions between 1853 and 2017. Chapters 3 and 4 examine the reasons behind the Executive's immigration policies during the administrations of Presidents Raúl R. Alfonsín and Carlos S. Menem, with special emphasis on the political and economic context of these policies and ideas about the appropriateness of certain groups for membership in the community shaping them. Chapters 5 and 6 scrutinize the role of Congress in immigration policy during the Alfonsín and Menem administrations, analyze the policies and other decisions approved by this body, and assess the extent to which this body provided a check on the power of the Executive. Chapter 7 explores the reasons for the historical immigration policy change in Argentina, which facilitated immigration to Argentina from most South American countries, and recent changes by the Macri administration. Finally, Chapter 8 offers some concluding remarks.

Argentine Immigration Policies in Comparative Perspective, 1853–2017

This chapter explores the events that shaped Argentine immigration policies between 1853 and 2017. It shows that economic, cultural, and international explanations need to be complemented with institutional explanations to fully account for immigration policy decisions. Economic factors, such as labor scarcity and unemployment, likely influenced the number of immigrants the country has been willing to accept. Also, cultural and other reasons explain why immigration policies prioritized certain groups of immigrants—those considered "ideal citizens"—over others. In turn, the division of labor between the Legislative and the Executive influenced policy making. More specifically, starting in 1923, the Argentine government made use of executive actions (*decretos*) to restrict immigration due to rapidly changing economic and international conditions. These executive actions were also used in nearly every decade that followed.

ARGENTINE IMMIGRATION POLICIES AFTER INDEPENDENCE

After Argentina became independent in 1816, Argentine elites wanted to create a modern state but felt the country lacked a large enough population.

The small size of the Argentine population, roughly above 400,000 people, was considered a problem for the creation of a modern state (Stahringer de Caramuti and Caramuti 1975). At first, due to postindependence fears of foreign influence, Argentine governments did not encourage European immigration (Douglass 2006). Later, however, this fear dissipated and, after the first immigration policies were approved, the population estimated at 1,000,000 in the 1840s (Lattes 1973) almost doubled by the 1870s (Solberg 1970). The census of 1869 revealed that 13 percent of the population of the country was foreign born.

Many countries in the Americas passed policies to attract immigrants during this period. The mercantilist doctrine that dominated the world when Europeans colonized the Americas warned against the prejudicial effect of a loss of population (Zolberg 2006). Thus, together with trade, colonial powers strictly controlled emigration. It is no surprise then that after independence, the United States rapidly annulled the British prohibition on migration, and soon immigrants contributed to the expansion of its agriculture and industrialization (Zolberg 2006). South American countries promptly reversed the restrictive colonial immigration policies and enacted legislation authorizing immigrants to settle and acquire property (Baily 1987; Mörner and Sims 1985). Argentina was among them (Germani 1994).

During an impasse in the confrontation between Buenos Aires and the interior, which would end ten years later, the confederation passed a liberal constitution in 1853 establishing a representative and federal republic not unlike that of the United States. Equally important, it delineated a number of clauses to help grow the country's population. Its preamble invited all the good-willed citizens of the world to immigrate to Argentina, and its Bill of Rights consecrated equal rights for all inhabitants and not just for citizens. However, Article 25 of the Constitution, still in effect today, stated that the "Federal government will encourage European immigration and may not restrict, limit, or burden with any tax whatsoever the entry into the Argentine territory of foreigners who arrive for the purpose of tilling the soil, improving industries, and introducing and teaching arts and sciences" (Honorable Senado de la Nación Argentina n.d.). An interpretation of both the preamble and these constitutional clauses leads to the conclusion that all migrants are welcome if the country is in need of their particular profession, industry, or art. However, Europeans are welcome (or sought after) by virtue of their origin (Romagnoli 1991). The Supreme Court has at times followed this interpretation (Corte Suprema de Justicia de la Nación 1932). However, in other cases, it has sustained broad sovereign power over the head of the federal government to restrict the entry of foreigners.[1]

Immigration policies are often related to ideas of nation in that they mark out the desirable members of the community (Behdad 1997; 2005; Brubaker 1992; Higham 1955; Hing 2004). Authors commonly refer to two types of national community: the Western or associational model and the non-Western, ethnic model. The first envisions the nation as an association of human beings living in a common territory under the same government and laws. This was the example that the founders of the United States used because, as Michael Banton (1998, 28) puts it, "what was to bind together the members of this new nation and distinguish them from the British, with whom they shared language, religion, culture and physical appearances?" Membership in this type of nation tends to be formal, and newcomers can be incorporated. The non-Western model, once associated with Germany, emphasizes a community of birth and a native culture. A nation in this view is primarily a community of common descent and is conceived in organicist terms.[2] One is born either inside the community or outside of it. Immigrants, in principle, do not have a place in this type of community. Although these models rarely exist in practice in their pure forms, they nevertheless provide a good starting point for analysis.

An examination of the 1853 Constitution in the light of these two models seems to indicate that, in principle, it adopts an associational type of community. However, the fact that the government encouraged only European immigration casts doubt. Why did the intellectuals at the time of Argentina's consolidation as a modern nation prefer European immigration? What role does descent play in the new Argentine community? To answer to these questions, I turn to the Argentine intellectuals who were most influential during this period, namely, Juan Bautista Alberdi and Domingo Faustino Sarmiento. These thinkers believed that Argentina needed agricultural workers to integrate into the world market as an agricultural exporter, although they also had other reasons to prefer European immigration. According to Jeane DeLaney (1997), both Sarmiento and Alberdi come closer to the Western model in that they privileged a political community above an ethnic one. Still, in my view, while this may be true for Alberdi it may not be true for Sarmiento, who was more skeptical of the capacity of the mixed-race population to improve.

Both Sarmiento and Alberdi, at least in their initial works, were inspired by Romantic (scientific) historicism (Sorensen 1996) and shared Rousseau and Montesquieu's Enlightenment ideas. As Romantics, they were skeptical that abstract solutions, which did not attend to history, could work. As Jeremy Adelman explains, "Human knowledge and consciousness had to account for ethnic, religious, and communal—in a word particularistic—features of human experience" (1999, 169). Sarmiento and Alberdi attempted to explain the failure of Argentina to unify after the 1810 Revolution by using history. But unlike the European Romantics, who appealed to an intrinsic and embedded *Volksgeist* for nation building, the Argentine Romantics put law at the service of constructing the state.

Born in a traditional family in Tucumán in the 1810s, Alberdi moved to Buenos Aires to study law. He became a student of comparative law and provided the blueprint for the 1853 Constitution. Alberdi argued that the Argentine postrevolutionary civil war was caused by the failure of the liberal elites to understand Spanish America's character and culture. True to his Romantic tradition, he thought that the confrontation between *Federales*, who wanted a federal system, and *Unitarios*, who wanted a unitarian, centralized system or, better, a synthesis of the two, should provide the bases for the organization of Argentina. The synthesis he devised was a moderate federalism. Unlike Sarmiento, Alberdi thought Juan Manuel de Rosas, a *Federal* who ruled Buenos Aires between 1835 and 1852, contributed to this synthesis by centralizing power in his own hands. The solution for Alberdi was to formalize what Rosas was doing in practice (Adelman 1999).

Alberdi's constitutional draft also included a progressive bill of rights mainly designed to attract European immigration. In his view, the native population was not ready for self-rule. Alberdi coined the famous phrase "to govern is to populate" to indicate that immigration should be the main instrument for the transformation of Argentina. He thought education should play a major role but was not enough to change the Argentine population. Alberdi believed that even if the "*gaucho*, the *cholo*,[3] fundamental share of our popular masses, [were to] go through the transformation of the best education system; not even in a hundred years will you get an English worker" (Alberdi, cited in Rosa 1963, 334). The main pedagogic force for Alberdi was immigration itself. Europeans, who had modern work and consumption habits, would educate the rest of the population by providing an example to follow (Alberdi 1966). In clear adherence to the Western model of nation, Alberdi also thought that *la patria* was not the territory but "freedom, wealth, order, and organized civilization on the native soil" (75). The Argentine gauchos and the indigenous population could be part of the imagined community if, through *mestizaje*,[4] they were educated on progress and freedom (Bletz 2010). Otherwise, they were considered inferior (Avni 1991).

One of Alberdi's main rivals, Sarmiento, was born in the province of San Juan, also in 1810. His early writings also partly adhered to historicism.[5] In his 1845 book *Facundo*, Sarmiento developed the first "cathedral" of the Argentine culture by setting out the terms of the debate through his "civilization or barbarism" dilemma (Sorensen 1996, 13). In *Facundo* he showed how environmental influences shaped the national character.[6] The vast extension of the Argentine territories and the dangers facing the population in the rural areas, Sarmiento thought, produced the barbarism of gauchos and caudillos (1988).[7] To be sure, the Spanish colonial system had caused considerable damage as well. But equally important was indigenous barbarism. Sarmiento thought that the gaucho, for instance, had all the faculties of the body but none of intelligence (1959). Even worse than the gaucho were the caudillos, who had, according to him, brought the country to ruin (Sarmiento 1988, 40).[8]

According to Sarmiento, the negative traits of the native population could be outweighed, in part, through education (1988). However, at times, Sarmiento showed little confidence in the capability of the local population to change. For instance, in 1849, reflecting on the population of Latin America, he wondered how many years, if not centuries, it would take to lift up the local population to the level of cultivated men (1959). Furthermore, in the 1880s Sarmiento's lack of confidence in the local population deepened and encompassed non-Anglo-Saxon Europeans. Inspired this time by Darwinian evolutionism, he attributed the United States' success to the Anglo-Saxon racial composition of its population. As these ideas show, Sarmiento's idea of nation had an ethnic component.

To be sure, other ideas of nation were also available in Argentina. The *Federales* in the interior disagreed with the idea that the Hispanic background and the racially mixed population were the main problems in Argentina. Also, some Argentine intellectuals became increasingly concerned with the status of the native population as immigration increased. José Hernández, for instance, defended the culture and cause of the gaucho and criticized immigrants in his *Martín Fierro*, published in 1872. However, his views did not become popular until several years later, when the nationalists took a similar stance and reclaimed some of his work. Other works critical of immigration took issue with Jewish immigrants (Castro 1995). The most renowned work against Jewish immigrants is Julián Martel's *La Bolsa* (1891), in which the author blamed Jewish financiers and businessmen for the Argentine crisis of 1890. Despite these alternative ideas, the liberal blueprint prevailed and all European immigrants were welcome in Argentina, at least for a while.

The Argentine State thus devoted muscular efforts to innumerable modernization and nation-building enterprises. To attract immigrants from Europe, Congress passed the Avellaneda Law in 1876, which established immigration offices in Europe and subsidized transportation[9] and land,[10] temporary lodging, and free transport inland from the port of arrival. According to this law, any immigrant who could prove his aptitude to develop an industry, art, or useful occupation could immigrate to Argentina. Between 1870 and 1914, 5.9 million migrants arrived in Argentina, and more than half of them settled permanently in the country (Rock 1987, 141). The national censuses of 1895 and 1914 show that the population rose from 3 million to 7.8 million (Rock 1987). Between 1904 and 1914, immigrant arrivals averaged more than 100,000 a year. However, the large numbers of Northern European immigrants that Sarmiento and Alberdi dreamed of did not materialize. Most migrants were Italian, followed by Spaniards (Moya 1998), French (Otero 1995), Russians (Solberg 1970), and Turks (which included anyone from the Ottoman Empire) (Klich 1998). By 1914 around one-third of the population of the country was foreign born, and in Buenos Aires that number was 50 percent. Despite the government dream of attracting immigrants to work the land, important numbers of them settled in Buenos Aires (Moya 1998).

Not unlike Argentina, the United States Congress sought to influence the ethnic composition of the country early on (Papademetriou and

Legomsky 1997). When the United States became independent, the 1787 Northwest Ordinance opened citizenship in the Northwest Territory to French Catholics, free blacks, Native Americans, and European Protestants. Three years later Congress restricted naturalization rights to free whites. Further, several states in the South and some in the North banned the immigration of free blacks, a ban later enforced by federal legislation. White plantation owners feared black people from places such as Haiti, where slave revolts started in 1791 (FitzGerald and Cook-Martín 2014). Thus, immigration selection started many decades before the Chinese Exclusion of 1882 (Segal 2010).

FitzGerald and Cook-Martín argue that Argentina, unlike the United States and other countries in the Americas, did not discriminate against immigrants because the former did not establish a ban (2014). Although this is true, Argentina also created a system in which European immigrants always had an advantage over other groups of immigrants considered undesirable at different points in time (Devoto 2003; Novick 1997; Romagnoli 1991). Thus, per Article 25, an interpretation of the Constitution followed by the Supreme Court has been that the government has an obligation to encourage European immigration but must refrain from restricting the immigration of persons who could be considered beneficial to the country because of their occupation or profession (Corte Suprema de Justicia de la Nación 1932).

Further, the Avellaneda Law defined an immigrant as a "foreigner who arrives on a steam or sail ship" (Albarracín 2004, 46), and immigrant ships were "those arriving from the ports of Europe" (Devoto 2003, 31). Who was an immigrant under the Avellaneda Law? The constitutional reform of 1860 laid out the requirements for naturalization. Law 346 included a special provision for the citizens of the former Viceroyalty of Río de la Plata, which encompassed the territories of Argentina, Bolivia, Uruguay, and Paraguay, allowing residents of these countries to become Argentine citizens (Rock 1987).[11] In 1895 some 120,000 residents of the Americas would not have qualified as immigrants under the Avellaneda Law (INDEC 1999). By 1914 that number almost doubled. Thus, while immigrants from the Americas were not considered immigrants under the Avellaneda Law, those who were born in the former Viceroyalty of Río de la Plata and aware of this little-known provision could find a way of immigrating to Argentina.

Other immigrants, including Arabs, arrived from the Middle East (Klich 1998; 2015). Many of the Arab immigrants were Christian (Marín-Guzmán 1997). Jewish settlers came from both Europe and the Middle East (Brodsky 2016; Avni and Seibert 1983). Despite these notable waves of newcomers, the government officially encouraged only immigration from Europe. FitzGerald and Cook-Martín use as an example encouragement of South Korean immigration by Argentina's military government in the 1960s (2014). As this chapter later shows, in the midst of the Cold War, the military government allowed the immigration of noncommunists fleeing communist countries. However, the General Law of Migration and Immigration Promotion (Law 22439) of 1981 drew a clear distinction between encouraged (European) immigration and spontaneous immigration (from other continents). It also stated that the government would encourage the immigration of those "whose cultural characteristics permit their integration into Argentine society." Further, in 1960 and 1961, another military government passed two decrees, 11619/60 and 5466/61, facilitating the immigration of Europeans residing in African countries who may have been interested in emigrating because of the decolonization of Africa. These decrees, however, remained silent about persons of non-European origin living in those former colonies.

"BRINGING BACK" TRADITION: NATIONALISTS AND PATRIOTIC EDUCATION

Soon after the enactment of the Avellaneda Law, Argentina faced a spectacular boom (Rock 1987). Exports grew exponentially, making Argentina the world's third-largest exporter of grain (Rapoport 2000, 74). During these years, a middle class and an urban proletariat emerged. By the 1880s Argentina had a modern and prosperous, though exclusionary, state.[12] An incipient commercial and industrial capitalism, controlled by foreigners, posed a threat to the dominance of the landowning elites. These elites also blamed immigrants, who comprised most of the emerging working class, for the increasing labor violence and activism in large cities. These and other factors contributed to the emergence of nationalist ideology that questioned the European immigration blueprint (Nascimbene and Neuman 2015). Due to the strong dependence of the Argentine economy on foreign labor, immigration policies remained generally unchanged. However, the definition of "ideal immigrant" changed and legislation was passed that banned certain ideologies and classes of people.

Argentina was not alone in reconsidering the benefits of European immigration. Political undesirables and other groups were also excluded in the United States' immigration legislation (Calavita 1994). In practice, though, these measures excluded about 1 percent of prospective immigrants because they were designed to "avoid measures so drastic as to cripple American industry" (57, quoted from Congressional Record 1902, 5763–64). The United States was going through a similar process of capitalist development, and there, too, immigrants comprised most of the working class. After years of labor unrest, "the European immigrant had developed a reputation of troublemaker, increasingly forming the backbone of strikes, and more often than not, remaining to become a permanent member of society" (Calavita 1994, 58). Like Argentina, the United States reconsidered the benefits of European immigration and opened the "back door" to immigration from Mexico.

In Argentina, the first waves of immigrants went predominantly to the rural areas, and in 1914 immigrants represented 57 percent of the population engaged in primary sector activities (Germani 1966, 170).[13] The settlement of the countryside was limited by two main factors: the traditional distribution of land ownership (latifundia)[14] and the methods used by successive governments to subdivide and allocate land (Bjerg 1995). Only in the northeastern provinces did colonization succeed. The process of land allocation was carried out through the intervention of commercial companies and individuals, both more interested in speculative activities than in distributing land to immigrants. This new entrepreneurial class became a strong interest group in the succeeding years. As a result, only 8 percent of immigrants were landowners by 1895, and by 1914 this number had increased by only 2 percent (Rock 1987, 140). The landowning elites were therefore successful in increasing their profits by controlling the land and exporting grain and meat. However, they had no control over the development of an urban industrial sector that could challenge the agricultural development model.

The Argentine two-strata system of the mid-nineteenth century was replaced by a much more complex system. Faced with the difficulties in acquiring land, a considerable portion of migrants settled in cities after the 1890s and took jobs in secondary and tertiary sectors (Silva 1998). Also, the middle sectors, now dominated by immigrants, expanded enormously. In 1895 migrants owned 80 percent of the industrial and commercial establishments (Germani 1966, 170). Nonetheless, with the rise of industrialization, not everyone was progressing at the same pace. Sixty percent of immigrants and a large portion of the native population lived in poverty and were subject to exploitative working conditions.[15] The urban proletariat, vulnerable to the cycles of the economy that heavily depended on foreign investment and imports, became gradually more active and organized. As Solberg puts it, "Eager to explain the sudden growth of social maladies, widespread labor violence and anarchism, the elites neglected the importance of the deep social and economic forces at work and instead focused their attention on one of the agents of change, the immigrant" (1970, 233). As in the United States, as labor unrest spread to Argentina, elites scapegoated immigrants. And Argentina likewise soon opened the back door to Latin American immigrants from the region (bordering immigrants).

The predominant labor unions in Argentina in the early 1900s professed socialist and anarchist ideologies.[16] Although in 1895 and 1896 they organized fewer than twenty strikes, the number of participants increased. At first Argentine legislators, fascinated with the success of the agricultural model, were reluctant to pass restrictive immigration policies. But when a strike in 1902 threatened to produce serious losses in grain for export, both chambers of Congress approved the Residence Law (Law 4144). This law allowed the Executive to deport any foreigners whose conduct compromised public order and to prevent the entry of those who, because of their ideologies, were deemed likely to become troublemakers (Baer 2015). As in the United States, this law in Argentina was probably a qualified action on the part of the state to allow the immigrant stream to continue by attempting to filter the undesirable elements. The Residence Law was rarely enforced[17] and, as in the United States, it did not significantly decrease immigration to Argentina (Novick 1992). Nor did the law weaken labor, which peaked in 1910 and 1919.[18]

Other selective immigration measures adopted during this period also related to changing social and economic conditions. In the late nineteenth and early twentieth centuries, the United States enacted several selective immigration measures that excluded the Chinese, those likely to become a public charge, those without prearranged work contracts, the criminal, and the diseased, together with the politically undesirable. As poverty and crime increased, the Argentine government also focused on restricting the immigration of paupers, people likely to become a public burden, and criminals.[19] Between 1906 and 1921, likely led by the United States, Brazil and Canada adopted similar measures (Timmer and Williamson 1996). Even though they did not significantly restrict immigration flows, these measures, together with the 1902 Residence Law, redefined the ideal immigrants.

Also, importantly, in Argentina these restrictions were passed by executive orders or decrees in 1916 and 1923 (Stahringer de Caramuti and Caramuti 1975). The passage of these decrees initiated a tradition of enacting immigration restrictions through executive actions, which became common in the rest of the twentieth century and into the twenty-first. Many times, these decisions have been of a symbolic nature, or, as Calavita puts it, a qualified action (1980). In this sense, the government has restricted immigration as a means of seeking national cohesiveness while appearing to respond to social problems, such as strikes, crime, and unemployment. In many of these cases, the real causes of those problems were ignored and immigrants were scapegoated for them. Executive decisions were also used in the 1930s, 1940s, 1960s, 1970s, 1980s, 1990s, and 2010s to pass immigration measures when getting congressional approval proved difficult. Further, in some cases immigration policies were enacted by second- and third-line bureaucrats.[20] This count does not include the military rulers who passed all decisions through executive orders.

Also of concern to the elites was Argentina's lack of unity (Nouwen 2013). Alberdi provided a political definition of *nation* as a group of citizens living in the territory of Argentina. As in the United States, immigrants failed to naturalize, which led Lucio Mansilla to call Argentina a nation without citizens (1907). How could the Argentine nation become cohesive if populated by a mass of un-naturalized foreigners? John Breuilly has asserted that nationalism helps fill a vacuum in the liberal state (1996). The hypothetical vacuum that nationalism fills is the gap left by the separation of state and society. It was only in the seventeenth century that politics was first linked to the idea of an abstract sovereign state, distinct from other parts of society (Jessop 1990). However, through the use of nationalism, states seek to abolish this distinction, therefore seeking obedience and conformity by merging personal identities with that of the nation (Migdal 2001). In this way, states make their nationals perceive their well-being and the well-being of the state as one and the same.

By 1914, even after the establishment of universal male suffrage in 1912, only roughly 2 percent of male foreigners in Argentina had naturalized (Solberg 1970, 42). Several factors explained why immigrants refused to become naturalized. For one thing, immigrants wanted to keep their home nationalities so that they could seek their home government's protection if needed.[21] As Otto Bauer (1996, 72) puts it, the desires to cast off foreign domination and to impede foreign intervention in domestic politics were driving forces of nationalism. For another, the establishment of mandatory military conscription in 1901, for the purposes of developing a modern army, teaching patriotism to the conscripts, and preparing for possible conflicts with neighboring countries, probably deterred immigrants from naturalizing.[22]

Public education is crucial for nations. Ernest Gellner (1996) believes that it serves the purpose of spreading standardized high cultures to prepare people to survive under conditions in which the division of labor and social mobility are highly advanced. Nationalist education also serves the purpose of shifting people's loyalty toward the nation and dissipating class identification or allegiance to other social or political units. Schools transmit traditions and history, forming future citizens and promoting patriotism in them. During the period of time under discussion, however, immigrant schools in Argentina imparted education in foreign languages and emphasized patriotic allegiance to their nations of origin. In response, the Argentine State established mandatory and secular education through Law 1420 in 1908. The government shaped education curricula to include Argentine history and geography, and after 1908 it gave impulse to the so-called Patriotic Education (Escudé 1992, 191).

IMMIGRATION POLICIES AFTER THE 1930s: REFUGEES AND NEIGHBORING IMMIGRATION

Several changes were notable during this period, including the increasing arrival of immigrants from European countries other than Italy and

Spain, refugees fleeing from Nazism and the Spanish Civil War, and immigrants from bordering countries. Immigration never reached its pre–World War I peak of more than 100,000 a year. Immigration during this period became increasingly non-Latin, which worried the nationalist elites who now believed in the easier assimilation of immigrants from Latin countries. Out of the 56 million Europeans who emigrated between 1820 and 1932, most came to the Americas. Almost 60 percent of them settled in the United States, 12 percent in Argentina, 9 percent in Canada, and 8 percent in Brazil. From 1920 to 1930, arrivals from Poland and Central Europe occupied third place, after Spaniards and Italians.

Jewish immigration from Russia had also become important after the 1880s, when President Julio Argentino Roca encouraged the migration of Russian Jews (Castro 1995). By the turn of the century, when the Residence Law was passed, Jewish immigrants had become progressively associated with labor activism. A wave of strong anti-Semitism followed the 1919 strikes, when a group of vigilantes attacked leftist unions' members and offices. Among those attacked was a sizable number of Russian Jews (Rock 1987). Anti-Semitic discourses engendered a paradox in that they simultaneously or successively portrayed Jews as potential revolutionaries and exploitative capitalists. Nationalist groups in Argentina attacked Jewish immigrants on both grounds.

The immigration of Jewish refugees became common during the 1930s. Anti-Semitism became a German state policy in 1933 (Wasserstein 1999). Following the Nazis' ascent to power, the half million German Jews were subjected to a series of legal enactments that excluded them from civic and economic life.[23] By 1939 Jewish emigration from the Reich had become a major European "problem."[24] Of the emigrants, about 57,000 went to the United States, 53,000 to Palestine, and between 60,000 and 70,000 to Britain. Before the outbreak of the war, refugees in substantial numbers went to Brazil, Argentina, and Canada. Nonetheless, some countries, notably Argentina and the United States, imposed several bureaucratic obstacles to the arrival of Jews.[25]

During the nineteenth century, most immigrants to Argentina had come from Italy, but after the 1910s they came from Spain (Da Orden 2010; Rapoport 2000). During the 1920s, 878,000 migrants entered Argentina. Then the Spanish Civil War (1936–1939), in which Republicans confronted Franco's forces, produced the largest emigration in Spanish history. Following the conclusion of hostilities, government forces arrested and tortured 15,000 to 30,000 people, and the leaders of the revolution were tried and executed (Bunk 2002). The large size of the Spanish community in Argentina facilitated the immigration of Spanish refugees from both sides of the war. However, the reception of Republicans after they lost the war was ambivalent at best (Figallo 2016). Many of them were feared as leftist troublemakers. Despite this, 13,000 Spanish refugees entered the country during the pre–World War II period (Albarracín 2004).

Immigration from bordering countries also became prominent during this period. Like the United States, Argentina has extensive borders with other countries, including Uruguay, Brazil, Paraguay, Bolivia, and Chile. These borders are costly to control, and the efficacy of increased enforcement as a means of curtailing illegal crossings is questionable (Cornelius and Salehyan 2007). Labor market forces are important in determining people's decisions to migrate. Quite simply, people move to places where jobs are available and wages are relatively higher than those in their country of origin (2007). In the case of Argentina, certain regional economies have drawn South American immigrants for almost a century. Whereas 43,000 immigrants from bordering countries lived in Argentina in 1869, in 1947 this number was 330,000 (Devoto 2003). To put it in perspective, while in 1914 migrants from the region represented almost 9 percent of the foreign population, in 1960 they comprised 18 percent.

The regional economies of Argentina are essential in explaining early migration patterns from bordering countries. The sugar mills and tobacco plantations of the northwest, in particular the provinces of Tucumán, Salta, and Jujuy, attracted increasing numbers of Bolivians, and the forestry industry and the production of cotton, yerba mate, and tea in the northeast attracted significant numbers of Paraguayan immigrants. Horticulture, fruit growing, wine production, coal and oil, construction, and cattle raising in the Patagonia region attracted Chilean immigrants (Villar 1984). For years, migrants from neighboring countries were recruited at the border by contractors and migration officials at the border would sometimes just count immigrants entering without any major scrutiny (Villar 1984). After the jobs in Argentina ended, migrants would leave the country in a similar way.

This book argues that economic conditions can shape immigration policies. The economic development of Argentina between the 1880s and

1914 was unprecedented; by 1914 the per capita income of Argentina equaled that of Germany. Labor for the construction of this new economy came mainly from the Mediterranean, but the capital was British (Rock 1987). This model of dependent capitalism relied strongly on world export markets and foreign investment. For that reason, it was highly sensitive to international economic cycles. While immigration restrictions at the beginning of the twentieth century did not significantly affect immigration flows, the Great Depression provided a justification for restricting immigration, and the influx of refugees from Europe in the 1930s and 1940s contributed to selective immigration restrictions that affected certain groups of immigrants and not others (Devoto 2003). As in the immigration restrictions of 1916 and 1923, the Executive made use of executive actions.

Most countries had abandoned their liberal immigration policies by the 1930s. Whereas rising unemployment rates provided a rationale for restricting immigration, an increased preoccupation with the assimilation of immigrants and the perceived threat posed by the potential massive arrival of refugees from Europe provided the rationale for enacting ethnic preferences in the Americas (Mármora 1988). The United States led this restrictive wave when it first established the literacy test in 1917 and passed the first nationality quotas in 1921. Bolivia prohibited the entry of Chinese, Jews, Roma, and blacks without special intervention from the highest authorities at the Ministry of the Interior (Senkman 1991). Mexico made the admission of foreign citizens conditional on the "national interest and their racial and cultural compatibility with the existing population" in 1936. Canada, in turn, established a literacy test in 1917, banned Chinese immigration in 1923, and seriously restricted all European immigration in 1930 (Timmer and Williamson 1996).

In December 1930 the new Argentine military government passed a decree that established a type of head tax for immigrants who were not coming to work the land (Rapoport 2000). In this way, the government created bureaucratic obstacles to restrict immigration (Devoto 2003). In October 1932 the conservative government that followed the military government attempted to deport some 4,300 unemployed immigrants who lived in improvised shantytowns in Buenos Aires (Albarracín 2004). Almost 40 percent of these unemployed were Polish, and the rest were Spaniards, Italians, Russians, Bulgarians, and Ukrainians. A census conducted in 1932 showed that Argentina had almost 334,000 unemployed, 25 percent of whom were in Buenos Aires (Albarracín 2004). Later, the Executive passed a decree requiring all prospective immigrants to have a job contract or somebody who could support them in order to apply for residence in Argentina; this cut immigration flow in half (Devoto 2003). Although further ethnic preferences were not made official in Argentina during the 1930s, most intellectuals agreed that immigrants should be selected according to their capacity to assimilate to Argentine society. While some spoke of encouraging rural immigration from a broad range of European countries, others believed that most desirable immigration had to proceed from Latin Europe (Italy and Spain). These positions were clearly stated during the First Population Conference, held in Buenos Aires in October 1940 (Museo Social Argentino 1941).

In 1938, following the occupation of Austria by Hitler's troops, U. S. President Franklin Roosevelt called an international conference to face the problems provoked by war refugees. Thirty-two nations sent representatives to this conference. The United States led with a view toward forestalling internal efforts to liberalize immigration laws (Perl 1995). The U. S. representative to the conference stated that something had to be done for the victims of the Nazi hatred and terror but immediately added that the U. S. government was not willing to change its quota law. The Argentine delegation, in turn, attempted to show that Argentina had proportionally received more Jewish refuges than any other country (Albarracín 2004). Argentine foreign minister Tomás A. Le Bretton, after explaining that the need for industrial labor was already satisfied, declared that the country was willing to receive agricultural workers. Le Bretton explained that Argentina did not welcome "migrants who were planning to remain attached to their countries of origin" (Albarracín 2004).

In 1938 rumors spread that Central European refugees were illegally entering Argentina from neighboring countries. Most newspapers, including *La Nación* and *La Prensa*, which had up to that point remained loyal to the slogan "to govern is to populate," turned their voices against immigration. A decree of the same year established that only agricultural workers could enter the country at a time when most refugees came from urban areas (Rapoport 2000). Minister of Foreign Affairs José María Cantilo further claimed that the refugees were not truly immigrants. Since these persons were fleeing political persecution, he reasoned, their decision to emigrate was not freely made and they would therefore be unwilling to assimilate into Argentine society (Senkman 1991).

Other provisions passed in 1938, in combination with the beginning of World War II, deterred migration. The provisions required immigrants to have a "permit to land" (*Permiso de Desembarco*), which could be obtained at the Argentine consulate in immigrants' countries of origin after completing extensive paperwork. According to Fernando J. Devoto (2003), this was an attempt by the Argentine government to reserve extensive discretionary power over who could migrate to Argentina. The permit to land had to be approved in Argentina by a committee composed of members of the Ministries of the Interior, Foreign Relations, and Agriculture. The Ministry of Foreign Relations, in principle, was reluctant to accept refugees. In practice, however, it signed agreements with several private companies to form agricultural colonies, some of them—such as the Jewish Colonization Association—suspected of corrupt practices. Despite the numerous obstacles to settlement of Jewish refugees, some 22,500 entered the country during the 1930s.

The government of Agustín Justo was supportive of the quasi-Fascist Franco and provided help to several of his followers during the first years of World War II. However, when Franco's troops marched into Barcelona in 1939, increased numbers of Republicans attempted to flee the country (Schwarzstein 1997). Members of the Argentine government believed Republican refugees were an "ideological threat" (Ministerio de Agricultura 19326, cited in Schwarzstein 1997). Further, some members of the Argentine government were more hostile to communist refugees than to Jewish refugees (Rapoport 2000). However, the state is not a homogenous actor, and not all members of the Justo government showed the same affinities toward the Franco regime. Under the influence of the British government, some members of the government worried about the expansion of Fascism in Europe. In addition, many of the children of Spanish immigrants who were already in Argentina sympathized with Republicans. Despite anti-communist sentiment and multiple legal restrictions, the mechanisms to allow for the arrival of Spanish citizens multiplied. Several refugees, for instance, were admitted as tourists (Figallo 2016).

In 1934 the Argentine State made the first attempt to officially regulate neighboring migration. Decree 34111/34 established that foreigners could enter the country as tourists, seasonal workers, and in-transit passengers (Villar 1984). To become a seasonal worker, foreigners had to apply for a visa at the Argentine consulate in their home country. Though contractors filed this paperwork, migrant workers who came to Argentina on their own usually entered the country with a tourist visa, which did not allow them to work. This tacit agreement between seasonal bordering migrants and Argentine authorities lasted several years. To be sure, the Argentine elites still had a strong bias in favor of European immigrants. Evidence of this is the fact that this decree did not allow neighboring immigrants to stay permanently in Argentina. In this sense, neighboring immigrants in Argentina played the role that Mexican immigration played in the United States, where, faced with increased labor demands from European-born workers, the Dillingham Commission noted some special advantages of Mexican immigrants in 1911: "The Mexican immigrants are providing a fairly adequate supply of labor.... While they are not easily assimilated, this is not of very great importance as long as most of them return to their native land. In the case of the Mexican, he is less desirable as a citizen than as a laborer" (U. S. Congress Senate 1911:690–91, quoted in Calavita 1994, 58). In Argentina, neighboring immigrants offered the same advantages: they constituted a less demanding labor force, and their desirability as citizens was not an issue until they started settling permanently in the country in the late 1940s.

IMMIGRATION POLICIES IN THE PERONIST ERA

At the end of World War II, most European countries and the United States embarked on interventionist economic policies. Argentina was not an exception under Juan Domingo Perón. Perón first became popular while occupying an important position at the Ministry of Labor. He participated in the military coup of 1943 but was elected president through popular and free elections in February 1946 (Rock 1987). Under his leadership, Argentina's industrialization process moved forward. Between 1939 and 1945, the state implemented strong intervention to expand local manufacturing and some heavy industries. In 1944 tertiary exports represented as much as 70 percent of the total exports (Rapoport 2000, 339).

Except for the year 1945, economic indicators during this period were over-all positive. Real salaries, employment, and per capita income all increased steadily (Rapoport 2000, 341). In turn, the well-being of the population in general and the working class in particular progressively improved.

Under Perón, Argentina went back to ambitious immigration poli-cies. Immigrants had an important role both in agricultural and indus-trial production. Nonetheless, the government showed a predilection for certain groups of immigrants. During this period, the preoccupation with the assimilation of immigrants continued. The government, likely in-fluenced by earlier nationalist movements and ongoing studies, sought to encourage immigration from Latin Europe. As in the preceding decade, the immigration of Jewish refugees and potential communists was dis-couraged and those who were already in Argentina had to abide by the new rules establishing Catholic education in all public schools (Rein 2010). In practice, corrupt practices in the Immigration Agency permit-ted the immigration of persons from Central Europe, political refugees, and Jews (Devoto 2003). For instance, the government facilitated the im-migration of refugees who had collaborated with the Nazis (Newton 1992). For the first time in history, the government also facilitated settle-ment of immigrants from bordering countries through amnesty decrees.

Many public officials within the Peronist administration considered opening the country to immigration to be a necessity. This belief was par-ticularly prevalent among those in charge of economic policy. However, the ministers of the interior and foreign affairs, with strong ties to unions, viewed immigration as a way of lowering the salaries of the working class. Despite this discrepancy, immigration had an important place in Perón's first five-year government plan (Plan Quinquenal), which called for the arrival of fifty thousand foreigners a year (Olivieri 1987). For the first time, the immigration policies of the Argentine State were directed to at-tract immigrants involved in a broad range of occupations and not just rural workers due to the labor scarcity produced by industrialization (Pérez Vichich 1988).

Government expectations regarding the number of immigrants were superseded by actual arrivals. Between 1947 and 1955, 829,846 immi-grants entered the country (Olivieri 1987, 244). Almost 60 percent of them were from Italy and 24 percent from Spain (Senkman 1992). To study the impact of immigration on the national character, the government created the Ethnic National Institute in 1946. Like the nationalist thinkers of the turn of the century, most researchers in this institute thought that immigrants from Latin Europe would more easily assimilate in Argentina. In their view, selecting for assimilation would avoid the creation of ethnic enclaves composed of people with a different lifestyle who could not integrate into Argentina (Senkman 1992).

Despite the significance of immigration during this period, which accounted for 17 percent of the population (see Figure 2.1), no comprehensive immigration policies were passed. The main instruments for the promotion of European immigration during this time were bilateral agreements signed with Italy (1947, 1948, and 1952) and Spain (1958). The agreement with Italy mirrored the Argentine policies from the end of the nineteenth century but was directed to attract all kinds of workers and not just agricultural ones. This agreement facilitated immigration in several ways. Both governments had an active role in the recruitment of workers, compiling data about labor needed in Argentina and Italian citizens interested in emigrating (Romagnoli 1991). In turn, both governments facilitated the transportation of immigrants to their final destination.[26] In 1954 the Argentine government approved the creation of the Intergovernmental Committee for European Migration (Law 13345). Its purpose was to finance emigration from Europe and facilitate later resettlement.

International factors may have facilitated the arrival of Nazi collaborators in Argentina at the end of World War II and deterred immigrants from communist countries. The U. S. government perceived Argentina as a refuge for Nazis until 1946 (Senkman 1985). However, Argentina received only middle-level scientists and military officers, leaving the top ones to the Soviets, the British, and the Americans (Steinacher 2011). In 1946 the United States launched the theory of containment, the set of strategies used to stop expansion of the Soviet Union (Gaddis 2005). In service of this radical change, the United States requested that the countries in the southern hemisphere join the anti-communist crusade. Eagerly, Perón's government joined this crusade and discouraged immigration from communist countries. Through secret instructions imparted to the Argentine consuls in Europe, Argentina forbade the immigration of persons from the Soviet Union and its satellite countries (Senkman 1985).

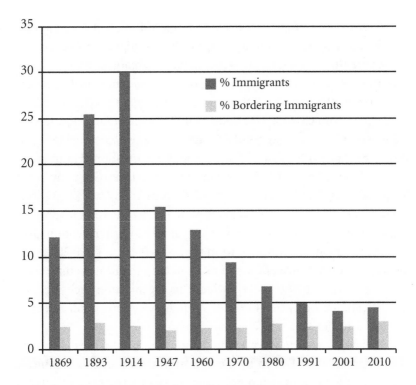

Figure 2.1. Proportion of Immigrants: Overall and from Brazil, Bolivia, Chile, Paraguay, and Uruguay (Bordering Countries), 1869–2010

Source: Censuses from the years indicated, INDEC, Argentina

As in the 1930s, the immigration of Jewish refugees was discouraged. Leonardo Senkman believes there was an unstated religious requirement for immigrants who arrived during this period. He bases this observation on the fact that Catholic immigrants represented 91 percent of total immigration (1992). Nonetheless, Devoto (2003) cautions that it was easy to lie about one's religion in the immigration forms. Further, different corrupt practices at the Immigration Agency allowed the immigration of Jewish refugees. When Argentina entered World War II in 1945 on the side of the Allies, it prohibited the entry of immigrants from Axis countries. When the Allies finally occupied Europe, some bureaucratic obstacles still deterred the migration of Jewish refugees. Argentine migration officials required immigrants to have official and legalized identification papers that many refugees lacked. Additionally, President Perón left the anti-Semite Santiago Peralta in charge of the Immigration Agency for a whole year after being inaugurated in 1946. Jewish organizations and the Argentine press denounced this public official's discriminatory practices.

Between 1947 and 1949 the country accepted a significant number of refugees from Croatia, Ukraine, Poland, Hungary, Austria, and Germany who had presumably collaborated with the Nazis during World War II (Senkman 1992). In addition to the above-mentioned immigrants from Italy and Spain, 10,286 immigrants came from Germany, 8,668 from Portugal, 5,867 from France, 3,255 from Yugoslavia, 2,733 from Poland, and 1,678 from Hungary (Senkman 1992). Perón's fascist style of government and leadership partly explains the warm reception given to Nazis in Argentina. Research from the 2000s (such as Goñi 2002) also highlights the existence of a secret and corrupt organization directed to find safe havens for Nazis in Argentina. This organization likely included the Vatican, the Argentine Catholic Church, Argentine public officials, and Swiss authorities.

After 1952 Argentina's bordering countries constituted the main source of immigrant labor. Drawn by the industrialization process, significant numbers of Paraguayans and Bolivians, and to a lesser extent Chileans, immigrated to the urban centers in the province of Buenos Aires and other places (Albarracín 2004). Unlike immigration from Europe, that from neighboring countries was spontaneous and unorganized. Between 1951 and 1960, Paraguayans represented 26.5 percent of immigrant arrivals, followed in number by Bolivians (11.3 percent), Chileans (9.7 percent), Uruguayans (4.3 percent), and Brazilians (4 percent) (Stahringer de Caramuti and Caramuti 1975). In the Buenos Aires metropolitan area, male migrants found jobs in the manufacturing and construction sectors, while female migrants worked in manufacturing and in the domestic work sectors. Despite the growing importance of bordering migration, no permanent laws were passed to administer it.

In July 1949 the government passed the first amnesty to regularize the status of undocumented immigrants (Decree 15972/49). While data on implementation are scant, this amnesty presumably favored an important number of immigrants from the Southern Cone.[27] In 1951 the Executive approved another amnesty (Decree 13721/51) favoring all foreign workers who had a job in Argentina. An economic plan of sustained growth, full employment, and extensive social policies made the integration of the migrants from the Southern Cone into Argentine society a smooth process, despite the negative reactions of certain sectors of society that mourned the end of the golden era of European immigration (Pérez Vichich 1988).

The same process of industrialization that attracted immigrants from bordering countries enticed migrants from the impoverished Argentine provinces after the 1930s (Oteiza and Aruj 1997). These migrants, who had indigenous or mixed racial origins, joined the working class and supported President Perón. They faced discrimination from the elites, who called them *cabecitas negras* (little black heads). The plan to decimate the indigenous population and to crowd the country with Europeans, intended to impose a dominant model of nation based on the legacy of white Europeans, surely fueled this racism. People of indigenous origin have been discriminated against in Argentina since the very first encounter with the Spanish during the conquest of the Americas. Economic motives likely played a role as well, as Perón and his model of industrial development challenged the agricultural export model of development and the power of the landowning elite.

IMMIGRATION RULES OF THE MILITARY
REGIMES AFTER 1955

Juan Perón was deposed by a bloody military coup in 1955. After this event, Argentina's history was dominated by instability and a recurrent military involvement in politics. Military regimes seized power in the periods 1955 to 1958, 1966 to 1973, and 1976 to 1983. In 1962 the military deposed the democratic government and attempted a coup. A government backed by the military was then elected and stayed in power for two years. Even when the military did not participate in politics in a direct way, the supposedly democratic governments lacked legitimacy because Peronists were banned from participating in democratic elections. Such was the case for Presidents Arturo Frondizi (1958–1962), José María Guido (1962–1963), and Arturo Illia (1963–1966).

CONTROL OF BORDERING MIGRATION

The different military governments were actively involved in immigration policies and generated several immigration rules and regulations. During these administrations, Congress was shut down and laws were passed by executive decree. Independent of the economic situation, successive military governments encouraged European immigration and strictly regulated bordering immigration, which had increased only slightly from 1947 to 1960 (see Figure 2.1). Despite some exceptions made for people fleeing communist countries, the military governments continued to imagine Argentina as a white nation and treated immigration from neighboring countries as a police matter. Several decrees defined the concept of an illegal immigrant and established penalties and strict deportation provisions. Also, the ideologies of the numerous military regimes were not identical. Some were more nationalist and believed in strong state intervention (for instance, President Juan Carlos Onganía), while others implemented neoliberal economic policies and encouraged foreign investment and imports. However, most of them shared a concern about fighting communism, which transpired in different immigration policies.

In 1963 the Guido administration (1962–1963)[28] enacted Decree 4805/63, which reflected a concern with the police aspects of immigration. This decree stated that Argentina had the right to control the admission of foreign citizens according to changing circumstances, including the power to deport those immigrants who did not comply with Argentine immigration policies. This decree did not clearly lay out who could be legally admitted in Argentina, but it defined as out of compliance those immigrants who entered the country without passing immigration controls, violated the conditions of their stay, or overstayed a visa. The Immigration Agency could order the immediate arrest and deportation of these immigrants, and its decisions could not be appealed. This decree also created penalties applicable to those who gave work or lodging to undocumented immigrants.

Similarly, one of the objectives of Onganía's (1966–1969) administration was to repress undocumented migration (Novick 1992). To accomplish this, the Executive enacted a measure called "Repression of Clandestine Immigration" in 1967 (Law 17294), which stated that Argentine immigration policies were inadequate to control undocumented migration and that the policy of amnesties for undocumented immigrants had failed.[29] It also explained that the extent of the Argentine borders with neighboring countries, coupled with the liberal regulations on the admission of tourists, increased undocumented migration. The law prohibited from working those who were unauthorized to work by the Immigration Agency (Novick 1992). At the same time, it required employers and hotels to check immigrants' documents and to report undocumented persons to the Immigration Agency.

The military dictatorship of 1976, also known as the National Reorganization Process, displaced the Peronist government and established a military junta. Unlike previous military governments, which were bureaucratic authoritarian regimes (as described by O'Donnell 1988) that sought to develop the country through selective industrialization, the military dictatorship of 1976 adopted strongly neoliberal economic policies in combination with repressive and authoritarian political policies. The military government encouraged population growth by prohibiting the use of contraceptive methods and promoting immigration that was both "healthy and culturally compatible" with the Argentine population (Decree 3938/77) in an era in which most nations had abandoned ethnic preferences in immigration (FitzGerald and Cook-Martín 2014). Following the elites that had consolidated the country in the 1880s, the military wanted to attract European migrants. However, European immigration had virtually ceased (Schneider 2000).

Immigration from neighboring countries remained at numbers comparable to the previous decade (see Figure 2.1). Despite this, the dictatorship believed that it should be carefully selected and controlled. As noted above, the 1981 General Law of Migration and Immigration Promotion (Law 22439) expressed the conviction of the military government that the country needed to increase its population and validated immigration as an instrument to achieve this goal. According to Gino Romagnoli (1991), this law followed constitutional provisions by distinguishing between encouraged immigration (European) and spontaneous immigration (the rest). This law gave ample powers to the Executive to design policies for both types of immigration.

Regarding encouraged immigration, the law established that the Ministry of the Interior would propose to the president the rules and procedures to foment immigration of foreigners "whose cultural characteristics permit their integration into Argentine society" (articles 2 and 3). In addition, this ministry would prioritize certain areas of the country as in need of population. The law also created a special fund for encouraged immigration and offered benefits to immigrants admitted in this category, including tax exemptions, subsidized transportation, and temporary lodging. Finally, it reiterated Executive powers to deport immigrants contained in previous decrees, stating that the Ministry of the Interior could deport foreigners who were sentenced to five years in prison or who engaged in activities affecting social peace, national security, or public order (Law 22439).

THE MILITARY, IMMIGRANTS, AND COMMUNISM

This book argues that the definition of ideal citizen changed over time. During the Cold War, military governments exhibited two preferences: the one for European immigrants just discussed and another for noncommunist immigrants. Due to fears about the spread of communism in the Americas, ideological considerations became crucial when selecting immigrants. The 1960s were an eventful decade in Latin America. Fidel Castro consolidated his power despite the Bay of Pigs invasion, the Cuban missile crisis, and attempts by the United States to destabilize his government. Not surprisingly, the United States worried that Cuba could export communism to the rest of Latin America. At the same time, a clamor for political inclusion and social justice arose throughout the hemisphere (McSherry 2002).

Within this context, the first guerrilla groups appeared in Argentina and other parts of Latin America. In Argentina, several organizations sought to emulate Castro's guerrilla movements by leading a revolution in Salta and Jujuy. These organizations included the Uturuncos, or Tigermen, in 1959, the People's Guerrilla Army in 1963, and the 17 de Octubre group in 1968 (Rock 1987) on the left, and Movimiento Nacionalista Revolucionario Tacuara on the right. Although accurate data are not available, many of these rural guerrillas were middle-class students who were captured and often killed by the police in large numbers (1987). Only in the 1970s did new revolutionary organizations emerge that remained active for more than a few years.

Despite the limited impact of the first guerrilla groups, the Argentine government enacted measures to prevent the rise of communism. In January 1963 the Executive approved a decree on Repression of Crimes against National Security (Decree 788/63). This highlighted the need to fight the "enemies of democracy and the free world" to preserve external security and guarantee internal peace. It also stated that some foreign doctrines threatened the Argentine way of life. Although this decree applied to the entire population, it contained some special provisions for foreigners. It specified a long list of crimes against national security and defined as treason the use of weapons against the Argentine nation or in aid of its enemies. This decree also repressed a long list of actions, including espionage, sabotage, and professing a doctrine that promoted the use of violence or attempted to change the Constitution or some of its basic principles. Punishments for these crimes ranged from a year in prison to a life sentence.

Decree 4214/63, Repression of Communism, prohibited the Communist Party and parties that professed communist ideologies. It stated that the Communist Party, due to its links to international communism, was prejudicial to the Argentine nationhood. A communist was defined as a person who was a member of the Communist Party, cooperated with any communist organization, or professed doctrines directed to institute a communist government. Persons considered to be communists were banned from the civil service and academia and could not receive government fellowships. Foreign citizens considered communists were forbidden from entering the country and could be deported automatically. This decree also punished naturalized foreigners who professed communism with the loss of citizenship and later deportation. Overall, this decree severely punished anyone who could be linked to the Communist Party in any way.

Decree 2457/63, passed in 1963, contained rules that applied only to immigrants from communist countries. Receiving immigrants fleeing communist regimes seemed like a safe option for a right-wing Argentina, and geopolitical interests dictated that anything that could improve the country's relationship with the United States should be encouraged. Immigrants from South Korea first arrived in Argentina in 1965 (Bialogorski 2004). In 1979 the government responded to a special call by the United Nations Secretary General, who begged countries to accept immigrants from Vietnam, Laos, and Kampuchea, by bringing some three hundred families from Laos, which had been under the control of communist forces since 1975 (Albarracín 2004).

Due to the "risks" associated with accepting immigrants from communist countries, the Executive enacted rules to strictly control them, requiring frequent check-ins with the government and limiting their initial visa terms to a maximum of three months, the length of time normally granted to a tourist. Further, upon arrival in Argentina these immigrants had to report to the federal police to receive a special identification to be used during their stay. In some cases, immigrants had to check in with the police monthly. In effect, this decree strongly restricted the constitutional freedoms granted to immigrants in Argentina.

In 1963 the profusion of measures for controlling subversive activities and communism increased. The guerrilla movements of the 1960s had had limited impact on society. In 1969, however, President Onganía grew weary of leftist movements. In late May the city of Cordoba erupted in a massive riot, primarily instigated by university students and automotive workers (Rock 1987). After declaring a strike, protesters swept into the city center, burning cars and buses along their way. As the riots developed, increasing numbers of people joined the protesters. For forty-eight hours, rioters clashed with police forces. After this event, known as the Cordobazo, leftist movements proliferated. Within only eighteen months, four highly professional guerrilla movements were active in Argentina.[30]

Although the Cordoba riots clearly resembled those of 1968 Paris, the government could not prove its contention that the Argentine disturbances had been caused by "outside agents" (Rock 1987). Nonetheless, Onganía's administration targeted immigrants. A law for the Deportation of the Undesirable (Law 18,235) was passed at the end of May; it declared that the "recent developments in the country [Cordobazo], have demonstrated that the Executive needs an agile and effective tool to deport undesirable foreigners." Accordingly, the Executive was awarded the power to remove foreigners who had been condemned by courts for serious crimes or who had engaged in activities that could threaten social peace, security, or public order. Of course, the Executive interpreted which activities qualified as a threat. These provisions were very similar to those of the 1902 Residence Law. It, like other laws repressing communism and approving deportation provisions, was unconstitutional on several grounds.

DEMOCRATIC GOVERNMENTS AFTER 1955

One immigration policy practice common to the democratic governments after Perón's first administrations (1946–1955) was amnesties enacted for immigrants from bordering countries. Strict rules for admission that could not be enforced generated significant numbers of undocumented immigrants. Without changing the permanent rules, democratic governments enacted amnesties to regularize the immigration status of bordering immigrants. Many of these amnesties were enacted following military regimes (Decree 3364 from 1958, Decree 49 from 1964, Decree 87 from 1974, and Decree 780 from 1983). Amnesties passed by later democratic governments include Menem's Decree 1023 from 1992 and Kirchner's amnesties in Decrees 836 from 2004 and 578 from 2005. Because Law 25871 from 2004 states the government has to provide the means for the regularization of immigration status of foreigners residing in Argentina, amnesties could become more common in the future.

After the 1930s, establishing rules to encourage immigration from certain countries became common. This was often done through bilateral agreements signed with immigrants' countries of origin. President Perón signed agreements for immigrants from Italy and Spain; President Frondizi for those from Spain (1960), Japan (1961), and for Europeans residing in the former African colonies (Decrees 11619/60 and 5466/61); President Illia for French citizens residing in North Africa (1964); and, more recently, President Carlos Menem for immigrants from Central and Eastern Europe (1994). In contrast, the Argentine government never signed accords to encourage permanent migration from bordering countries, and agreements for the immigration of people residing in former colonies in Africa benefited Europeans and not Africans. On various occasions, the government signed agreements with South American countries, but these agreements were signed with bordering countries to regulate the work of seasonal migrants, discouraging the permanent settlement of immigrants in Argentina. This type of agreement was signed by democratic governments with Paraguay (1958) and Bolivia (1964), and by military administrations with Bolivia (1978) and Chile (1971). In all, six democratic presidents enacted permanent rules for the admission of foreign citizens: Illia, Alfonsín (1983–1989), Menem (1989–1999), Néstor Kirchner (2003–2007), and Macri (2015–).

After the coup of 1955 deposed Perón, the military government, with the support of broad sectors of society, forbade him from competing in elections. In 1963 the Peronists, frustrated by this prohibition, decided to cast blank ballots, and Arturo Illia (of the Unión Cívica Radical—Radical Civic Union of the People) won the election. Unlike his predecessors, President Illia valued Congress and the democratic process. The Keynesian economic policies advocated by the United Nations Economic Commission from Latin America and the Caribbean (ECLAC), which included state intervention and planning, also influenced his government. The economic situation during Illia's short-lived administration was favored by industrial recovery and an increase in salaries.

President Illia made a serious attempt to systematize immigration policies. After annulling all the decrees dealing with immigration since the end of the nineteenth century, he issued Decree 4418/65 to establish new immigration rules in 193 articles. This decree has been described as the turning point in the immigration policies of democratic governments in that it included restrictive provisions together with moderately broad criteria for admission (CELS 2002). This decree distinguished between permanent immigrants (refugees, former residents, and relatives of Argentines) and nonpermanent immigrants (temporary residents, tourists, seasonal workers, persons in transit, awardees of political asylum, and daily border crossings). Spontaneous immigrants were admitted as long as they arrived in the country at their own cost.

Among the decree's restrictive facets was a long list of persons who were forbidden from immigrating to Argentina, including those with contagious or psychiatric illnesses, who lacked occupation or means of subsistence or had been involved in prostitution, persons addicted to drugs, and those who were condemned for crimes that were punished in Argentina with prison. It also followed the definition of illegal immigrants established by Decree 4805/63. Unlike this earlier measure, however, Decree 4418/65 gave undocumented immigrants the option of regularizing their immigration status before mandating deportation. It also raised fines for people who offered jobs or lodging to undocumented workers.

Partly because of problems facing the military government of 1976, Argentina made its transition to democracy in 1983 (Haggard and Kaufman 1995; Linz and Stepan 1996; O'Donnell and Schmitter 1986). Alfonsín, a member of the Unión Cívica Radical party, won the October 30 elections. The new president was a strong critic of the military government and committed to the construction of a new democratic order (Cavarozzi 1997). Together with punishment of human rights violations, Alfonsín's administration was committed to getting the country out of the serious economic crisis that affected Argentina and the rest of Latin America (Rapoport 2000). Despite the severe crisis, Alfonsín enacted an amnesty to resolve the situation of immigrants who had become undocumented during the military dictatorship. It is worth noting that while total immigration decreased by almost 3 percent from the previous decade, immigration from neighboring countries slightly increased (see Figure 2.1). But, like President Illia before him, instead of letting Congress modify or replace the law left in place by the military, President Alfonsín enacted several immigration provisions by decree.

Law 22439 of 1981 had left the requirements applicable to each immigration category up to the Executive. Restricting immigration, Decree 1434/87 established that relatives of Argentines or permanent residents, skilled workers, artists, and athletes of known solvency, religious workers, and migrants with investment capital could apply for residency. These requirements were to be removed once the country's situation had changed. Decree 1434/87 also stated that the National Directorate of Migration could pass regulations to specify or interpret the requirements established in it, according to new circumstances.

Any serious study of state policy needs to include the analysis of regulations passed by government agencies, which can specify or modify laws and executive orders in important ways. To regulate the decree of 1987, the Immigration Agency passed Resolution 700/88, which provided that this decree's requirements would not apply to European immigrants. "Most of the migrants that provided the base for the growth and development of our nation came from Europe," it explained, so these migrants deserved special consideration (Resolution 700/88). Once again, the Argentine government prioritized Europeans over other groups of immigrants, continuing with the tradition of promoting a white, European Argentina, even though countries around the world had mostly abandoned ethnic preferences by the 1960s (FitzGerald and Cook-Martín 2014).

IMMIGRATION POLICIES: 1990s

President Menem (1989–1995) was inaugurated early after Alfonsín resigned due to the severity of the economic crisis. After the application of
multiple market-oriented reforms, growth resumed and unemployment
went down (Pastor and Wise 1999). Within this context, the government
passed an amnesty that benefited immigrants from neighboring countries, the proportion of whom had decreased slightly compared to the previous decade (see Figure 2.1). In 1993 unemployment rates climbed and
economic growth slowed down (Rapoport 2000). During the same year,
the Executive passed Decree 2771/93, enabling it to deport immigrants
who committed crimes or illegally occupied dwellings. As with other measures with similar deportation provisions, this decree was questionable in
light of the rights awarded by the Argentine Constitution to all inhabitants and not just citizens.

In June 1994 the Executive passed Decree 1023/94, which regulated
the provisions of Law 22439 from 1981 and amended Alfonsín's Decree
1434/87. The considerations cited to justify immigration policy change
were highly contradictory. For one thing, the decree stated that the economic situation was better than in 1987. This observation was confusing
and seemed like a prelude for liberal immigration measures. The decree
also explained that the Executive was reformulating the population objectives of the country in the light of the new socioeconomic scenario and
the integration process with Mercosur countries. However, the decree also
stated that the government wanted to put an end to illegal immigration.

Decree 1023/94 was similar to Alfonsín's decree, but it was more permissive in one respect and more restrictive in another. It was more permissive in that it did not require migrants to be skilled. Instead, the decree
admitted all types of workers on the condition that they had a written job
contract from an Argentine employer (article 27). This last requirement,
however, made immigration policies stricter. Most migrants in Argentina,
as elsewhere, find jobs in informal sectors of the economy. In 1994 one-
quarter of male workers were employed in construction and as many as
half of female migrants worked in the domestic sector (Sana 1999). Many
employers were reluctant to sign job contracts for several reasons. For one
thing, employers feared legal and other obligations related to taxes and

benefits. For another, the immigration office's regulations demanded that employers provide proof that they did not have any debts to the federal government. These conditions made it highly difficult for migrants to get documented support from an employer.

In 1992 the Menem administration invited Central and Eastern Europeans to immigrate to Argentina, an overture celebrated by the right-wing media. Even though the government was unable to secure funding to support these families, the project moved forward and was formalized by the Ministry of the Interior's Resolution 4632/94. This resolution stated that immigrants from Central and Eastern Europe were not required to have a job offer. The resolution justified this measure by stating that the plan applicable to European citizens preceded the decree from 1994. The amnesty that benefited immigrants from bordering countries also predated the decree of 1994, but these immigrants were not exempted. Once again, in the midst of an economic crisis, the boundaries of the imagined community were redrawn to exclude immigrants from Latin America. As in 1987, analyzing regulations by the Immigration Agency seems crucial to understanding the immigration policies of Argentina. Some 8,944 immigrants benefited from this program in the 1990s (Cancillería Argentina 2002).

LAW OF 2004

In 2001 Argentina went through the most serious economic and institutional crises of recent decades, which led thousands of Argentines to emigrate (Albarracín 2004). In 2002 Mercosur presidents announced that they would allow for the free movement of people within the countries of the bloc (Mercosur n.d.). In 2003, when President Kirchner was in power, the Argentine Congress finally passed comprehensive immigration legislation to replace the law passed during the last military dictatorship in 1981. The new law, still partly in place as of this writing, represents a noteworthy departure from traditional immigration policies and has been characterized as one of the most progressive immigration policies in the world (Barbero 2016).

Law 25871, which was passed in 2003 and went into effect in 2004, grants an important bundle of rights to immigrants, including access to

health care education and the right to resort to judicial review when orders of deportation are issued by the Immigration Agency. This law also
prioritizes the immigration of citizens from Mercosur countries. For the
first time in history, Argentina passed a measure that gave preference to
immigrants from the Southern Cone. Not surprisingly, this law was passed
by Congress and not by executive order. As this work shows, with the exception of the amnesties common during democratic regimes, immigration rules passed by the Executive have usually been restrictive and have
responded to changing economic and political situations. This law was
the product of over a decade of dedicated work by Argentine legislators,
especially those who were members of the population committees created in the early 1990s (Albarracín 2004). The timing, however, was influenced by the progressive Kirchner administration, which passed further policy changes as well. In 2004 the Executive, through Decrees 836/04
and 1169/04, passed an amnesty to benefit immigrants from non-Merco-
sur countries. In 2005, through Decree 578/05, the program of regularization was extended to Mercosur citizens. Together these came to be known
as Great Fatherland (Patria Grande) programs (Dirección Nacional de
Migraciones 2010).

What made the enactment of a new law and executive order possible
in 2003? One explanation is that the progress of Mercosur pushed the passage of the new immigration policies. Kirchner and Brazilian president
Luiz Inácio Lula da Silva were both strong critics of globalization. Both
presidents also believed that Mercosur should occupy an important place
on their agendas. Against some predictions, Mercosur influenced immigration policies, and not just those regarding trade (Sassen 1996a; 1996b).
Other factors were also likely at play. Immigrant and human rights organizations actively lobbied Congress and the Executive for more liberal immigration policies for almost twenty years. The congressional committees on
population issues, created in the 1990s, worked actively with these organizations to agree on a new immigration law. Further, the work and dedica-
tion of Senator Rubén Giustiniani, who authored the law of 2003/4 in the
1990s and also chaired the Population and Human Resources Committee
of the Chamber of Deputies between 2000 and 2003, and the Kirchner administration's emphasis on Latin American integration and anti-imperial-
ism also helped the passage of the new immigration legislation.

THE IMMIGRATION POLICIES OF
THE MACRI ADMINISTRATION

President Mauricio Macri, leader of the center-right Republican Proposal (PRO) and president of the Change (Cambiemos) coalition, was inaugurated in December 2015 after winning the presidency in a runoff election. According to Jens Andermann (2016), one of Macri's objectives has been to reignite the liberal project of "republican" civilization devised by Bartolomé Mitre and Sarmiento. The 2010 census showed that the proportion of immigrants in Argentina remained unchanged (INDEC 2016). Almost 70 percent of the 1,805,957 immigrants living in Argentina in 2010 were from bordering countries, 13 percent from other countries in the Americas, 17 percent from Europe, 2 percent from Asia, and 1 percent from Africa (INDEC 2016). The main country of immigration from the Americas outside bordering countries (Brazil, Bolivia, Chile, Paraguay, and Uruguay) was Peru. One novelty during this period is that a somewhat significant number of immigrants came from Colombia (Dirección Nacional de Migraciones 2010). This is an important change because, as this work will show, drug trafficking became associated with immigrants from Colombia.

When Macri was inaugurated, he faced high inflation, economic stagnation, fiscal deficit, depressed foreign trade, and a downward pressure on the value of the currency (Yang 2016). In addition, homicide rates had increased over the past two decades and Argentina had become an important shipment point for cocaine headed to Europe (Dudley 2014). Certainly, increased crime rates have been common throughout the Latin American region. The Macri administration laid blame for crime, among other social ills, on immigration, even though the proportion of foreigners in Argentine prisons is 6 percent, only slightly higher than the proportion of foreigners in the country, at 4.5 percent.[31]

Early in his administration, Macri declared a public security state of emergency to correct organized crime and drug trafficking, greatly expanding the power of the military in internal affairs and border enforcement. The government has also passed policy measures affecting immigrants, including cutting back resources that facilitate documentation processes and opening an immigrant detention center in Buenos Aires

(Barbero 2016). In January 2017 the Executive approved important deportation provisions in Decree 70. This decree is framed as a decree of necessity and urgency (DNU), a last-resort mechanism laid out in Article 99 of the Constitution that allows the Executive to enact legislation in extreme situations (Honorable Senado de la Nación Argentina n.d.). Further, some have spoken of the Trump effect in Argentina, referring to U. S. President Trump's executive orders increasing border security and changing priorities for deportation to include persons who were suspected of having committed minor crimes (Barbero 2016).

This decree further delineates a number of cases in which foreigners are not allowed to enter Argentina, including having been sentenced for or accused of certain crimes (some of them without minimum prison sentences), having avoided immigration controls, and having been sentenced for or accused of participating in terrorist acts. It also rolls back the right to judicial review of deportation orders recognized by Law 25871 and establishes an expedited process for removal not unlike the one established by Trump through a 2017 executive order (Martin 2017). The DNU cites comparative legislation to justify the decision to establish the expedited removal but, probably to avoid comparisons to President Trump, mentions Spanish deportation rules and not those of the United States.

FACTORS SHAPING IMMIGRATION
POLICY DECISIONS 1853–2017

For several reasons, from right after independence from Spain until the 1930s, Argentine immigration policies encouraged immigration. Due to the sparse population, liberal elites sought agricultural workers to achieve their dream of turning the country into an agricultural exporter. Further, Northern European immigrants were supposed to have an important, beneficial cultural impact on the Argentine society. Reflecting these concerns, the 1853 Argentine Constitution was in principle open to immigration in general. However, the government was (and is to this day) only obligated to promote immigration from European countries. The immigration policies that followed the Constitution established immigration-recruiting offices in Europe and subsidized transportation and land for new arrivals. Immigrants from other Río de la Plata colonies, who did not qualify as immigrants, could take advantage of the naturalization rules designed for them. Unlike the United States, Argentina did not ban certain classes of immigrants from becoming citizens or from entering the country (FitzGerald and Cook-Martín 2014).

At the turn of the century, ideas about who constituted an ideal citizen changed (Behdad 1997; 2005; Brubaker 1992; Higham 1955; Hing 2004). The elites felt threatened because immigrants had acquired positions of influence in the rigid postcolonial society, failed to naturalize, joined unions, and organized strikes. Without seriously restricting immigration, the government enacted powerful deportation provisions to prevent the arrival and stay of potential troublemakers. It was during this time that Argentina initiated a tradition of passing immigration restrictions by executive order or decree. Later, a nationalist ideology emerged that exalted Spanish language and culture as desirable values to unite the national community. Although these ideas had an impact on education and the establishment of mandatory military service, they did not immediately affect immigration policies.

The Great Depression put an end to the era of mass migration and liberal immigration policies (Rock 1987). Most states during this period restricted immigration to preserve jobs for natives and selected groups of immigrants that could be easily assimilated into the different national communities. Argentina enacted several immigration restrictions during this period, mainly affecting Jewish and Spanish refugees. However, the Argentine government used economic rationales to justify these restrictions. Immigration from neighboring countries also became significant during the 1930s, and the government enacted the first measures to regulate it. Moreover, like the Bracero program in the United States, these regulations only allowed these immigrants to apply for temporary visas and merely tolerated their economic role, first in the regional agricultural economies and later in the industrialization process. In this sense, the role of Latin American immigrants in Argentina was similar to that of Mexican immigrants in the United States.

Why, then, does the state of the economy shape policies for certain groups of immigrants but not others? What determines this double standard for European and Latin American immigrants? Most authors agree that immigration is shaped by economic conditions. It is interesting to investigate whether this is true for the Argentine case. Restrictive immigration policies are negatively correlated to real gross national product (Albarracín 2004). Research indicates that the Argentine labor force has traditionally been educated and skilled and should thus face more competition from Europeans, for instance, than from regional immigrants.

In the Buenos Aires metropolitan area, home to one-third of the country's population, 50 percent of natives worked (and still do) in the service sector and another 20 percent in commerce (Sana 1999). Before industrialization they worked in the regional agricultural economies. Bordering immigrants seem to complement the native labor force fairly well because they occupy jobs that are not attractive to natives due to low pay and lack of benefits (Montoya and Perticará 1995). These jobs are concentrated in low-skilled, labor-intensive sectors of the economy: construction (25 percent) and manufacturing (16 percent) for men, and domestic service (50 percent) for women (Albarracín 2004, 51). For these reasons, Argentines should not feel competition from immigrants from the region (Maguid 1995).

In sum, economic concerns cannot account for the different consideration that the Argentine government has afforded European and non-European immigrants. This chapter tells a cultural-political story that is not completely independent from political economy (Behdad 1997; 2005; Brubaker 1992; Higham 1955; Hing 2004). In the case of Argentina, domestic closure against certain noncitizens does not rest on material concerns alone. This book argues that, although economic factors are important in explaining immigration policies and often determine *how many* immigrants a country is willing to accept, notions of the ethnic and/or cultural eligibility of certain immigrant groups for membership in the "imagined community" dictate *who* is admitted. Thus, Argentine immigration policies generally welcomed certain groups of European immigrants, regardless of the economic situation. At the same time, they tended to restrict Latin American (or Jewish or communist) immigration and further discriminated against it in periods of economic hardship.

During the Peronist administration (1946–1955), immigration policies occupied an important place in state planning. The government's emphasis on industrialization generated a growing need for workers (Rock

1987). Despite the economic role attributed to immigrants, the government did not promote immigration from different groups evenly. The Peronist administration negotiated agreements to encourage immigration only with Italy and Spain. Although the migration of citizens from bordering countries was facilitated through amnesty decrees, it was not encouraged through special agreements. Other ethnic preferences were also reflected in the Peronist immigration policies. As in the earlier period, the immigration of Jewish refugees from Nazi Europe was discouraged by multiple means. Instead, the country received refugees who had formerly collaborated with the Nazis in different parts of Europe.

The immigration policies of the several military governments that followed the fall of Perón in 1955 had several features in common. All of them showed a preference for European immigration and strict regulation of immigration from neighboring countries. Specifically, they combined lax policies for European immigrants with strict requirements and broad deportation provisions for neighboring ones. Additionally, ideological preferences complemented ethnic ones. The military regimes' geopolitical interests made them join the war against communism, and their immigration policies reflected this concern, allowing for the immigration of noncommunist persons from South Korean, Vietnam, Laos, and Kampuchea.

Finally, the democratic governments after 1955 had contradictory immigration policies (Novik 1992; 1997). All of them passed amnesties to regularize the status of immigrants from Southern Cone countries but did not pass permanent immigration laws to resolve the situation of these immigrants in a more decisive way (Albarracín 2004). It is worth mentioning that immigration restrictions, even during democratic governments, continued to be enacted by executive orders or decrees. Further, even though most countries in the Western Hemisphere had abandoned overt ethnic preferences, democratic governments in Argentina continued to express a bias in favor of European immigration. For instance, between 1983 and 2004, immigrants from Latin America were subjected to strict requirements to apply for a work visa in Argentina, but immigrants from Europe were exempted from these requirements. Several administrations negotiated agreements or passed special rules to favor the immigration of European citizens.

In 2004, for the first time in history, Argentina passed permanent immigration rules that benefited immigrants from Latin American countries. The weight of the Southern Common Market combined with multiple other factors to influence this decision. In 2017 President Macri's government reversed some of these policies by executive order, restricting entry to Argentina and immigrants' rights in important ways. It is true that economic considerations may have influenced this executive order; however, cultural factors also played a role because immigrants from Southern Cone countries, as this work shows, were scapegoated for drug trafficking and other crimes and for populating Buenos Aires's shantytowns. It remains to be seen if the Macri administration will continue to walk on the path of immigration restriction.

THREE

Immigration Policies after the Reestablishment of Democracy, 1983–1989

This book argues that ideas about the ethnic or cultural appropriateness of certain groups of individuals as members of what Benedict Anderson calls the "imagined community" (1991) can shape the immigration policies toward them (Brubaker 1992; Fitzgerald 1996; Ha and Jang 2015; Meyers 2000; Mukherjee, Molina, and Adams 2012). The effort to populate Argentina with Western Europeans as a means to foster growth represents a central, formative theme running through Argentine history. Paradoxically, while Argentina claimed to seek Western European immigrants to build an economically viable, "civilized" society, its policy proved open to a great many more local, Latin American immigrants.

This chapter explores the portrayal of immigrants in the Argentine press during the 1980s. During this period, Argentina faced severe economic crises. Despite economic hardship, the Executive enacted a generous amnesty through Decree 780/84, which benefited immigrants from all origins in 1984. The government needed to resolve the situation of 140,000 foreigners who had become undocumented under the strict immigration rules enacted by the last military government. The government likely also considered constitutional principles and human rights concerns. In 1984, despite the severity of the economic crisis, immigrants and immigration were portrayed overall in a positive manner in the press and not problematized as they would be in later periods. Further, the Argentine government seemed extremely preoccupied with the emigration of Argentine nationals due to the military dictatorship.

As different economic plans achieved sparse success and the economic situation worsened, rules for the admission of foreign citizens became more restrictive. In 1985 Resolution 2340/85, a questionable resolution by the director of the Immigration Agency, established new and stricter requirements to apply for a work visa. In 1987 these new requirements were passed by Executive Decree 1434/87. At first glance, economic hardship seems to have influenced the enactment of these new immigration rules. However, in 1988 another resolution by the Immigration Agency exempted European citizens from the strict new requirements. What explains this preference for European immigration? Again, it is likely that the perceived desirability of immigrants for membership in the community shaped immigration rules for them. This chapter explores the perceived desirability of different groups of immigrants as members of the imagined community in the six-month periods preceding immigration policy change via an analysis of their portrayal in two newspapers: *La Nación* and *Clarín*.

ARGENTINA'S FOREIGN-BORN POPULATION IN 1980

The census of 1980 recorded a total of 1.9 million foreigners living in Argentina. The concentration of immigrants in the city and province of Buenos Aires that started during the 1950s became more pronounced during the period under analysis. The total number of immigrants in the Buenos Aires region grew by 23.3 percent between 1970 and 1980, while in the rest of the country it grew by only 9 percent (Organización de los Estados Americanos 1985). The federal capital and the province of Buenos Aires remained the favorite destinations of immigrants, housing 53 percent of bordering immigrants and 80 percent of nonbordering immigrants (INDEC 1997). Areas with high proportions of bordering immigrants outside of Buenos Aires were the Patagonia region (16 percent) and the Northeast (15 percent). The only area with a high proportion of nonbordering immigrants outside of Buenos Aires was the province of Santa Fe (INDEC 1997). However, the "old" European immigration still represented a significant share of the foreign-born population of Argentina in 1980 (see Table 3.1).

Table 3.1. National Origin of the Foreign-Born Population in Argentina in 1980

Country of Origin	Percentage of the Foreign-Born Population
Italy	25.7
Spain	19.7
Paraguay	13.8
Chile	11.3
Bolivia	6.2
Uruguay	6.0
Poland	3.0
Other Countries	14.3
Total	100.0

Source: Census 1980, INDEC, Argentina

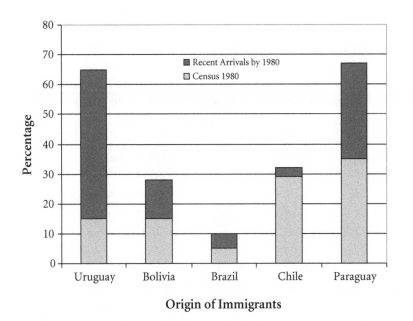

Origin of Immigrants

Figure 3.1. National Origin of Established Bordering Immigrants in 1980 Compared to Recent Arrivals by 1980

Sources: Census 1980, INDEC, Argentina, and Residency Decree 780/84

The European countries with the most significant numbers of immigrants were Italy (26 percent) and Spain (20 percent). Migrants from non-bordering countries still comprised 60 percent of the foreign-born population (INDEC 1997). Out of the 753,000 immigrants from bordering countries living in Argentina in 1980, 35 percent were from Paraguay, 29 percent from Chile, 15 percent from Bolivia, 15 percent from Uruguay, and 5 percent from Brazil (Figure 3.1). Despite the unstable economic situation, immigrant arrivals from the Southern Cone were steady after the reestablishment of democracy, with some 90,000 people of this origin entering the country in 1983 and 220,000 in 1984 (De Marco 1986, 335).

CULTURAL FACTORS SHAPING IMMIGRATION POLICIES: IMMIGRANTS IN THE PRINT MEDIA

Considerations about the perceived ethnic or cultural appropriateness of certain groups of immigrants for membership in the imagined community can also be at work when deciding the admission of these groups. In particular, if immigrants and immigration are considered in a problematic way, then immigration policies are likely to be restrictive. In what follows, I review the portrayal of immigration during the Alfonsín administration in two main Argentine newspapers: *La Nación* (center-right) and *Clarín* (center-left). *La Nación* was founded in 1870 and has a number of subscribers ranging from 180,000 to 350,000. *Clarín* was founded in 1945 and as of 2017 had 240,000 paper subscribers (see Appendix II).

The media coverage analyzed comprised two six-month periods right before an immigration policy change, October–March of 1983/1984 and March–August 1987. Decree 780 from March 12, 1984, approved a permissive amnesty for immigrants, allowing them to apply for residency by furnishing proof of identity and date of entry into the country. Decree 1434/87 from August 31, 1987, passed restrictive immigration rules stipulating that only skilled workers, artists, athletes, religious workers, and immigrants with investment capital would be admitted into Argentina.

A total of twenty-two articles were selected between the two newspapers (see Table 3.2). Three editorial pieces out of the seven identified for the periods under analysis were analyzed separately due to their higher

Table 3.2. Total Number of Stories Coded by Year, Newspaper, and Origin of
Immigration: 1983–1984 and 1987

	1983–1984		1987	
Origin of Immigrants	La Nación	Clarín	La Nación	Clarín
European	2	4	–	3
L. American	2	4	–	–
Other	–	1	1	5
Total	4	9	1	8

ideological content and biases. This study coded a total of thirteen articles
for the period 1983 to 1984 and nine for the year 1987. The salience of an
issue influences views about issue importance among the general public
and government policy makers (Cook et al. 1983). Further, the salience of
an issue creates a sense of urgency that may prompt policy makers to act.
As this study suggests, policy changes can happen during such periods.

The themes and topics of headlines constitute the most prominent
feature of news discourse, as they express the top of the semantic macro-
structure and define the situation (Van Dijk 1994). This study therefore
analyzed how this global level defined the overall meaning of the texts and
focused on mapping out and quantifying the themes and topics of the
headlines and stories. In the twenty-two stories analyzed, four main themes
and topics were identified in the headlines (see Tables 3.2 and 3.3). As this
analysis will show, the type and frequency of these themes and topics depended on the type of immigration covered (Latin American versus European), the social/economic context at the time of publication, and, to a
lesser degree, the newspaper under consideration.

The local-level analysis allowed for an examination of words, group
words, clauses, and sentences. The terms and themes used in the press to
talk about immigrants are also an indication of where immigrants stand
vis-à-vis members of the community (Hier and Greenberg 2002). These
terms and themes also have the important discursive function of sum-
ming the historically derived, culturally shared models and scripts about
people. This study traced the terms and themes used to characterize immigrants and immigration, which, according to Teun A. van Dijk (1994),
are key expressions that readers can easily recall. The terms were coded

Table 3.3. Topics in Headlines and Stories, by Year, Newspaper, and Type,
in Percentages: 1983–1984 and 1987

Topics	1983–1984		1987	
	La Nación	Clarín	La Nación	Clarín
Government actions/decisions	50 (2)	57 (4)	100 (1)	12 (1)
Problems w/ immigration	25 (1)	–	–	25 (2)
Immigration/descriptive	25 (1)	29 (2)	–	63 (5)
Call for action		14 (1)		(1)

as positive if they showed respect for immigrants as human beings and
negative if they disrespected immigrants and/or portrayed them as undesirable, treated them as objects (objectification), or exaggerated their
numbers (amplification) (see Table 3.4).

Additionally, the themes were classified as benefits if they attributed
positive social, economic, cultural, and political effects to immigration
and as problems if they attributed negative effects to immigration (see
Table 3.4). A total of 358 instances were coded in the two periods under
consideration, 82 percent of which were coded as positive and 18 percent
as negative (see Table 3.4). The terms and themes used to describe immigrants depended on the type of immigration covered (Latin American or
Asian versus European), the social/economic context at the time of publication, and, to a certain degree, the newspaper under consideration.

IMMIGRATION COVERAGE IN 1983

Most scholars treat the 1983 Argentine transition to democracy as a case of
so-called bottom-up democratization due to the collapse of the military
regime (Haggard and Kaufman 1995; Linz and Stepan 1996; O'Donnell
and Schmitter 1986). The military government in Argentina was unsuccessful on most fronts. For one thing, it left power in the midst of severe
economic crisis. Economic hardship had impoverished a large portion of
the population and later led to the bankruptcy of several business groups.
For another, the government became increasingly unpopular after the de-
feat in the Malvinas (Falkland) War against Great Britain in 1982. Further,

the armed forces faced several internal power struggles (Cavarozzi 1997). Alfonsín, a member of the Unión Cívica Radical, won the October 30 elections.[1] The new president was a strong critic of the military government and committed to the construction of a new democratic order (Cavarozzi 1997). Along with resolution of human rights violations and military questions, Alfonsín's administration was committed to getting the country out of the serious economic crisis.

In 1984 Alfonsín's administration passed Decree 780/84, which was intended to regularize the immigration status of migrants of any national origin who resided in the country before December 1983. Public officials estimated the number of undocumented immigrants to be somewhere between 300,000 and 800,000 (Sassone 1987, 263). Only some 142,000 foreigners, however, applied for residence under this so-called amnesty. Amnesties had become common in Argentina after President Perón's first administrations (1946–1955). For instance, 61 percent of the 858,000 foreigners who obtained permanent residence in Argentina between 1958 and 1985 did so through amnesty decrees (Sassone 1987, 267).

The 1984 amnesty decree stated that immigration policies during the military dictatorship "were detached from the socio-economic reality of the country and had left many people without legal documents" (Decree 780/84). As Raúl Galván, a high-ranking official of the Ministry of the Interior, explained in an interview published in *Clarín*, the law enacted during the dictatorship of 1976 to 1983 was "restrictive, oriented to ideological control, and disrespectful of our Constitution."[2] To evaluate the restrictiveness of the last military dictatorship's policy, it is helpful to consider that although an average of 26,000 bordering migrants obtained residency in Argentina each year from 1970 to 1975, that number for the period from 1976 to 1983 dropped by 60 percent.[3] According to Galván, democratic principles and human rights considerations influenced the enactment of the several amnesty decrees passed in Argentina.

Several economic issues are at stake in immigration policy. As Kitty Calavita puts it, it is difficult to identify and/or pursue "a national economic interest" when deciding on immigration policies (1994, 77). Decree 780/84 states that the amnesty will frustrate the "spurious interests of those employers, who taking advantage of migrants who lack of legal documents, pay them unfair salaries." However, it also explains that "clandestine labor represents unfair competition to the local labor, which is displaced by the migrant one." An officer of the Conferedación General del Trabajo, one of the most powerful unions in Argentina, representing workers of all sectors of the economy, explained that amnesties help decrease "the existence of informal labor markets."[4] Thus, the decree seeks to protect both the rights of immigrants and the native labor force.

During this period, the amount of media coverage on European immigration was comparable to that for Latin America (see Table 3.2). A global-level analysis allowed for an exploration of the headline topics by newspaper and shows no significant difference in the framing of immigration stories by right- and left-wing media. More specifically, both newspapers reproduced government decisions in most cases and had stories describing immigrants and immigration (see Table 3.3).

Most of the headlines coded during this period were mainly descriptive and not intended to produce a change of mind or reaction in the reader. For example, four headlines, two in each newspaper, announced the amnesty for immigrants with the words "Residence for Immigrants" (Radicación de Extranjeros). Using legal language, these stories explained the requirements for immigrants to regularize their immigration status under the new amnesty. However, one story in *Clarín* (10/18/1983),[5] titled "Migratory Pause" (Pausa Migratoria), was biased. In this sense, this story declared that the era of immigration was over, thus ignoring the contributions by the South American immigrants who still arrived in Argentina in important numbers. Except for this instance, the headlines for this period were not intended to produce a change or reaction in the reader.

The local-level immigration coverage analysis before the amnesty was enacted revealed a favorable portrayal of immigrants and immigration in both newspapers (Table 3.4). Moreover, the proportion of positive instances in *La Nación* was higher than in *Clarín*. Eighty-one percent of the instances coded used terms that showed respect for immigrants and/or spoke of beneficial impacts of immigration. Immigrants from all origins were treated in a respectful way and referred to as *immigrants* or *citizens*. I did not find terms such as *ilegal* and *clandestino,* which were often used in the press to refer to immigrants from bordering countries during the 1990s. The instances coded also attributed to immigration a beneficial impact on Argentine society. In this regard, the number of benefits coded was 30 percent higher than the risks.

Table 3.4. Instances Coded by Year, Newspaper, and Type, in Percentages and Absolute Numbers: 1983–1984 and 1987

	1983–1984		1987	
Instances	La Nación	Clarín	La Nación	Clarín
Total	35	115	3	205
Negative total	23 (8)	24 (28)		23 (45)
... Term	25 (2)	11 (3)		22 (10)
... Amplification	–	–	–	9 (4)
... Objectification	–	11 (3)	–	–
... Problems	75 (6)	78 (22)		69 (31)
Positive total	77 (27)	76 (87)	100 (3)	87 (160)
... Terms	52 (14)	70 (61)	100 (3)	61 (98)
... Benefits	48 (13)	30 (26)		39 (62)

Despite the overall positive portrayal of immigrants and immigration in the print press from 1983 to 1984, an examination of the media coverage by immigrant group shows a different picture. This study found quantitative and qualitative differences in the portrayal of European, Asian, and South American immigrants in the Argentine print press during this period. Whereas European immigrants were idealized as a group of brave people who contributed to the growth and prosperity of Argentina with their hard work, approximating the ideas by Sarmiento and Alberdi, immigrants from Asia and the Southern Cone were portrayed in a less positive light. Some stories that discussed the history of immigration to Argentina are illustrative in this respect.

When describing European immigration, one article refers to the "Italian and Spanish immigrants from all regions who joined their efforts in the expansion of Argentina" (*Clarín* 01/31/1984). In a similar vein, another story speaks of the "millions of immigrants arrived from all parts of the globe that invested their generous contribution in founding Argentina" (*Clarín* 10/18/1983). While these articles portrayed European immigrants in a heroic way, the print press failed to emphasize major contributions from Southern Cone immigrants. One of the stories mentioned above is a case in point. This story first explains that in the past few decades, while immigration from Europe decreased, immigration from Southern Cone countries became more important. "Since the 1930s," it continues, "Argentina has been attracting unemployed labor from bordering countries"

(*Clarín* 01/31/1984). Thus, whereas European immigration was said to have a major role in constructing Argentina as a modern nation, neighboring immigration was portrayed as a passive group of unemployed people that happened to be drawn to Argentina.

Perhaps more illustrative is a group of stories that detail the impact of immigration on Argentine society. One piece about the history of immigration to Argentina explains how European immigrants came to constitute the Argentine middle class and founded hospitals, schools, and orphanages (*Clarín* 10/18/1983). It also describes how these immigrants developed the wine industry in the west of the country and, in general, developed the productive structure of Argentina (*Clarín* 10/18/1983). However, this piece has nothing to say about Southern Cone immigration. This omission is especially significant if we consider that most immigration in the previous eighty years had originated in the countries that share borders with Argentina.

Even some articles that were supportive of neighboring immigrants provided a somewhat negative picture of the impact of neighboring immigrants on Argentine society. One story, which covers a request by the Catholic Church to grant residence to immigrants from the Southern Cone, exemplifies this (*Clarín* 01/22/1984). Although the bishops interviewed intended to support the cause for the regularization of these immigrants, they fell short in providing information about these immigrants' positive contributions to Argentine society. A Church document cited in the story first states that, due to their lack of papers, immigrants from Southern Cone countries are exploited and cannot exercise their rights to education, health, housing, and freedom (*Clarín* 01/22/1984). The same document then explains that Southern Cone immigrants live in marginal areas in the periphery, which makes it impossible for them to harmoniously integrate into society. As these instances demonstrate, a document supporting immigration from the Southern Cone for humanitarian reasons can fail to mention these immigrants' past or potential contributions to Argentine society.

Other groups of immigrants attracted even less admiration from the Argentine print press. Argentines in the period studied were ambiguous, to say the least, about immigration from Asian countries. Argentina has an old Japanese community that immigrated at the beginning of the twentieth century. Japanese immigrants in Argentina largely work in horticulture, though many run restaurants, dry cleaners, and other businesses. An above-mentioned article in the newspaper *Clarín* refers to the contribution of the Japanese community (*Clarín* 10/18/1983). The story first racializes these immigrants as "exotic." Specifically, it states that despite being "exotic, these Japanese immigrants had become part of the demographic peculiarities of Argentina" (*Clarín* 10/18/1983). The journalist seems somewhat perplexed that Japanese immigrants managed to integrate into Argentine society. In addition, the story minimizes the merit of Japanese immigrants for their economic success: it states these immigrants came to Argentina with no resources but later became independent businessmen. But instead of attributing this success to some type of "immigrant work ethic," as commonly cited when referring to European immigration, the journalist concludes that there is no explanation for this success.

In conclusion, during the years 1983 to 1984 the consideration of immigrants and immigration was generally favorable for their inclusion in the imagined community. Immigrants were talked about in a respectful way and not associated with unemployment, crime, and other ills of Argentine society. Further, Argentines associated economic prosperity and immigration to the point that the economic success of the country could be judged by the sheer numbers of immigrants. However, the preference for European immigration was still present in Argentina as several stories in this section show. Whereas immigrants from Europe supposedly played an important role in the construction of Argentina as a modern, prosperous nation, immigrants from other parts had a much more modest role, if any.

WAR ECONOMY: 1985 HARDENING
OF IMMIGRATION RULES

For a variety of reasons, the first economic plan did not bring about the desired economic well-being. In June 1985, when inflation rates were steaming ahead at an annual rate of 1,010 percent, the minister of economy announced the Plan Austral. This new plan included the launching of a new currency, salary and price freezes, controlled interest and exchange rates, and deficit reduction (Rapoport 2000, 911). Despite efforts by the Alfonsín administration, the recession hit Argentina in 1985, when the gross national product decreased by almost 5 percent, unemployment climbed almost 2 percent, and although real salaries slightly recovered, they declined again in the next year (927). During 1986 the economic plan brought some stability to prices and favored growth. By the last trimester of 1986, the economic plan was in need of new adjustments due to the decline in the international prices of wheat and corn.

The director of the Immigration Agency, Evaristo Iglesias, accompanied this "war economy" with restrictive immigration policy measures. Making use of the wide powers conferred to the Executive by Law 22439, he passed two resolutions that decreased opportunities for migrants to enter the country and to obtain legal residence once in it. Resolution 2340/85 established strict new requirements for applying for an immigrant visa in Argentina. (Its provisions were almost identical to those later approved by Decree 1434/87, described below.) Resolution 1089/85 established that immigration officers at the border should try to detect (and reject) tourists who intended to stay in the country and provided them with broad powers for evaluating and, if necessary, rejecting migrants who were likely to overstay their tourist visas. Guidelines for detecting these "false tourists" were not unlike those given to immigration officers in the United States and included checking that the person had a return ticket to his or her country, a certain amount of money available for the trip, and a place to stay in Argentina.

The Radical administration had promised to introduce a new immigration bill for congressional consideration.[6] The country, according to Interior Undersecretary Galván, needed a law that reflected the country's population needs. However, "Immigration Agency Director Iglesias thought that introducing a bill for congressional consideration would take too long," and thus, former agency director Silvia Lépore explained, "he decided to soften the police-like characteristics of the 1981 law through a set of rules enacted by presidential decree."[7] The Executive passed Decree 1434/87 in August 1987.

The law of 1981 had established that foreigners could be accepted in any of three categories—permanent, temporary, or transitory residents (article 12)—but left the requirements for each category to executive regulation. Decree 1434/87 stated that to apply for residence, potential immigrants had to demonstrate they were relatives of Argentines or permanent residents; skilled workers, artists or athletes of known solvency, or religious workers; or had investment capital. It also explained that these restrictive requirements would be removed once the country's economic situation improved. The following year, even though the economic situation had not improved, the director of the Immigration Agency passed Resolution 700/88, which provided that the strict requirements of Decree 1434/87 would not apply to European immigrants. Since "most of the migrants that provided the base for the growth and development of our nation came from Europe," the resolution explains, "these migrants deserve special consideration." Once again, the recurrent preference for European immigration had surfaced in legislation.

During this period, economic hardship appeared to be a factor shaping immigration policies for Latin American immigrants but not for European immigrants. In a public presentation in 1985, Iglesias, no longer director of the Immigration Agency, stated, "The country has had permissive immigration policies since the reestablishment of democracy and it was time for the government to reevaluate these policies" (1996, 190). Iglesias thought that the Argentine State should reassume its sovereign power in controlling immigration flows in a moment in which labor markets, public services, public hospitals, and schools were saturated (1996). However, he failed to explain why the new immigration restrictions did not apply to European immigrants.

President Alfonsín also provided a detailed justification for restrictive immigration policies for Latin American immigrants. In 1986 several Catholic bishops sent a letter to the president, begging him to reconsider his administration's immigration policies. In his reply, Alfonsín defended the government's decisions, stating that the enactment of exceptional immigration measures was justified by exceptional circumstances (quoted in Iglesias 1996, 198–99). This situation demanded, according to Alfonsín, the adoption of a "war economy," which had to be endured by Argentines and foreigners alike. Since the capacity of Argentina to receive immigrants was reduced to a minimum, according to him, immigration had to cease until circumstances changed. Overall, it seemed clear that there was an economic motivation for the immigration decisions of the period. However, Alfonsín also failed to explain why economic hardship should harden immigration rules only for non-European immigrants.

CULTURAL REASONS BEHIND IMMIGRATION POLICIES:
IMMIGRATION IN THE PRINT PRESS IN 1987

During 1987, the amount of media coverage on European immigration was comparable to that for Latin America (see Table 3.2). A global-level exploration of the headline topics by newspaper shows a significant difference in the handling of immigration by the right- and left-wing media. More specifically, whereas *La Nación* only reproduced government decisions related to immigration, *Clarín* ran several headlines on topics such as problems associated with immigration (from South Korea) and depictions of immigrants and their reality (see Table 3.3).

For instance, both of the stories from *Clarín* depicting problems associated with immigration refer to immigrants from South Korea and include headlines that are merely descriptive, free of the value judgments that became common later. The headlines of these stories are "Chinatown in Flores" (Chinatown en Flores) and "From Seoul to Once" (De Seúl at Once) (05/11/1987; 08/30/1987). Flores and Once are two neighborhoods in Buenos Aires with high concentrations of immigrants from South Korea. These stories are full of negative terms and references to problems associated with South Korean immigration, but the headlines themselves are relatively free of charged language intended to produce emotional reactions in the reader.

The local-level analysis of immigration coverage during this period in *La Nación* and *Clarín* revealed a favorable portrayal of immigrants and immigration. Eighty-one percent of the instances coded used terms that showed respect for immigrants and/or spoke of beneficial impacts of immigration. However, the favorability of the press toward immigration was inflated by two articles citing speeches by Pope John Paul II, which accounted for almost one-third of all the positive instances coded during this period. Still, immigrants were discussed in a respectful way and referred to as "immigrants" or "citizens" in most instances coded. Some groups of immigrants, however, were portrayed less favorably. The terms *illegal* and *second-class citizen* were used in reference to immigrants from Latin American countries. Also, several racialized terms and phrases were used in reference to immigrants from South Korea, who were described as having "Oriental faces," "slanted eyes," and "bronze-tone skin."

The media coverage also recognized immigration's beneficial impact on Argentine society. In this regard, the number of benefits coded was 50 percent higher than that of risks. Several positive traits and impacts were attributed to immigrants, including being hardworking, being good neighbors, and contributing to the common good and the cultural and economic richness of the country. However, the media also attributed negative impacts to non-European immigration. For example, some instances criticize South Korean immigrants for not learning the language, exploiting their employees, and taking over entire neighborhoods in Buenos Aires. Others denounce Latin American immigrants for bringing poverty to the country. Although the media coverage tended to describe the impact of immigration on Argentina as mostly positive, negative themes did emerge during the period under analysis.

In the early 1980s, the print media portrayed European immigrants more favorably than Latin American ones. In 1987 the media still gave European immigration a special place. The number of positive terms and impacts associated with European immigrants is almost six times higher than the number for Latin Americans. One article speaks of European settlers coming "from other lands to help build modern Argentina" and "enrich[ing] our culture through their harmonious integration to our national tradition" (*Clarín* 06/27/1987). In the words of a different journalist, European immigrants came "prepared for everything, to work nonstop" (*Clarín* 08/07/1987). Thus, the mythical contribution of European immigration to the construction of a great Argentina also appeared in the media in 1987.

Surprisingly, immigration from bordering countries drew little attention from the press in 1987. Only three newspaper articles during this period mentioned immigration of this origin. One article, which was similar to a story published in the previous period, depicted the history of immigration to Argentina while completely disregarding immigration from nearby countries. In this piece, the journalist states that "forty years ago, Spanish, Italians and families from diverse nationalities constituted the last immigration wave to Argentina" (*Clarín* 08/07/1987). Its author appears to ignore that there were close to a million immigrants from bordering countries living in Argentina by 1987 and that most of these immigrants had arrived in the country during those last forty years. One possible explanation for this omission is that Argentines are less optimistic about the contributions by recent immigrants to the country, a narrative also common in the United States.

Interestingly, discrimination against immigrants from Southern Cone countries in Argentina seemed to be a central preoccupation of Pope John Paul II in 1987. During a visit to Argentina, the pope made immigration the central topic in one of his addresses. In a speech delivered in Paraná, a northeastern city in a region once called *pampa gringa* because of its high number of immigrants, the pope first reviewed the history of immigration to Argentina. He then exalted the contributions of the different groups of European immigrants to the local cultural and religious heritage and praised the great disposition of Argentine society to accept and integrate diverse groups of immigrants. In contrast to this disposition, the pope notes, in "some places there are persistent prejudices against immigrants" (*Clarín* 04/10/1987). According to the pope, these prejudices could be observed in the lack of affection and even hostility with which immigrants from neighboring countries were treated (*Clarín* 04/10/1987). He also made a call for Argentines to keep their hearts open. "If you welcomed immigrants from the Old World before," the pope claims, "do welcome your less privileged neighbors now" (*Clarín* 04/10/1987).

One immigrant group that was becoming increasingly visible in Argentina was Koreans. Unlike immigration from the Southern Cone, immigration from South Korea received attention from the press in 1987. South Korean immigration to Argentina became significant during the 1970s (Jeon 2005). At first, most Korean immigrants were of modest social background and settled in shantytowns in some Buenos Aires areas. During the 1980s, many of these immigrants came to the country with investment capital and formed a business class. Although devoted to diverse economic activities, they soon excelled in the textile industry, which had earlier been dominated by the Jewish community. At first, South Korean immigrants used Argentina as a stepping stone for their immigration to the United States. However, some thirty-six thousand South Korean immigrants lived in Argentina by 1985. Most of them settled in Buenos Aires and its surroundings.

The view of these settlers in the Argentine press was ambivalent, as a best-case scenario. For instance, one article describes the concentration of

South Korean immigrants in the neighborhood Flores Sur as the creation of a "Chinatown" in Buenos Aires (*Clarín* 05/11/1987). While this story positively portrays this new ethnic district as "colorful," "full of the magic characteristic of millenarian cultures," "bright," and "enigmatic," the author nevertheless seems concerned by the way Koreans are taking over this area of town. Examples of this concern are commenting that South Koreans had "invaded" Flores Sur or were "taking over the whole neighborhood." To prove these statements, the journalist provides a paragraph summarizing "what anyone who visits this Koreatown" could see: "gracious and seductive Korean ladies, Korean schoolchildren, Korean babies, female and male Koreans of all ages, sizes and condition appear everywhere." In this instance, the journalist uses iteration (Korean . . . , Korean . . . ,) to create the image that Korean immigrants are "everywhere." Likely, this statement is intended to produce a feeling of disapproval in the reader.

The ambivalence of the journalist can also be seen in another instance where he provides the reader with contrasting characterizations of Korean immigrants. On the one hand, the journalist describes these immigrants as "good neighbors, good people, and hardworking." He also points out that they are peaceful people who pay for everything with cash. On the other hand, he repeats several times that Korean immigrants do not speak Spanish and need the help of other members of their communities to get by in Argentina. He also explains that, while most Korean stores have signs both in Spanish and Korean, others exhibit signs in only Korean. After providing some success stories of South Koreans, he closes the story by saying, "They multiply. They multiply . . ." Once again, the journalist insinuates the idea that Korean immigration is somehow out of control.

Another story featuring South Korean immigration during this period is less ambiguous and more openly critical. Entitled "Koreans Advance over Businesses and Small Industries: From Seoul to Once," the article devotes half a page to describing illegal and semilegal ways in which South Korean immigrants are achieving economic success in the textile industry. According to the journalist, Korean businessmen have managed to lower costs by engaging in some illegal practices, like disregarding labor agreements and evading taxes. For this reason, the journalist states, the textile workers' union has been keeping an eye on these

Korean entrepreneurs. Apparently, certain union leaders maintain that Korean-owned businesses pay salaries at least 30 percent below the legal minimum, make people work between fourteen and sixteen hours a day, and employ children.

This story may have shocked readers in several ways. For starters, it alleges that Korean immigrants were breaking the law. As Gilroy (1991, 74) puts it, the law and the ideology of legality express and represent the nation and national unity. According to this concept, law is a national institution and adherence to its rule symbolizes the imagined community of the nation and expresses the fundamental unity and equality of its citizens. It therefore follows that if South Korean immigrants do not respect this national institution they could (should) be excluded from the national community. This story probably also outraged unions and working people alike over the way in which Korean businessmen allegedly treated workers. Overall, the view of South Korean immigration in the Argentine press in 1987 was not positive.

Argentine predilection for European immigration remained intact during this period. This region accounted for the substantial majority of the positive instances used to describe immigrants and their impact. At the same time, immigrants from the Southern Cone were largely ignored and their contributions overlooked. In turn, the press became progressively more critical of immigrants from South Korea. Overall, we can hypothesize that the ideas about European immigrants' appropriateness for membership in the national community may have influenced the enactment of special immigration rules for them.

EDITORIALS

This study identified seven editorial pieces during the periods under analysis, three of which are analyzed in this section. One of them, entitled "The Laotians in Argentina," was published in La Nación on October 17, 1983, and discusses the situation of Laotian refugees in the country. The various military governments during the Cold War had welcomed refugees fleeing communist regimes. In 1979 some three hundred families arrived from Laos, which had been under the control of communist forces since 1975, following a civil war further complicated by U. S. involvement in Southeast Asia during the Vietnam War (Vizcarra 2016). The story starts by recalling how the first Laotian immigrants arrived in Argentina in response to a special call by the United Nations Secretary General asking countries to accept immigrants from Vietnam, Laos, and Kampuchea (currently a territory of Cambodia).

Soon after their arrival in Argentina, these Laotian families received considerable attention from the press because of some complaints by neighbors that these immigrants were eating dogs. The author of the article, however, dismisses these stories as "isolated events that were given sensationalist tones." The journalist continues, "It is true that some of these immigrants have shown some adaptation problems, but these problems are common in cases of forced migration" (*La Nación* 10/17/1983). Later, the editorial goes on to describe some successes achieved by the Laotian refugees in Argentina, including that 85 percent of the chiefs of household were employed and their children had learned Spanish and were performing well in school. However, instead of praising the Laotian immigrants for integrating into society, the journalist gives credit to Argentines for not discriminating against them. According to the journalist, Argentines were hospitable because they do not discriminate against the Laotian immigrants on the basis of race or religion.

A second editorial piece, entitled "The Migratory Trend," was published in *Clarín* on October 23, 1983, and discusses emigration from and immigration to Argentina. The piece begins by lamenting that professionals, skilled workers, businessmen, and workers alike had emigrated from Argentina in previous years due to the economic situation and discrimination. I imagine that, by "discrimination," the author is referring to the persecution and killing of political opponents by the military government; however, the press was still censored at the time this piece was published and the author could not have been more explicit. In the preceding several years Argentina had lost hundreds of thousands of persons, the article explains, reversing the tendency of the country to attract immigration.

Next, the writer describes the different waves of immigration to Argentina, including those of Italians and Spaniards, Poles, people fleeing World War II, and immigrants from bordering countries. Unlike other stories on the history of immigration that ignored immigration from Latin

American countries, this one portrays an evenhanded picture of the different groups of people who have immigrated to Argentina over the years. After describing the "exodus" of Argentines from the country, the author makes a call to reestablish the conditions that once made Argentina an attractive country for immigration. "It is the responsibility of future rulers to create the conditions for [Argentines] to return to the country and to turn it into an appealing place for those who want to work" (*Clarín* 10/24/1983).

Another editorial, entitled "Argentina and Its Immigrants," published in *Clarín* on June 27, 1987, reflects on the newly announced opportunity for foreigners to vote in local elections in Buenos Aires. Like the article previously described, this piece provides a balanced picture of immigration to Argentina by praising the contributions of all immigrants, not just Europeans. The story opens with the criticism that even though Argentina proclaims to be open to all "the men of the world," in reality it does not support the civic incorporation of immigrants. According to the journalist, the country fails to promote the naturalization of those who become a fundamental part of the country.

"The contribution of men and women arrived from other lands has been consubstantial with the construction of Argentina as a modern nation," the writer continues (*Clarín* 06/27/1987). Despite this, he laments, Argentina does not follow other counties that promote naturalization and make it an automatic right, but instead remains respectful of immigrants' wishes and lets them decide if and when to become naturalized. Further, the author continues, calling these persons "foreigners" is utterly inappropriate and giving them the right to vote in local elections is just a first step in acknowledging that these immigrants have become an integral part of the Argentine nation.

As these editorials show, the portrayal of immigrants of non-European origin was less favorable than that of immigrants from Europe. However, an ideological divide between newspapers also became evident during this analysis. Whereas the pieces from *Clarín*, the center-left newspaper, were more positive about all immigration, the piece from *La Nación*, the center-right newspaper, was ambivalent about the contributions and integration of immigrants from Laos. The divide between the right- and left-leaning media would become more pronounced during later periods.

FACTORS SHAPING IMMIGRATION
POLICY DECISIONS IN THE 1980S

The immigration policies enacted during Alfonsín's term attempted to regularize the immigration status of all foreigners in 1984. This occurred despite the severity of the economic crisis. Human rights considerations and an Argentine tradition of granting residency to foreigners during democratic regimes likely influenced this decision. In addition, the existence of a positive view of immigrants and immigration in the press, coupled with a preoccupation with the emigration of Argentines, likely encouraged the enactment of the amnesty decree. Further, headlines and stories during this period did not problematize immigrants and immigration to Argentina.

As economic conditions worsened, Argentine immigration rules became stricter. While economic factors help us understand the approval of the general immigration rules in 1985 and 1987, they cannot account for the special immigration regime for European citizens passed in 1988. The persistence of a favorable view of Europeans for inclusion in the Argentine community likely shaped the immigration rules applicable to them. At the same time, less favorable treatment of South American and Asian immigration in the press possibly influenced the rules affecting non-European immigrants.

FOUR

Immigration Policies during Menem's Administration, 1989–1995

After the reestablishment of democracy in 1983, Alfonsín's government approved an amnesty for immigrants from neighboring countries. As the economic conditions worsened, however, the Argentine immigration rules became stricter (Calavita 1994; 2010). The persistence of a favorable view of European immigrants when compared with South American immigrants, however, may have influenced subsequent Argentine immigration policies, which exempted European immigrants from these stricter rules. This chapter explores the portrayal of immigrants in the Argentine press during the 1990s. Decree 1033/92 from June 26, 1992, approved a permissive amnesty for immigrants from neighboring countries, allowing them to apply for residency by furnishing proof of identity and date of entry into the country. The International Organization for Migration and the Catholic Church had lobbied for this measure during the first years of Menem's presidency.

In the midst of an economic crisis after the implementation of neoliberal economic policies, Menem's administration sought obedience and legitimacy (Breuilly 1994). In combination with other social groups, the

Argentine government signaled that Latin American immigrants were undesirable by scapegoating them for unemployment, crime, and most of the ills of Argentine society.[1] More specifically, the government tightened immigration controls in 1993 when Decree 2771/93, effective January 6, 1994, gave the Executive branch of the government extensive powers to deport immigrants caught in flagrante in the commission of a crime or engaged in the illegal occupation of dwellings, and mandated raids on suspected undocumented immigrants' dwellings. Further, Decree 1023/94, from July 5, 1994, approved new rules for the admission of foreign citizens and required a written job offer for immigrants seeking to reside in Argentina. However, a number of European countries were exempted from these strict new requirements. The Ministry of the Interior's Resolution 4632/94 formalized a plan from 1992 to facilitate permanent residency for immigrants from twenty-one countries of Central and Eastern Europe; these immigrants were required only to furnish proof of identity to migrate to Argentina. This plan was renewed until 2000, when it was replaced with a plan that benefited only Russians and Ukrainians.

ARGENTINA'S FOREIGN-BORN POPULATION IN 1991

The census of 1991 recorded 1,628,210 foreign-born citizens living in Argentina, 52 percent of whom were citizens from bordering countries, namely Brazil, Uruguay, Paraguay, Bolivia, and Chile (INDEC 1997). As shown in Table 4.1, in 1991 the rest of the foreign-born population was mainly composed of Italian (20 percent) and Spanish (14 percent) immigrants. Of the immigrants from bordering countries, one-third were from Paraguay and a similar proportion from Chile. These groups of immigrants were followed in importance by Bolivians (18 percent) and Uruguayans (16.5 percent). The pattern of new arrivals, however, changed during the 1990s. Paraguayan immigrants lost their first place to Bolivian ones (Texidó et al. 2003), while immigration from Uruguay and Chile became less pronounced. At the same time, the total number of immigrants increased between 1991 and 1992 by almost one million (Oteiza and Aruj 1997, 21). Fifty-six percent of the immigrants from bordering countries lived in either the city or the province of Buenos Aires.

Table 4.1. National Origin of the Foreign-Born Population in Argentina in 1991

Country of Origin	Percentage of the Foreign-Born Population
Italy	20
Paraguay	16
Chile	15
Spain	14
Bolivia	9
Uruguay	8
Poland	2
Other Countries	16
Total	100

Source: Census 1991, INDEC, Argentina

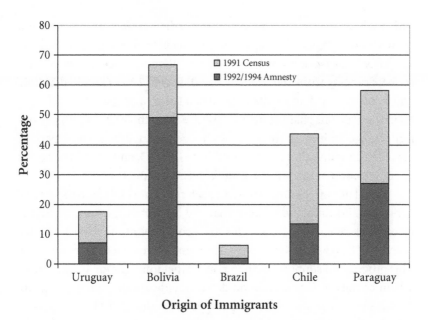

Figure 4.1. National Origin of Bordering Immigrants in 1991 and New Arrivals 1992/1994

Sources: Census 1991 and 1992 amnesty

Table 4.2. Total Number of Stories Coded by Year, Newspaper, and Origin of Immigration: 1992, 1993, and 1994

Origin of Immigrants	1992		1993		1994	
	La Nación	Página 12	La Nación	Página 12	La Nación	Página 12
European	6	5	–	–	–	3
L. American	5	6	10	21	18	15
Other	2	1	–	2	–	–
Total	13	12	10	23	18	17*

*The numbers don't add up because one story discussed both European and Latin American immigrants.

CULTURAL FACTORS SHAPING IMMIGRATION POLICIES: IMMIGRANTS IN THE PRINT MEDIA

This analysis investigates the Argentine media coverage on immigration in two main Argentine newspapers: *La Nación* (center-right) and *Página 12* (leftist). *La Nación* was founded in 1870 and has a number of subscribers ranging from 180,000 to 350,000. *Página 12* was founded in 1987 and as of 2017 had approximately 20,000 subscribers (see Appendix II). As in the previous chapter, media coverage from three six-month periods right before an immigration policy change was analyzed. These periods preceded executive decrees approved in 1992, 1993, and 1994. (For details about selection of stories and analysis, see Appendix II.)

A total of ninety-three articles was selected from both newspapers (see Table 4.2). Editorial pieces were analyzed separately due to their higher ideological content and biases. This study coded twenty-five articles for the year 1992, thirty-three articles for 1993, and thirty-five articles for 1994. This progression supports the observation that immigration became more salient as the economic situation deteriorated (Epstein and Segal 2000). As this study suggests, restrictive policy changes during 1993 and 1994 resulted from "collaboration" between journalists, unions, and government staff members.

Print media represent a fertile ground for exploring how "appropriate" certain groups are for inclusion in the Argentine imagined community. Again, per Foucault, language is an active political force "composed

Table 4.3. Topics in Headlines and Stories, by Year, Newspaper, and Type, in Percentages: 1992, 1993, and 1994

Topics	1992 La Nación	1992 Página 12	1993 La Nación	1993 Página 12	1994 La Nación	1994 Página 12
Government actions/decisions	73 (8)	18 (2)	20 (2)	35 (8)	50 (9)	17 (3)
Problems w/ immigration	18 (2)	–	70 (7)	30 (7)	50 (9)	11 (2)
Mocks/criticizes gov't policy	–	73 (8)	–	21 (5)	–	61 (14)
Other	9 (1)	9 (1)	10 (1)	13 (3)	–	11 (2)

of practices that systematically form the objects of which they speak" (1972). In the ninety-three stories analyzed, four main themes and topics were identified in the headlines (see Table 4.3). As this analysis will continue to show, the type and frequency of these themes and topics depended on the type of immigration covered (Latin American versus European), the social/economic context at the time of publication, and the political bias of the newspaper under consideration.

As in the previous analysis, this study traces the terms and themes used to characterize immigrants and immigration, key expressions that readers can easily recall (Van Dijk 1994). The terms were again coded as *positive* or *negative,* while the themes were classified as *benefits* or as *problems* (see Table 4.4). A total of 693 instances were coded in the three periods under consideration, 12 percent of which were coded as positive and 88 percent as negative.

Finally, the last part of this chapter covers the analysis of open editorials by guest writers about immigration that appeared in *La Nación* and *Página 12* during the same periods. As the numbers show, the frequency of editorials increased over the years as the sense of an "immigration crisis" that started in 1993 deepened. Because *La Nación* had no open editorials for 1992 and 1993, the analysis is limited to one editorial from *La Nación* from 1994 and two from *Página 12,* one from 1992 and one from 1994. The content of the editorials depended on the agenda and characteristics of the author, but, more importantly, on the newspaper that published them.

WELCOMING ARGENTINA: MEDIA COVERAGE IN 1992

President Alfonsín resigned in 1989 because of the intense economic crisis, and President Menem, who had already been elected, assumed power early. Alfonsín's economic policies had failed to keep hyperinflation in check. Following advice by multilateral organizations, Menem embarked on several market-oriented and labor reforms. The establishment of peso–dollar convertibility in March 1991—which made possible the exchange of one peso for one dollar—provided macroeconomic stability (Pastor and Wise 1999). In addition, broad privatizations provided Argentina with a cash flow that kept the economy running. The gross domestic product grew by 9.6 percent in 1992 (Rapoport 2000). Within the stable macroeconomic scenario of 1992, the Argentine government passed two favorable policy decisions affecting immigrants: a plan to encourage immigration from Central and Eastern Europe and an amnesty for immigrants from neighboring countries.

During this period, media coverage was evenly split between European and Latin American immigrants and was, overall, positive about immigration, at least in comparison to later periods (see Table 4.2). An exploration of the headline topics by newspaper sheds light on the differing treatment of immigration groups by the right- and left-wing media. More specifically, whereas *La Nación* (right wing) celebrated the plan to bring Central and Eastern Europeans to Argentina, *Página 12* (leftist) supported the amnesty for immigrants from neighboring countries. As Table 4.3 shows, the topics of the headlines during this period were of three main types: government actions and decisions regarding immigration, problems related to immigration, and mockery or criticism of government actions and decisions.

While *La Nación* applauded government decisions or measures related to immigration in 73 percent of the articles coded (see Table 4.3), *Página 12* tended to mock government decisions in the same proportion of articles. For instance, *La Nación* was optimistic about the government's proposal to bring immigrants from European countries and employed headlines such as "Argentina Will Receive European Immigrants" (*La Nación* 01/25/1992) and "The Proposal to Receive Immigrants from the Former USSR" (*La Nación* 01/31/1992).[2] These articles enthusiastically described the government's plan to bring in one hundred thousand European immigrants and evoked the economic growth and development Argentina had witnessed during the golden years of European immigration. The plan to bring European immigrants was supposed to include financial support for immigrant families as well as language classes. It is worth noting that never in the history of Argentina was there a plan to provide Latin American immigrants with government funds.

Página 12, on the other hand, was skeptical about the government's proposal to bring in European immigrants and implied it was unrealistic, unfeasible, or directed to attract white immigrants. One headline, stating "Here Come the Russians but Broke," referred to the difficulties the government faced in obtaining financial support from the European Economic Community (EEC) for its plan (*Página 12* 01/25/1992). In this article, Foreign Affairs Minister Guido Di Tella explained that, if financed by the EEC, the plan to bring Europeans to Argentina could represent a solution for everyone: Argentina could receive financial support and Europe would solve the "problem of immigration" from former communist countries. The Argentine government never obtained financial support for its plan to bring in Eastern and Central Europeans. Nonetheless, the plan was approved by the minister of the interior in 1992 and extended multiple times until 2000. When Decree 1023/94 approved the new, stricter immigration rules, Eastern and Central Europeans were exempted.

On February 14, 1992, another *Página 12* story, called "Not the Brown People" (Morochos Inviables), reported the Argentine government's presentation of its plan to bring Central and Eastern Europeans before the European Parliament. During this presentation, the Argentine government claimed this plan would help the "immigration crisis in Western Europe," purportedly caused by an actual or potential massive influx of Central and Eastern Europeans. The Belgian prime minister responded to the Argentine delegation by stating that, if Argentina wanted to help Europe, it should recruit the Algerian and Moroccan immigrants living in Europe instead of the immigrants from former communist countries the Argentine government wanted. The Argentine government turned down the offer.

Página 12 mocked the Argentine government's lack of acceptance of this offer and used the headline to imply their decision was racist. In the same story, the undersecretary of population, Germán Moldes, justified the government's decision by saying that immigrants from Africa were not a "good fit" because Argentina needed immigrants who could bring capital, were from a country with technology similar to that of Argentina, and had a community of co-ethnics already established in the country (*Página 12* 02/14/1992). The Argentine government was looking for immigrants of European background similar to those whom Sarmiento (1959) and Alberdi (1966) had dreamed about. These headlines are a first indication that, while *La Nación* tended to idealize European immigrants like the Argentine intellectuals of the 1800s, *Página 12* was less likely to do so and used humor to criticize the government's preferential treatment of European immigration.

The positions of the newspapers were reversed when it came to the coverage of immigration from other Latin American countries. *La Nación* conveyed problems associated with immigration in its headlines, but *Página 12* did not. For example, during a cholera outbreak in Argentina's neighboring countries, a February 10, 1992, article from *La Nación* alarmingly reported an incident in which immigrants from Bolivia were deported as "Illegal Emigrants." The article details an event in which thirty immigrants from Bolivia were arrested and given medical treatment for cholera. These immigrants had paid a coyote to find work in Argentina. After treatment, the Bolivians were to be deported to their home country. *Página 12* responded on February 20, 1992, by mocking the Argentine government's scapegoating of Bolivians for transmitting cholera as "The Plague: Bolitas Go Home."

The first part of the *Página 12* response headline seems to make reference to Albert Camus's novel *The Plague*, which tells the story of a cholera outbreak that swept the Algerian city of Oran. *Bolitas* is a pejorative term used by Argentines to refer to immigrants from Bolivia. "Go Home" seems to allude to stories about Mexicans painting the legend "Greens Go Home" during the Mexican American War, asking American soldiers to leave the country. The phrase "Bolitas Go Home" clearly conveys the message that Bolivian immigrants are not welcome in Argentina. This article explained, "Those [in the government] with a sickening nationalism take advantage of this opportunity to discriminate against Bolivian immigrants." Another article, entitled "About Discrimination," reinforced this last point (*Página 12* 02/22/1992).

On April 5, 1992, *La Nación* announced the amnesty for Latin American immigrants with a headline stating "Immigrants in Argentina: Chronicle of an Amnesty Foretold." This headline references Gabriel García Márquez's novel *Chronicle of a Death Foretold*. Although a literary analysis of the novel is beyond the scope of this work, suffice it to say that the word *amnesty* could be replaced with the word *death* in the headline. This article is very nostalgic about the old waves of European immigration. "Maybe the legend of a generous land keeps attracting immigrants to Argentina, but let's be honest, they are not those colonist immigrants from the past but a handful of people in search of new horizons," the article explains.

On the other hand, *Página 12*'s headlines broadcast the amnesty for immigrants from neighboring countries with neutral expressions, such as "Immigrants: Amnesty from Las Leñas," from the March 15, 1992, issue. This article describes how the government decided to grant amnesty to undocumented immigrants living in Argentina to avoid situations of "injustice and exploitation." However, it also states that undocumented immigrants present unfair competition to Argentine labor. The article discusses public opinion polls among the general population, commissioned by the government, which show that there was "a high degree of receptivity" to the idea of granting amnesty to undocumented immigrants. This article is overall more positive about the idea of granting residency to Latin American undocumented immigrants than the article from *La Nación*.

An examination of the themes and terms used to refer to immigrants reveals similar findings. As mentioned before, these themes and terms influence the consideration given to immigrants by the public (Hier and Greenberg 2002). Thus, if immigrants are defined as illegal and associated with problems, they will likely not be welcome in the community. Out of the 117 instances coded, 48 percent were positive and 52 percent negative (see Table 4.4). Although the majority of instances were coded as negative, the coverage of immigration during this period was favorable to immigrants compared with the later periods, during which the proportion of negative instances went up to 96 percent and 95 percent.

An analysis of immigration coverage by newspaper and immigrant group showed, once more, that *La Nación* was substantially more optimistic about European immigration and much less so about Latin American

Table 4.4. Instances Coded by Year, Newspaper, and Type, in Percentages and Absolute Numbers: 1992, 1993, and 1994

Instances	1992			1993			1994		
	La Nación	Página 12	Total	La Nación	Página 12	Total	La Nación	Página 12	Total
Total	46	71	117	84	254	338	132	106	238
Negative total	48 (22)	55 (39)	52 (61)	98 (82)	95 (242)	96 (324)	93 (123)	96 (102)	95 (225)
. . . Term	45 (10)	33 (13)	38 (23)	24 (20)	26 (62)	25 (82)	25 (31)	19 (19)	22 (50)
. . . Amplification	14 (3)	5 (2)	8 (5)	6 (5)	8 (20)	8 (25)	8 (10)	5 (5)	7 (15)
. . . Objectification	14 (3)	28 (11)	23 (14)	5 (4)	7 (17)	6 (21)	8 (10)	2 (2)	5 (12)
. . . Problems	27 (6)	33 (13)	31 (19)	65 (53)	59 (143)	61 (197)	59 (72)	74 (76)	66 (148)
Positive total	52 (24)	45 (32)	48 (56)	2 (2)	5 (12)	4 (14)	7 (9)	4 (4)	5 (13)
. . . Terms	42 (10)	22 (7)	30 (17)		50 (6)	43 (6)	22 (2)	75 (3)	38 (5)
. . . Benefits	58 (14)	78 (25)	70 (39)	100 (2)	50 (6)	57 (8)	78 (7)	25 (1)	62 (8)

immigration than *Página 12*. Seventy-one percent of the positive instances coded in *La Nación* referred to European immigrants, while that number for *Página 12* was 50 percent. In turn, 91 percent of the negative instances coded in *La Nación* were used in reference to Latin American immigrants, while that figure for *Página 12* was 69 percent. In addition, qualitative differences existed between the coverage of both groups of immigrants in the two newspapers under consideration.

In 1992 migrants were generally treated respectfully compared to later periods. Thirty percent of the positive instances coded corresponded to positive terms used to refer to immigrants and 70 percent to benefits (see Table 4.4). Out of the instances showing respect for immigrants, stories referred to immigrants as "immigrants," "citizens," or "brothers"—for instance, "immigrant families" (*La Nación* 06/19/1992), "citizens of Bolivia" (*Página 12* 02/20/1992), or "our brothers." The impact of immigration on Argentine society was also considered advantageous during this period. Further, benefits associated with immigration were mentioned twice as frequently as risks. Among the desirable impacts of immigration, the most common was economic growth and prosperity, which appeared in 54 percent of the cases.

Not all immigration, however, was considered equally beneficial. The favorable impact on the economy was attributed to immigration from Europe. As mentioned above, in the period between January and June 1992, the project to bring immigrants from Central and Eastern Europe was intensely debated in the newspapers. Some of the opinions supporting this plan resemble ideas of Sarmiento and Alberdi: ideas that Argentina needed European immigration to improve or replace the racially mixed Argentine masses. For instance, on three occasions in 1992 (February 13, February 20, and April 1), Alberdi's famous phrase "to govern is to populate" appeared in *La Nación* to support the government plan to attract European immigration.

Foreign Minister Di Tella, when asked about reasons to encourage European immigration, stated, "In Argentina as well as in the United States, immigration is associated with a process that was very positive in the past" (*La Nación* 02/13/1992). Or, in the words of Vice Minister of Foreign Affairs Fernando Petrella, "Immigration from fast-growing countries brings some of that push with it" (*Página 12* 02/05/1992). As these quotes show, European immigration was expected to foster growth and economic prosperity as it had in the nineteenth and early twentieth centuries. However, immigration from Latin American countries was not.

Were other immigrants also romanticized? An analysis of the benefits attributed to Latin American immigration during the discussion of the amnesty favoring Latin American immigrants that passed in 1992 sheds light on this question. In comparison to the coverage of European immigration, the portrayal of migrants from Latin America was less favorable. Some instances, however, expressed some constructive, though modest, effects of Latin American immigration. These discourses did not link immigration from the region to the development and/or economic growth of the country. In general, they limited themselves to an acknowledgment that neighboring migrants "did work" and made a contribution to the Argentine economy.

For instance, one *La Nación* story stated, "The majority of those persons, even without the necessary legal documents, develop activities that are useful for the country" (*La Nación* 06/27/1992). As we can see, most favorable statements call for "tolerating" immigrants from Latin America. Also telling is a statement by the Bolivian minister of the interior, in *Página 12*, that "immigrants [from Bolivia] come to work in Argentina and they do not deserve to be treated as criminals" (*Página 12* 03/31/1992). I believe this plea by the Bolivian official reveals the discriminatory attitudes and actions toward Latin American immigrants that were common at the time.

Negative references to immigrants during this period included 69 percent negative terms and descriptions and 31 percent problems (see Table 4.4). Further, 77 percent of these negative references were used in connection to immigrants from the Southern Cone. The most common negative terms used to describe immigrants were *illegal* and *clandestine* (*ilegal* and *clandestino*) (52 percent of the negative terms coded). In addition, words describing and exaggerating the numbers of immigrants (amplification) in Argentina comprised 8 percent of the negative instances coded. For example, "massive" was often used in reference to immigration, and *La Nación* used the word *exodus* on February 10, 1992, to refer to a small number of Bolivian undocumented immigrants deported from the north of Argentina.

Also, newspapers reported undocumented immigration numbers without justifying these numbers (Van Dijk 1994). Both newspapers, for example, reported an estimate of 500,000 undocumented immigrants while only 230,000 regularized their immigration status through amnesty. As these numbers show, the number of undocumented immigrants present in Argentina in 1992 was overestimated. Finally, 23 percent of the negative instances coded treated immigrants as objects, animals, or plants. Stories referred to the "import" and "export" of immigrants, the "herd of immigrants," and the "implantation of immigrants" on Argentine soil. Perhaps the depiction of immigrants as objects has a dehumanizing effect, which allows the formation of negative attitudes about immigration among readers.

The themes used to describe immigrants, as discussed previously, are also an indication of where immigrants stand in relation to the imagined community (Hier and Greenberg 2002). The discussion of problems associated with immigration was four to five times less frequent in 1992 than in 1993 to 1994, appearing in 31 percent of the negative instances coded (see Table 4.4). Additionally, this study found no specific negative themes that repeatedly appeared in the news articles associated with immigrants. This evidence, together with the moderately low occurrence of negative terms and themes, shows that a structured exclusionary discourse was not working to keep immigrants out of Argentina.

In *La Nación*, problems associated with immigrants were exclusively limited to Latin American immigrants and included entering the country illegally, running away from cholera, and not providing education for their children. In contrast, *Página 12* showed a degree of compassion toward Latin American immigrants by portraying problems "affecting them" (Van Dijk 1994) and not just "caused by them" (38 percent of the total number of problems coded in this newspaper). For example, some stories explained that immigrants worked long hours and suffered inhumane conditions, including bad nutrition, poor housing, and poor health conditions. This higher degree of compassion toward Latin American immigrants illustrates the differences between the right-wing and more liberal presses (Van Dijk 1994).

JULY TO DECEMBER 1993: THE PERIOD BEFORE THE NEW DEPORTATION PROVISIONS WERE PASSED

Menem's government had adopted neoliberal economic policies at the onset of the decade, and in 1993 unemployment rose from 6.9 to 9.9 percent (Rapoport 2000, 1019), signaling the beginning of an economic downturn. In December the government passed Decree 2771/93, enabling the Executive to deport migrants who broke the law. Possibly, this decree was the consequence of a kind of immigration crisis fostered by interactions between certain state officials, labor unions, and the media (Cook et al. 1983). State officials, reacting to demands from the unions, blamed immigrants for most social ills during a successful campaign to disguise the failure of the economic plan. "It is always easier to blame outsiders," a high-ranking official of the Immigration Agency told me.[3] Sometimes public officials were reacting more to the "political temperature of immigration" than to what was truly occurring with immigration.[4] *Página 12* stated that when the deportation provisions were passed, nine out of ten Argentines thought immigration was hurting local labor (*Página 12* 12/09/1993). Immigration restrictions became instrumental for the state in that they helped dissipate fears that the economic plan was failing.[5] Even though the Catholic Church resisted the scapegoating of immigrants, it did not stop.[6]

In this climate, the media coverage on immigration became highly negative and almost exclusively about Latin American immigration. The main themes reproduced in headlines during this period were government actions and decisions regarding immigration, problems related to immigration, and mockery or criticism of government actions and decisions (see Table 4.3). As in the previous period, the occurrence and frequency of these themes depended on the newspaper under analysis. For example, whereas 70 percent of the headlines from *La Nación* portrayed immigration as problematic, this number for *Página 12* was only 35 percent. *La Nación*'s article of October 25, 1992, "Many Immigrants Don't Dare to Show Up [to regularize their status]," made the unlikely implication that many immigrants who could have benefited from the amnesty just refused to do so.

This October 25 *La Nación* article portrays the amnesty process as a big, corrupt business. To be sure, corruption scandals related to amnesty existed at the time and several middlemen offered their services outside of the National Directorate of Migration building. But the article also describes immigrants in a stereotypical and somewhat racist way. For example, it talks about immigrants as an "army of bags who land in the city every morning." This statement likely refers to the many bordering immigrants who work in construction and carry a bag with a change of clothes.

Another article, entitled "Seven out of Ten Immigrants Are Still Illegal," also problematizes immigration from neighboring countries (*La Nación* 10/25/1992). It estimates the number of undocumented immigrants in the country at close to half a million and claims that only one-third of them had processed their paperwork. At the end of the amnesty period in December 1992, however, it became clear that the numbers estimating undocumented immigration were inflated.

Thirty-five percent of *Página 12*'s headlines responded to the problematization of immigration by mocking, ridiculing, or criticizing government actions (30 percent of the headlines) (see Table 4.3). One headline of this type stated, "The Government Blames Immigrants for the Illegal Occupation of Dwellings: Little Black Heads" (*Página 12* 07/31/1993). The phrase *little black heads* (*cabecitas negras*) is a pejorative term used to refer to a person of mestizo origin and was used by the Argentine elites in the 1940s when President Perón's industrialization attracted migrants from the provinces of Argentina, many of indigenous origin. In this case, the addition of this phrase implied that the journalist believed the government's scapegoating of immigrants was racist. This story reproduced declarations by government officials in relation to a decision by the government to evict some illegal occupants of dwellings—supposed to be immigrants—without a court order. These headlines show that a process of defining immigrants as problematic, and contestation of that definition, took place between the two newspapers.

In addition, while another 20 percent of *La Nación*'s headlines discussed actions and decisions by the government in response to immigration, *Página 12* tended to mock, ridicule, or criticize those decisions as well. For example, when *La Nación* announced on November 21, 1993, "The Government Will Regulate the Admission of Foreign Workers," *Página 12* reported the same event on the same day with the phrase "The Sound of Broken Chains." These articles covered the government announcement of the future passage of Decree 1023/94, which would require a written job contract in order to be eligible for a work visa. The story by *La Nación* reported this government decision to restrict immigration in a celebratory way. It quoted Minister of the Interior Carlos Ruckauf as stating that the objective of the new immigration rules would be "to put an end to the immigration drawn to a successful country that receives mass immigration and is not ready for it" (*La Nación* 11/21/1993). The headline in *Página 12*, on the other hand, was critical of the government decision. More specifically, it alluded to a part of the national anthem which refers to the freedom gained after independence from Spain and implied that the national ideal of freedom does not include Latin American immigrants under the new government regulations (*Página 12* 11/21/1993).

An examination of the terms and themes used to characterize immigration reveals an even more negative picture. Of the 338 instances coded during this period, 4 percent were positive and 96 percent negative (see Table 4.4). Overall, immigrants during this period were considered much less favorably than in the previous period. Of the few positive instances, 43 percent were terms and descriptors and 57 percent were references to benefits associated with immigration. Further, 88 percent of these positive instances occurred in *Página 12*: positive words used to characterize immigrants included *workers* (appeared on November 20 and 21, 1993) and *citizens* (appeared on August 13, 1993).

Benefits linked to immigration encompassed two quotes from the decree granting amnesty to Latin American immigrants, which stated that even though immigrants lack the necessary paperwork (to work in Argentina) they "develop activities that are useful for the country" (*La Nación* 10/25/1993; *Página 12* 11/05/1993). Another benefit attributed to immigration outlined the advantages of low-cost labor by stating, "Cheap labor allows for a better service" (*Página 12* 07/16/1993). As these numbers and examples show, the positive coverage of immigration during this period was both quantitatively and qualitatively slim.

Negative instances concerning immigrants during this period included 39 percent negative terms and descriptions and 61 percent problems (see Table 4.4). Not only did the proportion of negative instances rise from 52 to 96 percent, but the proportion of problems reportedly linked to immigration also climbed from 31 to 61 percent from the previous period (see Table 4.4). The most common negative words employed to identify immigrants continued to be *illegal* and *clandestine*, appearing in 32 percent of the cases. In addition, the word *slaves* appeared in 10 percent of the cases in *Página 12* in reference to Latin American immigrants. The use of this term, which first turned up in 1992 and became more pronounced in 1994, established a dichotomy between "free-Argentine labor" and "slave-migrant labor." Also, because of the history of slavery, the word *slave* implies that immigrants were highly racialized.

The most important problems associated with immigration were increased unemployment, displacement of the native labor force, and depressing salaries (71 percent). Immigrants were accused of taking jobs from Argentines, accepting lower salaries, and presenting unfair competition for Argentines. Once immigrants are blamed for taking jobs from Argentines and creating additional hardships, they become "undesirable" members of the community. But these problems were not established in an objective or scientific way. Furthermore, even public officials have acknowledged that they were aware of studies that showed the impact of immigration on unemployment was minimal. In general, a nationalistic rhetoric accompanied the statements that served to create a boundary between "us" and "them." Ruckauf, for instance, declared that the government "will regulate the admission of foreign citizens with the objective of prioritizing jobs for Argentines" (*La Nación* 11/21/1993). The government then implied that immigration restrictions would benefit Argentine labor (Andreas 1999).

Also, the minister of the interior stated in *La Nación*, on December 3, 1993, that "the 45,000 new jobs that the government expects to create next year are an important political motivation to put an end to illegal immigration." As we can see, these statements not only hold immigration responsible for Argentina's economic problems but also aim to draw a line between "us," Argentines, and "them," immigrants who cause trouble. Even more divisive is the comment by Gerardo Martinez, leader of the construction workers' union, that "many times foreign workers take more the side of the employer than the side of the union" (*Página 12* 08/03/1993). Therefore, while at least part of the government was aware that the impact of immigration on unemployment was not significant, immigrants were scapegoated to keep the public believing that their government was acting in their interest when policy changes took place (Migdal 2001).

While the supposed negative impact of immigration provided the reason to discursively marginalize immigrants, the reference to them as "slave labor" added legitimacy by casting the cause as "protecting natives from the unfair competition" produced by "these slaves." The portrayal of immigrants as slave labor legitimizes the exclusion of immigrants in the name of the higher value of freedom. For instance, Alberto Mazza, minister of health, said of immigrants, "These workers are highly marginal since if that wasn't the case, they wouldn't agree to work as slaves" (*Página 12* 12/03/1993). Or, as Ruckauf put it in the same story, "We don't want more slave workers to come [to the country], because they cause us serious labor, sanitary, and security problems." It is also interesting that this discourse appeared at the moment when the government was pressuring the unions to accept a labor law reform, which would take away many of the social rights won during the postwar period.

IMMIGRATION COVERAGE IN 1994: NEW AND STRICT RULES FOR ADMISSION OF FOREIGN CITIZENS

The economic situation in 1994 continued to deteriorate. The gross domestic product contracted by 4.4 percent, and by the end of the year, Argentina had entered a recession. As a result, the newspaper coverage of immigration issues in 1994 mostly showed a continuation of the "immigration crisis" theme initiated in 1993. However, in *La Nación* the problematization of immigration in the headlines increased and the types of problems associated with immigration became more serious.

The contrast in immigration coverage between both newspapers continued to be noteworthy. During this period, as the problematization of immigration in *La Nación* increased by 20 percent, the criticism or mockery of government decisions and actions in *Página 12* almost tripled (see Table 4.3). For example, on January 29, 1994, *La Nación* again exaggerated the number of undocumented immigrants living in the country, stating that "Four Hundred Thousand Illegal Immigrants Still Live in Argentina," though the number of immigrants who applied for residency under the amnesty was 230,000. Although it is possible that new immigrants entered the country after the amnesty started, it is unlikely, if not impossible, that the number of undocumented immigrants could have increased by so much, so quickly, especially considering that new immigrants could not benefit from the amnesty. But it seems equally improbable that so many eligible immigrants would have decided not to apply.

Also, 50 percent of the immigration-related headlines by *La Nación* denounced problems related to undocumented immigration. For instance, one article, entitled "Illegality and Promiscuity Coexist One Step Away from the City," attempted to create a sharp contrast between immigrant living conditions and the upscale Buenos Aires financial district (*La Nación* 08/19/1994). The article created this contrast by using the English word *City* to refer to the financial district, a practice of the English-speaking upper classes in Argentina, after mentioning the supposedly widespread problems created by immigrants. This story discussed the problems created by Peruvian (and some Argentine) squatters who lived in an old hotel that had been raided the previous week. It portrayed the hotel as a place where poverty was intertwined with illegality. It also described some of the residents, one of whom had a "dark complexion," as people who seemed fearful and distrustful.

In contrast, *Página 12* continued to be critical of the poor treatment of immigrants by the government and others. One article, headlined "They Call Us Thieves," stated that immigrants were accused of being thieves and quoted complaints by Chilean immigrants about discrimination experienced in Argentine society (*Página 12* 02/06/1993). This article discusses an incident during which a Chilean flag was burned. The ambassador from Chile is featured in the story. Chilean immigrants describe different discriminatory comments Argentines made to them, such as, "Chilean thieves, if you have something it is because you stole it" and "What are you doing here, why don't you go back to Chile?" The Chilean ambassador, however, reports being satisfied with the Argentine government's condemnation of the burning of the Chilean flag.

In general, the newspaper coverage of immigration issues in 1994 recapitulates that of 1993, but some differences are apparent upon closer inspection. Although the negativity of the overall coverage decreases very slightly, from 96 to 95 percent, the content of the negative instances changes. For one thing, the mention of problems associated with immigrants increases from 61 to 66 percent of the total negative instances (see Table 4.4). For another, there is an increased criminalization of migrants, including a more widespread use of the term *illegal,* which encompasses 62 percent of the negative terms used to refer to migrants. Also noticeable is a change in the definition of the risks linked to immigration, especially crime, which grows from 40 to 55 percent as articles stress the association between crime and immigration.

The generalizing discourse leads the reader to associate immigration with illegality, breaking the law, and disrespecting national institutions. As Paul Gilroy states, the law and the ideology of legality express and represent the nation and national unity. Law is "primarily a national institution, and adherence to its rule symbolizes the imagined community of the nation and expresses the fundamental unity and equality of its citizens" (Gilroy 1991, 74). As soon as the association between immigration and lawbreaking is established, migrants can be excluded from the national community without regret. To reinforce the association of immigrants and illegality, newspaper articles in this study constantly referred to the legal problems created by immigration. Examples include Minister of the Interior Ruckauf's justification for increasing immigration controls to prevent "tourists from becoming illegal workers" (*Página 12* 09/12/1993) or as "thwarting any opportunity for criminal acts" (*Página 12* 12/23/1993). The criminalization of immigrants, however, reached its apogee in the press coverage of 1994, when 55 percent of the references to risks associated with immigration pertained to illegal or criminal activities.

Providing a legal justification for such exclusion, the government passed Decree 2771/93. This decree was "intended to cope with the serious problems posed by the illegal occupation of houses and other crimes that disturb social peace," supposedly caused by immigrants from the region. To face this "serious problem," the Executive needed an "agile and effective methodology that facilitates the immediate deportation of illegal immigrants" (Decree 2771/93). According to *Página 12,* with the passage of this decree "the government puts in the same bag both migrants and the reports regarding the illegal occupation of dwellings" (*Página 12* 01/07/1994).

Increasing association between immigrants and crime was also related to irregularities detected in some visa applications involving government officials, diplomats, and some middlemen used by immigrants to file their paperwork. As reported by *La Nación* on December 11, 1993, on that date the government prohibited the participation of middlemen for the remainder of the amnesty period. Several articles in *La Nación* (January 26, January 28, and January 31, 1994) and *Página 12* (January 27, January 28, and February 1, 1994) expanded on different details of these irregularities.

As immigrants became increasingly criminalized, the discourse of public officials became more threatening in its tone. Ruckauf emphasized in *La Nación* on January 11, 1994, that "any illegal foreigner who is discovered violating the law will be repatriated." Ruckauf further observed that the Executive would intensify border controls and would solicit competitive bids to computerize the posts of immigration entry at the border. Additionally, Decree 2771/93 increased control powers of the Executive, facilitating inspections that would become common in the second half of 1994. As is often the case, those inspections rarely targeted employers; rather, most of them were conducted in hotels, apartments, and other places where immigrants lived. Such immigration controls may help demarcate the boundaries of the imagined community.

The government accompanied these discursive practices with control measures. In 1994 the Immigration Agency signed an agreement with the Argentine Tax Agency to conduct joint inspections at workplaces and hotels, as the Immigration Agency did not have enough resources to conduct inspections.[7] This was intended to increase the Immigration Agency's capacity for controlling undocumented work without devoting more resources to it.[8] After this agreement was signed, enforcement of immigration regulations increased. Out of the 115 inspections conducted in 1994 and 1995, 80 were done in combination with the Tax Agency.[9] During these inspections, the government detected 151 infractions of immigration regulations. At the same time, the auxiliary immigration police force, Gendarmería Nacional, likely increased its enforcement as well. While it detected 816 undocumented workers in 1994, this number climbed to 3,092 in 1995 and to 5,259 in 1996.[10]

Some articles show the role of immigration controls and inspections in marking out nonmembers of the community. One story in *Página 12* referred to the decree containing deportation provisions as "a way of putting in black and white the problem of illegal immigration" (*Página 12* 01/07/1994). As soon as the decree was passed, thirty citizens of Peru were deported; this was followed by Ruckauf's threatening message in *La Nación* that those deportations "were meant to teach a lesson" (*La Nación* 01/11/1994). In a similar vein, Foreign Affairs Vice Minister Fernando Petrella stated that "these deportations are framed in the new immigration policy that the country will have, and these persons were not only not complying with the immigration regulations, but were also committing an infraction" (*Página 12* 01/16/1994). These visible controls have strong symbolic meanings that project a favorable image of statehood and relegitimize the boundaries of the imagined community (Andreas 1999).

The beginning of 1994 coincided with the deadline to apply for the amnesty benefits. Several newspaper articles accordingly devoted space to describing the long lines and other difficulties facing immigrants applying for residency. Many of these articles also featured interviews with immigrants. Following Van Dijk's (1994) argument that, in part, immigration news coverage is unsympathetic to immigrants because journalists rarely ask immigrants or immigrant groups for information, I expected to find a correlation between news that relies on immigrants and immigrant groups as sources of information and a more sympathetic treatment of immigration. Surprisingly, I did not find a correlation between the two. Furthermore, some articles that at first sight seemed to show concern for the problems facing migrants applying for residency turned out to be offensively racist. For instance, the following appeared in *La Nación*:

> The spectacle of some 60 people lying on the street is pretty sad. Darkness and lack of hygiene are not good company for the night. They know it better than anyone: "and . . . what do you want me to do?" they seem to justify themselves; "If I don't come at this time I will be left out of my papers," explained a man who wasn't above 30, bag in hand, just out from the construction site. (January 24, 1994)

> Yesterday could be nominated as the Day of the Undocumented Migrant, when during the day a great amount of "irregulars" crowded the surroundings of the National Directorate of Migration . . . , joining the ones that had preferred to spend the night there. (February 1, 1994)

> This open space [yard inside the National Directorate of Migration building] resembled a camping site, with groups of families sitting or lying under trees while alleviating their thirst with cold drinks. Bits of conversation in Quechua intermingled with the noise from portable radios, the crying of babies, and the noise of the parrots. (February 1, 1994)

> The day after the amnesty deadline aimed at the regularization of migrants from neighboring countries, the National Directorate of Migration closed its doors to conduct a more than symbolic task: disinfect the environment. (February 6, 1994)

These articles are interesting because they do not emphasize major impacts of immigration. By merely describing with contempt the disorderly situation produced by migrants in front of the Immigration Agency, they are intended to shock the white population of Argentina. I consider these articles to belong in the category of traditional racism (Gilroy 1991).

SPEAK UP: EDITORIALS ON IMMIGRATION

Eight open editorials were identified in both newspapers during the period under analysis. The editorial entitled "Those of Us from the North" was published in *Página 12* on February 22, 1992. Its author was a Radical Party representative, Normando Alvarez García, from Jujuy, a northern province. This article clearly supports immigration from other Latin American countries. Alvarez García begins by showing that the cholera outbreak had triggered xenophobic reactions. He is especially alarmed by a statement about bordering immigrants made by Peronist Party representative Irma Roy to the press days earlier that "these populations are not cultured, have no education; what can we expect from them?"

Representative Alvarez García goes on to explain that maybe, in the north of Argentina, a more conservative and insulated area of the country, some businesspeople's pejorative attitudes toward indigenous populations were not uncommon. However, he points out, a member of Congress expressing similar attitudes undermines the role assigned to democratic state powers. According to him, Representative Roy's statement is proof of her own intellectual limitations. He goes on, "It is the role of those in power to defend cultural diversity, the right of each community to its own social customs, and above all, equality before the law." As this statement shows, Alvarez García took diversity and equality seriously. Further, he describes Roy's statement as belonging to a type of thinking that is totalitarian, dogmatic, and dictatorial. To be sure, Roy was not the only one making accusations against immigrants. For instance, the minister of health blamed Bolivia for a cholera outbreak in *Página 12* on February 20, 1992. Alvarez García, however, characterizes cholera as a serious disease that affects the poor populations and should be a cause for concern. He later states that observing how public officials contradict themselves highlights the importance of scientific opinions based on experience, knowledge, and altruism for those living outside of the First World.

The article entitled "Terrifying Numbers" appeared in *La Nación* on April 21, 1994. This editorial was written by Amílcar Argüelles, a former health minister from the military dictatorship, and offered some thoughts about Argentine health issues. Argüelles begins by stating that two-thirds of public hospitals' budgets are spent on Latin American immigrants. Public hospitals in Argentina are free and open to anyone, but because employers are obligated by law to provide health insurance, people who are employed can access private health services. For the most part, those working in the informal economy and the unemployed are the main users of public health. Despite this, it is hard to believe this figure.

Referring to the increase in disease and cases of Chagas, meningitis, tuberculosis, and cholera in Argentina, Argüelles writes in his editorial, "This alarming increase in deaths is related to the arrival of illegal immigrants in the country, who live 'herded' and promiscuously in the periphery of Buenos Aires, other cities, and rural areas." He continues, "Even if for humanitarian reasons we wanted to keep accepting this ignorant and poor population, our resources would not allow it, and if we don't stop it we will be divided into two countries: one developed and the other one from the Third or Fourth World." He then adds that the 1994 rebellion against the North American Free Trade Agreement in Chiapas, Mexico, should teach readers a lesson about what could happen in Argentina.

The ensuing paragraphs of the editorial become even more stereotypical and racist. For example, Argüelles asserts, "The number of births among immigrant families, of lower intellectual capacity, will lead to a noticeable decrease in the average intellectual capacity of our population." After rallying for an immigration policy for immigrants from Central and Eastern Europe, and France, as well as white South Africans "fearful of the reaction by the African population," to populate Patagonia and other rural areas, he concludes, "Postponing these actions will put our national sovereignty at risk and will bring a monstrous growth of contaminated Third World neighborhoods, populated with retarded people, which will hurt our national intellectual capacity and the development and competitiveness of the country in the 21st century." As these statements show, the author of this editorial had a clear preference for white immigrants and was willing to support his position with any kind of unfounded statement.

Finally, the editorial entitled "Xenophobia" was published in *Página 12* on February 6, 1994. Written by Ema Cibotti, a history professor from the University of Buenos Aires, the article opens by pointing out that the xenophobic reactions against immigrants in Argentina were not new. The arrival of the nineteenth-century wave of immigrants that settled in big cities and some rural areas in the northeast also produced a reaction from the elite, which coined pejorative terms such as *gringo* and *Napolitano* to refer to them. Later, immigrants joined anarchist and socialist unions that protested and organized strikes seeking to improve the living conditions of the working class. The elites, instead of questioning the social conditions in which the working class lived, blamed immigrants for social unrest.

Within this context, Law 4144 of 1902, also known as the Residence Law, authorized the Executive to deport immigrants without the due process guaranteed in the Argentine Constitution for all inhabitants, not just for citizens. Nonetheless, according to Cibotti, social mobility in Argentina at the time allowed for the relatively smooth integration of immigrants. Later on, the elites discriminated against migrants from the provinces of Argentina, pejoratively named little black heads. Again, economic growth and the fight for inclusion eased the integration of these immigrants into Buenos Aires's society. Unlike then, the author explains, Argentina in the 1990s was bankrupt and faced increased class segmentation, individualism, and xenophobia. Without a policy for social cohesion, therefore, xenophobia could take deep root in Argentine society.

FACTORS SHAPING IMMIGRATION POLICIES DURING THE 1990s

According to Zolberg (1999), from the capitalist perspective, immigrants of any kind are first and foremost workers and secondly a political and cultural presence. This multiple character of immigration helps shed light on the complex interests that are at stake when a state makes a decision about the selection and admission of foreign citizens. In that regard, this chapter argues that, although economic factors are important in explaining immigration policies and often determine how many immigrants a country is willing to accept, notions of the ethnic and/or cultural eligibility of certain immigrant groups for membership in the imagined community (identity politics) dictate *who* is admitted. Although Argentina's history shows a recurrent, even if qualified, preference for European immigration, millions of immigrants of indigenous origin have arrived in the country since the 1930s. Nonetheless, the attitude of Argentines toward these migrants remains ambiguous. As soon as economic conditions become uncertain, these immigrants become a "problem" for Argentine society and the doors of Argentina close to them.

Also, during times of deep economic transformation, an opportunity arises to redraw the boundaries of the imagined community. In this process of exchange, both traditional and new discourses about the appropriateness of certain immigrants for inclusion into the imagined community are renegotiated. This happened in Argentina between 1993 and 1994. Labor unions called attention to the supposed worsening of the economic situation due to immigration from neighboring countries. While overlooking other possible weaknesses in its own economic model, the government blamed immigrants for the ills of Argentine society. States seek obedience and conformity through the use of nationalism by merging personal identities with the collective self-consciousness of the nation. In this way, states make their nationals perceive their well-being and the well-being of the state as one and the same (Breuilly 1994). Consequently, when the state deported "criminal immigrants" it appeared to be taking care of internal security. The following year, the state limited immigration instead of making structural changes to the economic plan.

FIVE

Gridlock or Delegative Democracy?

Congress and Immigration, 1983–1989

Institutions are important in accounting for the success and failure of democracies (March and Olsen 1983; Peters 2011). Government institutional designs for representative democracies affect the ways in which the political process operates (Shugart and Carey 1992). Understanding the constitutional division of powers between the Executive and the Legislative in immigration policy is crucial. However, analyzing whether these constitutional powers reflect the reality of the policy-making process is as important (Levitsky and Murillo 2009; Waylen 2014). The Argentine Constitution empowers Congress to rule on the admission of foreign citizens. Despite this, the immigration decision-making process in Argentina was centralized in the Executive until 2003. What are some of the reasons for this centralization?

A body of literature derived from the work of Juan Linz argues that presidential systems have problems and these problems affect the survival and functioning of democracies. According to Linz (1990), situations of divided government—that is, situations in which different political parties control the Executive and the Legislative in presidential systems—can lead to gridlock. For example, during the Obama administration the U. S. Congress was unable to approve comprehensive immigration reform due to a case of divided government and gridlock. President Raúl Alfonsín faced a situation of divided government wherein his Radical Party never controlled the Senate and lost control of the House in 1987. Is it possible that the Alfonsín administration also faced gridlock? This chapter analyzes this question.

Scholars argue that presidents in certain countries rule as they see fit, bypassing Congress whenever necessary. Guillermo O'Donnell (1994) cites Argentine President Menem as the paradigmatic example of this type of government. This chapter finds that, when it comes to immigration policies, Alfonsín centralized powers in an important way. However, Argentina from 1983 to 1989 was a case of congressional inaction more than a proactive Executive. This chapter first places the Argentine division of powers in historical context and delineates congressional powers in matters of immigration policies. Then, it explores the reasons underlying this centralization both theoretically and empirically.

The fact that Congress did not pass a comprehensive immigration law between 1983 and 1989 does not mean that this body remained inactive in matters of immigration. Until the 1990s, the Argentine Congress had no standing specialized committees on immigration policies, and committees on agricultural and foreign affairs dealt with immigration issues and policies. As the next chapter shows, interest in and activity on immigration issues increased dramatically after the creation of standing congressional committees on immigration and population issues in the early 1990s. Nonetheless, between 1983 and 1989, the Argentine legislature considered forty-three decisions or resolutions regarding immigration matters (see Table 5.1).

The Argentine Congress, not unlike the U. S. Congress, approves different types of resolutions in addition to traditional bills. For instance, it can approve a resolution requesting information from the Executive. Further, Congress can also request that the Executive take a certain course of action. During the years 1983 to 1989, one-third of all congressional decisions considered were bills with minor immigration policy changes. Another 26 percent were directed to request information from the Executive and 44 percent to influence the latter to take a certain course of action. Finally, 2 percent of proposed declarations were directed to express opinions or endorse events. The following questions are analyzed in this chapter: How did Congress interact with the Executive? Did the policies initiated in Congress differ from those followed by the presidency? What was the content of the information requests to the Executive? Were they responded to in a timely manner? Did they represent a check on presidential power?

Table 5.1. Immigration Bills and Other Decisions Considered by the Argentine Congress: 1983–1989 (Absolute Numbers and Percentages)

Decisions Considered	House	Senate	Total
Total	34	9	43
Number of Bills	9 (27%)	3 (33%)	12 (28%)
Number of Information Requests	11 (32%)	None	11 (26%)
Number of Courses of Action	14 (41%)	5 (55%)	19 (44%)
Number of Declarations	None	1 (11%)	1 (2%)

Note: Decisions having only an internal administrative impact on Congress are not included in this table. The House proposed two decisions of this nature during the period 1983–1989.

IMMIGRATION POLICY MAKING:
INSTITUTIONAL FRAMEWORK

The 1853 Constitution established a federal system and a division of powers between an executive branch headed by a president, a bicameral legislature, and a judiciary. Although the Argentine division of powers closely resembles that of the United States, the Argentine Executive is stronger than its U. S. counterpart (Morgenstern, Polga-Hecimovich, and Shair-Rosenfield 2013; Shugart and Carey 1992). Juan Bautista Alberdi, who set the blueprint for the 1853 Argentine Constitution, was fully aware of this difference (Alberdi 1966). While writing the Argentine Constitution, he followed the example set by the American Constitution for the most part; however, Alberdi (1966) thought that the United States executive branch was not strong enough. For this reason, and with the purpose of avoiding anarchy, he replicated the Chilean Executive. The Argentine constitutionalists thus conceived the presidency as the motor of the government (Llanos 2001).

For example, unlike the American president, the Argentine president has proactive powers to initiate legislation (Shugart and Mainwaring 1997), which is then submitted for congressional consideration. As in the United States, the reactive power embodied in the institution of veto allows the president to participate in the legislative process by approving or rejecting legislation. However, Argentine presidents can also cast amendatory or partial vetoes (Morgenstern, Polga-Hecimovich, and Shair-Rosenfield 2013). When it comes to passing statutes and regulations through executive orders, the president of Argentina is also stronger than the president of the

United States. According to Article 99.2 of the Argentine Constitution, the president "approves the statuses and regulations necessary for the implementation of the laws, without altering their spirit by enacting statutory exceptions" (Honorable Senado de la Nación Argentina n.d.).

Further, the Argentine president can issue a DNU. These decrees were used for many years and are now regulated under the 1994 Constitution. According to Article 99.3, a DNU can be issued in exceptional circumstances and cannot legislate on issues related to criminal, tax, electoral, or political parties' legislation (Honorable Senado de la Nación Argentina n.d.). This article also establishes that these decrees need to be submitted for congressional consideration. However, Law 26122 regulating these exceptional measures was passed on July 27, 2006. Thus, Presidents Carlos Menem, Fernando de la Rúa, Rodolfo Rodríguez Saá, Eduardo Duhalde, and Néstor Kirchner did not have to abide by any rules when issuing DNUs. All the powers described above explain why Matthew S. Shugart and John M. Carey (1992) classified Argentina as one of several countries with the strongest presidential power, together with the German Weimar Republic and surpassed only by Chile in 1989 and Paraguay.

Despite the existence of the strong Executive established by the 1853 Constitution, Article 75.18 of this document states that Congress has exclusive legislative power to rule on the selection and admission of foreign citizens. Yet the Argentine Congress has seldom exercised this power. Law 817 of Immigration and Colonization was passed in 1876 (see Appendix I, Table A.1). Between that year and 2003, the Argentine Congress passed partial modifications to this law on various occasions but never a comprehensive immigration law. Passed during the last dictatorship without congressional debate, Law 22439 of 1981 (see Appendix I, Table A.1), strongly concerned with the police aspects of immigration control, provided the context within which constitutional governments framed their immigration policies between the reestablishment of democracy in 1983 and 2003.

Also, because immigration from Latin American countries increased after the 1930s and the policies were highly restrictive, democratic governments approved permissive rules (amnesties) to benefit these immigrants through executive decrees in 1949, 1951, 1964, 1974, 1984, 1992, 2004, and 2005 (see Appendix I, Table A.1). Thus, even during democratic governments, Argentina's Executive enjoyed a high degree of power in matters of immigration. The acceptance of this centralization of immigration policy on the Argentine Executive contrasts with the lack of consensus about what the U. S. president can do in matters of immigration. The standard conception of the presidency in the latter country is that the office is constrained by the separation of powers and the general weakness of the chief executive's formal powers.

Executive orders are not defined or described in the U. S. Constitution, but they have been used as an implication of the vesting of executive power in the president from the Washington administration forward (Rudalevige 2012). The Executive Vesting Clause grants executive authority to the president. In November 2014, President Barack Obama, tired of the congressional inability to pass comprehensive immigration reform, passed the executive order known as Deferred Action for Parents of Americans,[1] granting quasi-legal status and work permits for undocumented parents of American citizen children who entered the country before 2010 (Kagan 2015; Kandel et al. 2015).

This executive order drew immediate objections from Republican lawmakers, who asserted that the president's actions provided grounds for impeachment (Kagan 2015). Two federal district courts reached opposite conclusions about the constitutionality of Obama's executive action. At the same time, a coalition of twenty-six states filed a complaint in another federal district court challenging the president's constitutional authority to implement new immigration policies. Some legal scholars alleged that the president's executive actions indicated a refusal to faithfully execute the law as required by the Constitution, but the White House and a number of immigration law scholars argued that the Obama administration was exercising prosecutorial discretion and that there are many examples of previous presidents taking similar actions (Kagan 2015). This executive action was successfully blocked in the courts.[2]

LEGISLATURES IN LATIN AMERICA: THE DEBATE

Scholars have argued that the presidential form of government contributes to problems in Latin America (Linz 1990; Shugart and Mainwaring 1997). This argument states that presidentialism can lead to government gridlock and paralysis in cases of divided government. In Argentina, this paralysis in turn can prompt the Executive to take unilateral action through the enactment of decrees (Mustapic 2002). Alfonsín's administration faced a case of divided government because it never controlled the Senate and, after the election of 1987, also lost control of the House.

However, gridlock in matters of immigration never existed. Further, neither the presidency nor Congress generated a comprehensive immigration bill. Instead of submitting an immigration bill for congressional consideration, Alfonsín's administration enacted Decree 1434 in 1987 to regulate the provisions of Law 22439, which made immigration rules stricter (see Appendix I, Table A.1). Was Alfonsín a president prone to circumventing Congress by the use of decrees?

O'Donnell (1994) used the case of Argentina under President Menem as a paradigmatic example of the delegative democratic model. A discretionary Executive is the cornerstone of this distinctive type of democracy, in which presidents rule free of mechanisms of horizontal and vertical accountability, except from post-facto electoral verdicts (Peruzzotti 2001). In this way, presidents supposedly overcome opposition to their policies by bypassing entrenched interests and appealing directly to the people (Panizza 2000). It is clear that the Menem administration fits the delegative model of democracy, but does Alfonsín's?

It is important to distinguish between the different presidential periods in Argentina. President Menem (1989–1999) ruled by decree on 166 different occasions (O'Donnell 1994). However, President Alfonsín did so in only ten cases. In addition, Alfonsín's style of government was more democratic and respectful of the separation of powers than Menem's. As Enrique Peruzzotti (2001, 148) states, "Both in its rhetoric and political practices, the Radical government disconfirmed the delegativeness argument." Alfonsín respected both the Congress and the judiciary. His administration made a conscious effort for self-limitation. For example, he did not bypass Congress through executive decrees on other significant rulings. Alfonsín had to share power with a Congress partly dominated by the opposition. Also, according to Peruzzotti (2001), there was a high degree of cooperation between the majority parties in Congress.

Alfonsín offered the presidency of the Argentine Supreme Court to a leader of the opposition to ensure the independence of the judiciary. Overall, a process of institutional differentiation in the direction of a separation of powers took place during the Alfonsín administration. However, the picture that emerges from the immigration decision-making process is different. In the case of immigration policy, Alfonsín's style was not highly respectful of Congress and immigration decisions were also made by executive decree. Furthermore, during Alfonsín's administration the director of the Immigration Agency also enacted immigration policies.

As mentioned above, Congress was somewhat active in immigration matters between 1983 and 1989. The centralization of the decision-making process during the years 1983 to 1989 was not caused by executive action alone.[3] The Argentine Congress could have passed immigration legislation any time after the reestablishment of democracy in 1983. However, it chose not to do so. For this reason, I believe it is also important to assess the reasons why Congress was unable to agree on a new immigration policy for so many years. Thus, the next section draws on interview data with Argentine legislators and key actors in immigration policy in Argentina to shed light on this puzzle (for details about these interviews, see Appendix III).

WHAT LED TO CENTRALIZATION OF THE DECISION-MAKING PROCESS?

Two political parties dominated Argentina between World War II and 1999: the Unión Cívica Radical (UCR) and the Partido Justicialista (PJ, called the Peronist Party). The composition of Congress also tended to reflect the dominance of these two parties. While Radical president Alfonsín was in office (1983–1989), his party enjoyed a plurality in the House that ranged from almost 45 to 51 percent (see Table 5.2). However, due to the strong influence of the PJ in the Argentine provinces, the UCR did not dominate the Senate (see Table 5.3). As mentioned above, although Alfonsín's administration faced a situation of divided government, this fact alone does not explain congressional inability to pass comprehensive immigration legislation.

One possible explanation for the lack of comprehensive immigration reform during the Radical administration was that, due to the lack of specialized committees, Congress did not generate comprehensive immigration reform bills. The structure of the Argentine Congress mirrors that of the United States; both chambers have standing committees that deal with

Table 5.2. Composition of the Argentine House of Representatives by Political Party: 1983–1989

Political Party	Period (Percentages)		
	1983–1985	1985–1987	1987–1989
PJ	43.7	24.4	38.2
UCR	50.8	50.8	44.9
Other	5.5	24.8	16.9
Total	100.0	100.0	100.0

different policy issues. Today, the Argentine House of Representatives has forty-five standing committees and the Senate has thirty-six. Until the 1990s the Argentine House and Senate lacked a specific committee on immigration. Therefore, the agricultural or foreign affairs committees dealt with all issues related to immigration. The Senate Committee on Population and Human Development was created in 1990 by Resolution 275-S-90, and the House Committee on Population and Human Resources in 1991 by Resolution 516-D-91 (see Appendix III). Before these committees were created, interest on immigration matters appears to have been limited.

Evidence of this is found in the small number of bills and other decisions on immigration issues generated by Congress before 1989, compared to the later period. For instance, while both chambers discussed forty-three proposals dealing with immigration issues in the period 1983 to 1989 (see Table 5.1), this number climbed to 108 for the period 1989 to 1995. On the reason behind the lack of comprehensive immigration reform, former director of the Immigration Agency Jorge Gurrieri explained, "During Alfonsín's administration there was no interest in enacting a new immigration law, and this circumstance did not change until the early 1990s."[4] As the next chapter shows, soon after the creation of specialized committees on immigration, the Argentine Congress produced comprehensive immigration bills.

O'Donnell's (1994) argument regarding the causes of delegative democracies states that these models of democracy emerge in countries affected by serious economic and political crises. In Peruzzotti's (2001) view, the phenomenon of delegativeness is intimately associated with processes of collective learning triggered by the experience of successive hyper-

Table 5.3. Composition of the Argentine Senate by Political Party: 1983–1989

Political Party	Period 1983–1989 (Percentages)
PJ	45.7
UCR	39.1
Other	15.2
Total	100.0

inflationary crises that culminated in the dramatic riots and lootings of 1989. According to Peruzzotti, hyperinflation left a deep cultural imprint on Argentine society, comparable only to the one previously left by state terrorism (2001). Demands for political accountability were postponed in the face of a more immediate need to reestablish normal economic conditions. Is it possible that immigration and political crises determined the effect of centralization of immigration policy making in the Executive?

This chapter argues that economic and other crises are important in explaining the centralization of the immigration decision-making process in two ways. First, they acted as an obstacle for passing immigration legislation, since more urgent matters got in the way. In addition, economic crises were said to make the centralization of power convenient, giving the Executive the flexibility to respond promptly to economic and other demands. During 2003 and 2004, I interviewed a sample of twenty-seven Argentine legislators (approximately 8 percent of the total number of legislators) and asked them to assess the reasons why the Congress had been unable to agree on a new immigration law for some twenty years.[5] This section analyzes the findings of these interviews together with a number of interviews with key policy officials.

Almost one-third of the legislators interviewed thought that urgent economic and political problems had delayed the passage of a new immigration law. Members of Congress believed that the body had prioritized more pressing matters at the expense of immigration policies. In this regard, a PJ congresswoman thought that "the serious economic problems combined with the lack of institutional stability deferred the enactment of a new immigration law."[6] In a similar vein, a UCR legislator stated, "Legislators gave priority to other laws that at the moment were considered more urgent."[7] Concurring with these Argentine legislators, a representative of the Peruvian community in Argentina thought that successive crises in South America had led the Argentine State to postpone the enactment of immigration legislation.[8] As these comments show, interviewees agreed that the economic and institutional crises facing Argentina had come before new immigration law.

In addition, the same crises made it convenient for the Executive to pass immigration policies by decree. Some opinions emphasized the flexibility enjoyed by the Executive to rule on immigration matters according to changing circumstances. One congressman believed that this flexibility could lead to permissive immigration policies, noting that "the law is open enough to facilitate and foment the residence and integration of immigrants in Argentine society."[9]

Most interviewees, however, argued that this flexibility made it easy and convenient for the Executive to restrict the entry of foreigners into the country. For instance, a representative from a provincial party noted that the flexibility awarded to the Executive facilitated the enactment of immigration restrictions when the economic situation worsened.[10] Other key actors involved in immigration policy issues also shared this view. The director of an Argentine graduate program in immigration law, Professor Gabriel Chausovsky, explained that the 1981 law permitted the Executive to exploit the weak position of immigrant communities.[11] Former Immigration Agency director Gurrieri also stated that the Executive found it unnecessary to pass a new immigration law because it enjoyed broad powers to restrict immigration thanks to the one dating from the last military dictatorship.[12]

One important question concerns the beliefs of Argentine legislators about the role that Congress should have in immigration policies. As mentioned above, the Argentine Constitution empowers Congress to rule in matters of immigration. However, some legislators believed that Congress should have a limited role in immigration issues. This belief may have played a role in this body's inability to pass wide-ranging immigration legislation for twenty years. For instance, almost 31 percent of the legislators interviewed believed that the Executive should have a strong role in immigration policy.[13] Some legislators thought that Congress could not enact a new immigration law because the Executive did not provide enough guidance. In this sense, a legislator from the Frente Grande (Broad Front), a left-leaning political party, explained that Congress was unable to agree on a new immigration law "because the state did not dictate a strategy on the matter."[14]

Three other UCR congressmen also shared this view. One explained that Argentina lacked "a state policy in immigration matters."[15] Another said, "In reality, the Executive lacks a clear immigration policy."[16] The third made the argument more explicit, explaining, "If we agree that immigration policy is a state policy as is also, for instance, foreign policy, it then makes sense for the Executive to have the last say on immigration matters."[17] Clearly, some Argentine legislators believed that the Executive and not Congress should be the main engine in immigration policy.

If the Executive creates policies, what should Congress do? Some legislators thought Congress should exert only post-facto control on the Executive's actions. One UCR legislator explained, "The role of the Executive should be central in matters of immigration, and the Congress and judiciary should guard individual rights."[18] In reality, the Argentine Congress did exercise its supervisory role when showing its distress with the Executive's immigration policies after 1985. For instance, in 1986 Congress asked the Executive to revoke its immigration policy and to establish more liberal immigration rules until Congress could agree on a new immigration law.

Another legislator from the UCR assigned an even more limited role to Congress. This person explained, "Congress should control and follow up on presidential immigration policies, thus obtaining fresh information about immigration flows and on the efficacy of the immigration policies implemented by the Executive."[19] According to this version of the role of the legislature, this body would only update itself on the policies implemented by the Executive and their consequences. As becomes obvious from these comments, an important number of congresspersons in Argentina believe in a limited congressional role regarding immigration. This belief may partly explain this body's low commitment to producing comprehensive immigration legislation.

Concurrently, Argentine legislators did not believe that the Executive had a high level of discretion regarding the powers attributed by the 1981 law. This law establishes a preference for European immigration and allows the Executive to create norms and procedures to encourage the immigration of foreigners whose cultural characteristics permit integration into Argentine society (see Appendix I, Table A.1). In the above-mentioned questionnaire, congresspersons were asked to assess their agreement with the statement that immigration legislation in place was attributing excessive power to the Executive (answers ranging from 1 to 5, 1 being *completely disagree* and 5 *completely agree.*). The average response to this question was 2.86, just above the indifference level. Further, no partisan differences were found.

One possible explanation for the belief in a limited role of Congress is of a historic and cultural nature. Military governments dominated the Argentine political scene after World War II. Between 1930 and 1983, Argentina had more military governments than civilian, democratic ones. During these military governments, Congress was shut down and the Executive approved policy decisions by presidential decree. Further, democracy and democratization are easier in countries with previous experience with democracy (Schmitter 1994). Thus, Argentina's limited experience with democracy may have influenced legislators' beliefs about the limited role of Congress in immigration issues.

CONGRESSIONAL ACTIVITY

This section analyzes the kind of immigration bills and other decisions this legislative body did produce. As in the United States, the House represents the population of Argentina and the Senate represents its provinces and federal district (Honorable Senado de la Nación Argentina n.d.). The House has 257 members and the Senate has 72, 3 from each province and 3 from the Autonomous City of Buenos Aires (Ciudad Autónoma de Buenos Aires). Not unlike the U.S. Congress, the Argentine House and Senate have standing specialized congressional committees for issues they discuss and decide upon. The House and Senate committees that deal with immigration issues today are both named Population and Human Development Committee. The House committee has 30 members and the Senate committee has 17. However, during the Alfonsín era, these specialized committees did not exist.

The committees' task is generally limited to issuing opinions regarding proposed legislation and other decisions. In some instances, however, committees can issue binding decisions. For example, the unanimous members of House committees (Albarracín 2004) or two-thirds of the members of the Senate committees can approve information requests. Such approvals are valid without further discussion or voting in the chamber. In other instances committees can be highly influential on the rest of Congress. The House can vote on a bill without debate and deliberation once the project has received a unanimously favorable opinion from committee members. In turn, the Senate can approve a bill in general and delegate the deliberation and voting of each article to the committees.

TYPES OF DECISIONS CONSIDERED BY CONGRESS

The Argentine Congress deals with different types of decisions that may have an impact on the design of policies. Representatives can propose bills (*leyes*), resolutions (*resoluciones*), and declarations (*declaraciones*). A bill is a proposed law, which has the purpose of establishing or changing government policy. Declarations are expressions of the body's opinions about certain matters. Resolutions are administrative decisions and other pronouncements of mandatory character. For instance, the House asks the Executive to provide information or to follow a certain course of action through resolutions.

In the Senate, legislators can propose bills, decrees (*decretos*), resolutions, communications (*comunicaciones*), and declarations (see Table 5.4). Decrees are decisions that permit the Senate to make determinations that have an administrative impact within this legislative body. Resolutions are similar in nature to decrees; through resolutions the Senate communicates certain plans or decisions that do not affect other government bodies. Communications are of central importance for this study: through them, the Senate can request that the Executive provide information about certain matters or follow a certain course of action. Finally, declarations are expressions of the body's opinions about different issues.

Because this terminology can become confusing, this study simplifies the vocabulary for the sake of clarity. The term *bill* poses no problem since both chambers use it in the same way. The terms *resolution* and *communication* will be replaced by the effect sought by each decision. For instance, if the decision requests information from the Executive, it will be referred

Table 5.4. Degree of Effectiveness of Each Chamber: 1983–1989 (Ratio of Decisions Approved versus Proposed)

Type of Decision	House	Senate
Percentage of Decisions Approved	40 (14/35)	44 (04/09)
Percentage of Laws Approved	33 (03/09)	66 (02/03)
Percentage of Information Req. Approved	36 (04/11)	N/A
Percentage of Course of A. Approved	50 (07/14)	25 (01/04)

to as an *information request*. If it intends to make the presidency take a certain course of action, it will be called *course of action request*. In turn, if the resolution simply makes a resolve of a different kind, I will explain the nature of this *resolve*.

ACTIVITY OF CONGRESS RELATING TO
IMMIGRATION ISSUES: 1983–1989

This analysis considers the Radical administration of President Alfonsín (1983–1989)[20] (see Appendix IV for details on documents included). Between 1983 and 1989, both houses considered a total of forty-three decisions relating to immigration issues (see Table 5.1). Bills are important instruments for creating policies. Out of the total number of decisions discussed during this period, Congress considered a modest number of bills (28 percent). It also made use of the so-called information requests to require the Executive to account for different actions (26 percent). Information requests cover a broad range of issues and can constitute an important check on the Executive. They generally contain an exhaustive number of questions followed by statements regarding the congress members' point of view on how affairs should be conducted. These requests are not limited to requiring information and are usually intended to produce a change in Executive behavior.

Requests for a course of action were the most numerous (see Table 5.1). These instruments were very popular during Alfonsín's administration, comprising 44 percent of the immigration affairs considered. Between 1989 and 1995, the use of this type of request decreased to 21 percent. This decrease was compensated to some extent by the increase in information requests. Perhaps, in their search to make the presidency more accountable, Argentine legislators opted for the latter because they provide a more effective check on the Executive. These instruments can provide Congress with detailed information about the Executive's affairs.

The Senate was less productive than the House during the period under consideration (see Table 5.4). The number of actions dealing with immigration considered in the House was between two and four times higher than in the Senate, as previously documented in the literature (Molinelli, Palanza, and Sin 1999). The data provided by that study show that between 1984 and 1995, the House generated around 31 percent of the bills that became laws, while the Senate produced only 17 percent of them. It is true that the House is more than three times the size of the Senate. However, despite the difference in size, the standing committees of the Senate have sizes similar to those in the House.

The Senate was, however, more effective than the House (Table 5.4). Effectiveness can be defined as the number of projects that are approved as a percentage of the total number proposed. Further, the Senate's effectiveness increased for the period 1989 to 1995, growing from 44 to 59 percent. Based on data provided by Molinelli, Palanza, and Sin (1999), this study estimated the effectiveness of both chambers of the Argentine Congress in all decisions considered during the periods under study.[21] The Senate's effectiveness ranged from 58 to 68 percent and that of the House ranged from 23 to 29 percent.

The number of proposals generated also varied by political party (see Table 5.5). During the period 1983 to 1989, the PJ initiated more than twice as many proposals as the UCR. The UCR's productivity on immigration issues was low considering that during that period this party held from 45 to 51 percent of the seats in the House (see Table 5.2). In addition, third parties initiated a number of proposals that equaled the number of proposals by the PJ and UCR combined. In the Senate, the PJ initiated 55 percent of the projects considered while the UCR contributed only 22 percent. This speaks well of the PJ, considering that the party held more seats in the Senate during this period than the UCR (see Table 5.3).

It is also important to consider the effectiveness of each political party in passing the proposals initiated. The PJ managed to pass 33 and

Table 5.5. Immigration Decisions Proposed by Political Party: 1983–1989

Political Party Proposing	House	Senate
PJ	12 (34%)	5 (55%)
UCR	5 (14%)	2 (22%)
Other	15 (43%)	None

Note: This table does not include bills originating in a different chamber or the Executive.

Table 5.6. Immigration Decisions Approved by Political Party: 1983–1989

Political Party Initiating	House	Senate
PJ	4 (33%)	2 (40%)
UCR	3 (60%)	None
Other	5 (33%)	None

40 percent of those actions it proposed in the House and Senate, respectively (see Table 5.6). The UCR, probably leveraging the majority it enjoyed in the House, passed 60 percent of its proposals in this chamber.[22] In contrast, the UCR could not pass any of its proposals in the Senate. As mentioned before, the UCR never controlled the Senate due to the strong influence of the PJ in the provinces. This fact may explain the UCR's lower effectiveness in this chamber.

BILLS INTRODUCED, 1983–1989

Creating legislation is a main function of legislatures. Although the Argentine Congress was unable to agree on a comprehensive immigration law until 2003, it nevertheless produced and considered different bills on immigration issues. This section analyzes these bills, paying particular attention to those that received more support from the Argentine Congress. It also compares these proposals with Executive immigration rules that were in place during this period. What type of immigration decisions did the Argentine Congress approve? What were the characteristics of the proposals that did not obtain approval? Were the Argentine congresspersons more liberal than the presidency when it came to immigration policies?

In the period 1983 to 1989, the Argentine Congress considered eight bills, three of which, initiated by the Executive, became law (see Tables 5.7 and 5.8).[23] The House considered a total of eight bills, but only three became law. In turn, the Senate considered three bills, two of which became law.[24] The UCR was more active in both chambers, being responsible for two-thirds of the legislation considered in the Senate and half of the legislation considered in the House. The PJ did not initiate any legislation in the Senate and proposed one piece in the House. Third parties were more active in the House than in the Senate (see Tables 5.7 and 5.8).

The purpose of the legislation proposed varied. Almost 75 percent of it proposed small changes to immigration legislation, such as updating the amounts of penalties assessed for immigration offenses, revoking rules applicable to immigrants originating in communist countries, or imposing HIV tests on immigrants. An important number of them proposed amnesties for immigrants from Latin American countries. One group of bills dealt with issues related to immigration in a less direct way. One such case proposed the creation of different development regions in the country and another approved the constitution of the Intergovernmental Committee for Migration (ICM), the antecedent of the International Organization for Migration.

Of the bills introduced between 1983 and 1989 by both chambers of the Congress, coding identified three that would have made immigration policies stricter, seven that would have made them more permissive, and one that would have produced no significant change (see Tables 5.7 and 5.8). As these numbers show, almost 65 percent of the proposals aimed to make Executive immigration policies more liberal. Examples include three bills proposing an amnesty for immigrants from Latin American countries and one bill eliminating fees for border crossings. Thus, it is safe to assume that if approved, congressional immigration policies would have been more permissive than Executive policies. This finding seems to go hand in hand with the observation by some interviewees mentioned above that the centralization of the immigration policy-making process made it more convenient for the Executive to enact immigration restrictions "as needed." Had Congress been able to pass comprehensive immigration reform, it would likely have been more liberal than the policies enacted by presidential decree.

Table 5.7. Bills Introduced in the House: 1983–1989

ID No.	Year	Approved	Party	Description	Permissive?
638-D	1983		Other	Residency for immigrants from bordering countries	+
900-D	1983		PJ	Residency for immigrants from bordering countries	+
1339-D	1984		PJ	Creation of development areas away from Buenos Aires Metropolitan Area	+
1590-D	1985		PJ	Residency for immigrants from bordering countries	+
2876-D	1986	L. 23564	UCR	Updates the amounts of penalties for immigration offenses	–
3802-D	1986		Other	Residency for immigrants from bordering countries	+
1470-D	1988		UCR	Eliminates fees for border crossings with bordering countries	+
161-PE	1989	L.23768		Revokes norms applicable to immigrants originating in communist countries	+
48-PE	1989	L. 23816		Migration	0

Table 5.8. Bills Introduced in the Senate: 1983–1989

ID No.	Year	Approved	Party	Description	Permissive?
503-S	1985		UCR	Impedes foreigners who are HIV-positive from applying for a permanent visa	–
2876	1986	L. 23564	UCR	Updates the amounts of penalties for immigration offenses	–
161-PE	1989	L. 23768		Revokes norms applicable to immigrants originating in communist countries	+

BILLS PASSED, 1983–1989

Three bills that originated between 1983 and 1989 were passed (see Tables 5.7 and 5.8). The ideological record of the immigration decisions passed during this period was mixed. One bill (2876-S-86) was directed to improve the enforcement of immigration rules by raising the penalty amounts charged for immigration offenses.[25] This bill was considered "of vital importance for preventing the proliferation of undocumented immigrants in the country" (2876-S-86). This modification to the existing legislation also provided a mechanism for an automatic adjustment of penalty amounts according to inflation. In sum, this bill sought to enforce immigration rules by strengthening the coercive mechanisms established in the 1981 law.

One bill (161-PE-89) passed during this period was clearly intended to make immigration rules more liberal.[26] It was initiated by the Executive and aimed to revoke the strict controls that applied to immigrants arriving from communist countries. These controls had been approved by Decree 2457 of 1963 and subjected these immigrants to strict checks before and after arriving in the country. The revocation was necessary "because it [the decree] implied an unacceptable ideological discrimination, which was no longer justified." Further, this measure "could improve Argentina's relationships with communist countries, in a context in which the Cold War was almost overcome" (161-PE-89). At this point, most of the controls that this norm was supposed to eliminate were no longer in place. Nonetheless, it was a healthy, though symbolic, reaffirmation of the democratic principles that should guide immigration policies.

OTHER BILLS INTRODUCED, 1983–1989

What other actions did the Argentine Congress consider during this time? Examination of the bills on immigration topics that Congress considered between 1983 and 1989 that did not become law is important (see Tables 5.7 and 5.8). One of these bills was aimed at enacting health-related immigration requirements. It would have prevented HIV-positive people from applying for a visa in Argentina by requiring an HIV test for persons from areas of the world in which this disease was widespread. This bill

Table 5.9. Permissiveness of Immigration Legislation: 1983–1989

Impact of the Bill	More Restrictive	More Permissive	Neutral
Proposed	3	7	1
Approved	2	2	1

was not passed, but the rules in place until the 1990s prevented the immigration of people with certain diseases and disabilities. It took a scandal involving the immigration of a girl with Down syndrome to change this legislation in 1993.[27]

The other unsuccessful bills introduced during the period (638-D-83, 900-D-83, 1590-D-85, 1339-D-84, 3802-D-86, and 1470-D-88) sought to enact more liberal immigration policies (see Table 5.9). For instance, a number of representatives proposed bills to regularize the immigration status of undocumented immigrants (638-D-83, 900-D-83, 1590-D-85, and 3802-D-86). These bills sought to award residency either to immigrants from bordering countries or immigrants from any Latin American country. Even though the Constitution gives the power to legislate on immigration to Congress, the Executive again passed an amnesty for undocumented immigrants soon after the reestablishment of democracy (see Appendix I, Table A.1, Decree 780/84). These bills, in a way, reclaimed these legitimate congressional powers.

In 1984 some PJ legislators prepared a bill for the creation of four development regions in the country—Northeast, Northwest, West, and South—in order to encourage migration and immigration (1339-D-84). Another bill introduced between 1983 and 1989 intended to encourage migration and tourism by eliminating all fees applicable to border crossings with neighboring countries (1470-D-88). As this analysis shows, the majority of the bills introduced by Congress were considerably more liberal than the immigration policies the Executive enacted after 1985.

Further, on three occasions, Argentine legislators requested that the Executive annul the immigration policies passed through the Immigration Agency Resolution 2340/85. Although these requests were not passed, they show a congressional discomfort with the immigration policies of the Executive (137-S-86, 4549-D-85, and 2882-D-86). The first of these requests originated in the Senate and was written in a categorical tone.

After noting that Argentines had reconquered democracy, it recalled that the Constitution invited "all good-willed citizens of the world" to immigrate to Argentina if they wished. "It is clear," it continued, "that the Constitution did not discriminate based on economic, religious, professional, racial, or political reasons" (137-S-86). This resolution went on to state that the government discriminated against foreigners on the basis of their profession (by requiring them to be skilled workers) and economic condition (by requiring them to have investment capital).

A decision that requested the Executive annul immigration policies passed through the Immigration Agency Resolution 2340/85 was also persuasive. Authored by a legislator from a center-left party, this request stated that the resolution "arbitrarily restricts the entry and settlement of immigrants in Argentina" (4549-D-85). It estimated that after the January 1986 deadline to apply for amnesty there would still be some two hundred thousand immigrants in Argentina who needed to regularize their immigration status. It also mentioned that the governments of some bordering countries and several human rights organizations had expressed concern about Immigration Agency Resolution 2340/85 and added that many of the migrants affected came from poverty and performed the roughest jobs in Argentina.

A PJ representative proposed the third decision that the Executive annul its 1985 resolution (2882-D-86). This request was innovative in two respects when compared to the other two. First, it acknowledged that Congress had to enact new immigration legislation to replace that passed by the last military dictatorship. It then added that the Executive should pass another norm for the regularization of immigrants residing in the country (2882-D-86). Second, the request explained that Congress was willing to cooperate with the Executive in finding temporary solutions for these immigrants. Overall, this resolution provided a blueprint for the ideal immigration decision-making process.

INFORMATION REQUESTS

The Argentine Congress can create legislation and influence policy in a direct way. In addition, it can influence policy in more indirect ways.

Table 5.10. Information Requests Approved: 1983–1989

Chamber	No. IR	PJ	Party Proposing UCR	Other	% Responded	Avg. Delay in Response
House	4	2	None	2	50	64 days
Senate	None	None	None	None	None	N/A

Table 5.11. Information Requests Proposed Not Approved: 1983–1989

Chamber	No. IR	PJ	Party Proposing UCR	Other
House	7	2	None	5
Senate	None	None	None	None

Through information requests, Congress asks the presidency to answer questions related to a policy issue or to change its position on an issue (see Tables 5.10 and 5.11). In theory, the questions relate to information that Congress may need to exercise its legislative function. In practice, Congress exercises this power broadly and does not need to justify this action in any specific way. An information request simply describes a problem that has been identified and poses questions to gather information about it. These questions function as a check and send the message that the Executive is being watched.

Argentine legislators also use information requests as a way of expressing their position on how certain official affairs should be conducted. In these cases, the intent of legislators goes beyond mere familiarity with a given issue. For instance, on several occasions Congress requested that the Executive provide information about the entry of immigrants to Argentina and its control (for instance, 4962-D-93, 1082-D-94, 2432-D-94, and 1587-S-92). These requests included a number of questions related to the ways in which entry of immigrants was controlled at the border, data on legal and illegal entries, and measures adopted by the Immigration Agency to prevent undocumented immigrants from working. These information requests were not just directed to obtain information but also constituted a way of telling the Executive about a problem that needed attention.

Following this distinction between the purposes of the information requests, this study classifies them into two main groups (see Tables 5.12 and 5.13). The first group, called *oversight* in this study, comprises those requests aimed at acquiring information about certain events and provides a general overview of the Executive's task. The second group, termed *critique/change*, encompasses requests that are critical of a particular situation and aimed at changing Executive's behavior. This study argues that this second type of request has potential for enhancing congressional control over the Executive. All information requests under analysis for the period 1983 to 1989 were of the critique/change type. Most of the information requests under analysis for the period 1989 to 1995 were also of the critique/change type (74 percent), but over a quarter of them (26 percent) were of the oversight type.

NUMBER, INITIATION, AND TOPICS
OF THE INFORMATION REQUESTS

For the period 1983 to 1989, the House initiated eleven information requests and four were approved (see Table 5.12). The information requests comprised 25 percent of the total number of immigration-related issues (see Table 5.1). The Senate remained less active during the first period under analysis and proposed no information requests. Perhaps because information requests play an important role in exercising oversight over the Executive, opposition parties usually initiated information requests. For instance, while a Radical president was in office between 1983 and 1989, the PJ or third parties initiated all information requests.

The information requests covered a broad range of issues (see Tables 5.12 and 5.13). For the period 1983 to 1989, most of the information requests related to irregularities detected in the Immigration Agency and the rest concerned more general aspects of immigration policies. The Immigration Agency has had serious corruption problems over the years, and several information requests addressed these problems. Several information requests in the House addressed aspects of the administration of the Immigration Agency.

Table 5.12. Information Requests House: 1983–1989

ID No.	Year	Approved	Responded?	Party	Description	Objective
General						
3142-D	1985			PJ	Entry of immigrants to the country / Data about visas awarded	Critique/change
3629-D	1985			Other	Policy of the Immigration Agency that requires capital to apply for residency / discriminates against Latin Americans	Critique/change
2486-D	1986			PJ	Agreement with Soviet Union to bring Jewish immigrants to Argentina	Critique/change
3594-D	1988			Other	Entry of immigrants who are HIV positive	Critique/change
2233-D	1989	Y		Other	Control of entry of tourists in the south of Argentina	Critique/change
Regarding Irregularities at Immigration Agency						
2787-D	1987			Other	Permits awarded to Asian immigrants to migrate to Argentina	Critique/change
195-D	1988	Y	Y	PJ	Indictment of Immigration Agency Office in Formosa related to Asian immigrants	Critique/change
407-D	1988	Y	Y	PJ	Indictment of Immigration Agency Office in Formosa related to Asian immigrants	Critique/change
642-D	1988			Other	Indictment of Immigration Agency Office in Formosa related to Asian immigrants	Critique/change
1649-D	1989			Other	Indictment of Immigration Agency employees & other middlemen regarding illegal activities related to visas for Asian & neighboring immigrants	Critique/change
2228-D	1989	Y		Other	Executive lack of compliance with projects for the immigration of Asians	Critique/change

Table 5.13. Information Requests Senate: 1989–1995

ID No.	Year	Approved	Responded?	Party	Description	Objective
General						
0234-S	1990	Y		PJ	Implementation of immigration legislation	Oversight
1083-S	1991			UCR	Inviting ministers of economy & interior to inform about fees paid at international bridges	Critique/change
71-S	1992	Y		UCR	Regulations for issuing visas & passports	Critique/change
1587-S	1992	Y		Other	How the entry of immigrants to the country is controlled (neighboring & Asian)	Critique/change
1966-S	1993	Y	Y	Other	Extent to which the 1991 census data has been processed	Oversight
Central & Eastern European						
1383-S	1992	Y	Y	Other	Plan to bring Central & Eastern Europeans	Critique/change
Neighboring Migration						
749-S	1993	Y		Other	Entry of Brazilian citizens to the country	Critique/change
1408-S	1993	Y	Y	PJ	Employment of Brazilian workers in an electrical plant	Critique/change
1692-S	1993	Y		UCR	How the amnesty passed by Decree 1033/92 is being implemented	Critique/change
1967-S	1993			Other	Partial outcome of Amnesty Decree of 1992	Oversight
341-S	1995		Y	Other	Immigration policy the Executive is implementing	Oversight
745-S	1995			Other	Control measures at the borders	Critique/change
1951-S	1995	Y		Other	Official estimates regarding the existence of 800,000 illegal immigrants	Critique/change
1979-S	1995	Y	Y	Other	Data about neighboring immigrants residing in the country	Critique/change
Illegal Activities						
193-S	1992			Other	Visas issued at the Argentine consulate in China	Critique/change

Executive's Response to the Information Requests

Information requests can be an effective way of supervising the Executive, but legislators do not have a way of compelling the Executive to respond. For the period 1983 to 1989, the Executive responded to half of the requests approved (see Table 5.12). For the following presidential period, however, this number was lower. The Executive took an average of over two months to respond to these requests. Because the number of requests referring to immigration issues during the period was so small (N=4), it is possible to speculate that Congress did not exercise a strong check on the Executive in matters of immigration during the period under analysis.

UNDERSTANDING CONGRESSIONAL ACTIVITY DURING ALFONSÍN'S ADMINISTRATION

The Argentine Congress faced no gridlock on matters of immigration policy (Linz 1990). The literature on delegative democracy sheds light on the Alfonsín administration's immigration policies. More specifically, O'Donnell (1994) tells us about a proactive Executive that overrides the legislature. However, the literature falls short in accounting for cases in which the delegation patterns arise as a consequence of congressional inability to pass legislation. In immigration policy, the Argentine Executive ruled on the admission of foreign citizens because the Congress did not legislate in this policy area.

Scholars of democratization argue that economic and institutional crises shape the pattern of centralization of power in the Executive. Presidents in such cases generate institutional responses to problems perceived as urgent by decree. In the cases under analysis, however, Congress failed to act. Economic and institutional crises likely played two roles in this congressional inability. First, the crises gave rise to more urgent matters that required congressional attention, so other legislative responsibilities were given priority over immigration. Second, the crises awarded the Executive flexibility to rule on immigration and, as this study shows, a significant number of legislators were comfortable with this flexibility.

Overall, the immigration policies of the Argentine Congress differed from those of the Executive. Between 1983 and 1989, 65 percent of the proposals contemplated in the Argentine legislature aimed to make immigration rules more liberal. Furthermore, when the Executive enacted restrictive immigration policies, Congress expressed its distress through several information requests and attempted to make the Argentine Executive more accountable. The range of topics covered, as well as the depth in which these topics were discussed, attest to this. Even though the Executive was somewhat slow to respond to these requests, a mechanism for checking its power was in place after the reestablishment of democracy.

SIX

Delegative Democracy Revisited

Congress and Immigration, 1989–1999

The Argentine Constitution empowers Congress to rule on the admission of foreign citizens. Despite this, the immigration decision-making process in Argentina was centralized in the Executive until 2003. Multiple reasons accounted for this centralization. The literature on delegative democracy sheds light on the Menem administration's policy-making style. O'Donnell argues that presidents in these models of democracy rule as they see fit, bypassing Congress whenever convenient (1994, 59). However, the literature falls short in accounting for congressional inability to pass (immigration) legislation. This study argues that in immigration policy, the Executive ruled on immigration policies because the Congress did not take up this responsibility.

Economic and institutional crises likely played a role in this congressional inability in two ways. First, they gave rise to more urgent matters that required congressional attention. Second, they made it convenient for the Executive to enjoy flexible powers to rule on immigration. Further, most legislators thought the Executive should take the lead on immigration policies, leaving Congress as a supervisor of Executive action. The creation of the legislative committees on population in 1990 and 1991 put immigration issues on the legislative agenda, increased congressional activity on immigration, and created an opportunity for the passage of comprehensive immigration reform. However, Congress was unable to agree on a new comprehensive immigration law until 2003.

Congress, however, was otherwise active in matters of immigration, generating bills, submitting information requests for the Executive, and making policy declarations on different subjects. Through some of these proposals, Congress played a role in supervising the Executive. This chapter explores this congressional activity during Menem's two administrations, 1989 to 1995 and 1995 to 1999.

POPULATION AND DEVELOPMENT COMMITTEES

Resolution 275-S of 1990 created the Senate Committee on Population and Human Development, and Resolution 516-D of 1991 created the House Committee on Population and Human Resources (see Appendix III). After the creation of these standing committees, interest in immigration issues increased significantly, as did the likelihood of passing a comprehensive immigration reform. For instance, three comprehensive immigration reform bills were introduced between 1994 and 1995. An additional two were introduced between 1996 and 1998. It is likely that the restrictive Executive immigration policies that followed a xenophobic outburst triggered by some public officials and unions at the end of 1993 (analyzed in chapter 4) made Argentine legislators aware of their responsibility for producing immigration policies.

COMPOSITION OF CONGRESS

As mentioned before, two political parties dominated Argentina between World War II and 1999: the UCR and the PJ. Only in 1999 did an alliance between the UCR and the Front for a Country in Solidarity (Frente País Solidario, or Frepaso) win the presidency. Therefore, until then, the composition of Congress tended to reflect the dominance of the PJ and the UCR. When PJ president Menem was in office (1989–1999), he enjoyed a plurality in the House for most periods and a comfortable majority from 1995 to 1997 (Table 6.1). Further, the PJ clearly dominated the Senate, with a majority ranging from 54.2 to 62.5 percent (Table 6.2).

Table 6.1. Composition of the Argentine House of Representatives by Political Party: 1989–1999

| Political Party | Period (Percentages) | | | | |
	1989–1991	1991–1993	1993–1995	1995–1997	1997–1999
PJ	47.2	45.1	49.4	52.1	46.7
UCR	35.4	32.7	32.7	26.9	26.5
Other	17.4	22.2	17.9	21.0	26.8
Total	100.0	100.0	100.0	100.0	100.0

Source: Jones 2002

Table 6.2. Composition of the Argentine Senate by Political Party: 1989–2001

| Political Party | Period (Percentages) | | | |
	1989–1992	1992–1995	1995–1998	1998–2001
PJ	54.2	62.5	55.7	55.7
UCR	29.2	22.9	28.6	30.0
Other	16.6	14.6	15.7	14.3
Total	100.0	100.0	100.0	100.0

Source: Jones 2002

CONGRESSIONAL ACTIVITY, 1989–1995

This analysis considers two Menem administrations, 1989 to 1995 and 1995 to 1999. (See Appendix IV for details about documents included.) After the creation of the population committees in the Senate and House in 1990 and 1991, respectively, the numbers of immigration decisions introduced more than doubled, climbing from 43 in 1983 to 1989 to 108 in 1989 to 1995 and 75 in 1995 to 1999 (see Tables 6.3 and 6.4).[1] Bills that become laws are important instruments for creating policies. During the latter two periods, Congress considered an important number of proposals, ranging from 28 to 44 percent of the total issues examined, directed at creating new or modifying existing legislation, including comprehensive immigration reform.

The Argentine Congress also generated important numbers of information requests, ranging from 19 to 47 percent of the total issues examined,

Table 6.3. Immigration Bills and Other Decisions Considered by the Argentine Congress: 1989–1995

Decisions Considered	House	Senate
	Absolute Numbers and Percentages	
Total	76	32
Number of Bills	25 (33%)	9 (28%)
Number of Information Requests	23 (30%)	15 (47%)
Number of Courses of Action	18 (23%)	5 (16%)
Number of Declarations	2 (3%)	1 (3%)

Note: Decisions having only an internal administrative impact on Congress are not included in this table.

Table 6.4. Immigration Bills and Other Decisions Considered by the Argentine Congress: 1995–1999

Decisions Considered	House	Senate
	Absolute Numbers and Percentages	
Total	54	21
Number of Bills	24 (44%)	6 (29%)
Number of Information Requests	12 (22%)	4 (19%)
Number of Courses of Action	4 (7%)	1 (5%)
Number of Declarations	14 (26%)	10 (48%)

Note: Decisions having only an internal administrative impact on Congress are not included in this table.

demanding that the Executive provide information about different policies and actions. The information requests covered a broad range of issues, from specific immigration policies to alleged illegal activities, generally including an exhaustive number of questions followed by statements regarding the desired Executive behavior.

Congress considered requests for a course of action. These instruments are intended to produce a change in Executive behavior and were broadly used during Alfonsín's administration. For the period 1989 to 1995, the use of this type of request decreased to 16 to 23 percent, and for the period 1995 to 1999 it decreased to 5 to 7 percent. The decrease in course of action requests was likely compensated to some extent by the increase in information requests. Congress also issued declarations on a

Table 6.5. Degree of Effectiveness of Each Chamber: 1989–1995 (Ratio of Decisions Approved versus Proposed)

Decisions Considered	House	Senate
Total Decisions Approved	28	19
Bills Approved	7 (25%)	5 (26%)
Information Req. Approved	11 (39%)	12 (63%)
Course of Action Approved	9 (32%)	2 (11%)
Declarations Approved	1 (4%)	0

Table 6.6. Degree of Effectiveness of Each Chamber: 1995–1999 (Ratio of Decisions Approved versus Proposed)

Decisions Considered	House	Senate
Total Decisions Approved	17	11
Laws Approved	1 (6%)	3 (28%)
Information Req. Approved	6 (35%)	2 (18%)
Course of Action Approved	1 (6%)	1 (9%)
Declarations Approved	9 (52%)	5 (5%)

broad variety of topics, ranging from establishing national holidays to commemorating immigrants and their contributions to Argentina, and to a meeting on issues of interest related to immigration. Whereas these accounted for just 3 percent of congressional activity during the first Menem administration, they accounted for 26 to 48 percent during the second one. Legislators' interest in immigration issues seems to have broadened just a few years after the creation of the congressional population committees.

Patterns in the productivity and effectiveness of the two chambers of the Argentine Congress similar to those noted during 1983 to 1989 were obvious in the later periods under analysis. The Senate was less productive than the House (see Tables 6.3 and 6.4). For both periods, the number of decisions dealing with immigration in the House was more than twice that number for the Senate. In turn, the Senate was more effective in approving the decisions originating therein (see Tables 6.5 and 6.6). The majority held by the PJ may partly explain this higher degree of effectiveness of the upper chamber.

Table 6.7. Immigration Decisions Proposed by Political Party: 1989–1995

Political Party Proposing	House	Senate
PJ	27	8
UCR	29	4
Other	13	10

Note: This table does not include the bills originating in a different chamber or the Executive.

Table 6.8. Immigration Decisions Proposed by Political Party: 1995–1999

Political Party Proposing	House	Senate
PJ	17	10
UCR	7	7
Other	27	2

Note: This table does not include the bills originating in a different chamber or the Executive.

During both periods under consideration, the PJ generated more issues for congressional consideration than the UCR (see Tables 6.7 and 6.8). This dominance of the PJ was particularly noteworthy in the Senate from 1989 to 1995, when the productivity of the PJ was double that of the UCR (see Table 6.7). The influence of third parties increased, becoming especially important during the period 1995 to 1999 in the House, where third parties generated 53 percent of the proposals considered. This increased influence is explained by the growth of Frepaso, which went from holding 3 percent to 16 percent of the seats in the House (Jones 2002). Further, Juan Pablo Cafiero, a member of Frepaso and son of former presidential candidate Antonio Cafiero, headed the House Committee on Population and Human Resources and personally signed or cosigned fourteen bills and decisions between 1995 and 1999.

BILLS INTRODUCED, 1989–1995

Although Congress was unable to agree on a comprehensive immigration law until 2003, it nevertheless produced, debated, and sometimes approved bills related to immigration policy. During the period 1989 to 1995, congressional pronouncements on immigration issues increased immensely.

Both houses considered a total of thirty-four bills, almost three times the number considered for the period 1983 to 1989 (see Table 6.3). The House was much more productive than the Senate, generating all but one of the twenty-five bills introduced. The Senate, on the other hand, initiated none of the nine bills it considered, 80 percent of which originated in the lower house and 20 percent in the Executive.

Most of the bills initiated between 1989 and 1995 related strictly to immigration policies, including changes to existing immigration legislation in areas such as the admission of persons with disabilities, deportation of immigrants, amounts charged for immigration offenses, rules for the admission of foreigners in higher-education institutions, and jobs that could be held by foreigners (see Tables 6.9 and 6.10). Other bills dealt with the Immigration Agency's delegation of functions to the regional offices and creation of an administrative service. The remainder addressed a diverse set of topics, including the creation of a federal committee for migration and the approval of an agreement with the International Organization for Migration.

BILLS PASSED, 1989–1995

Five bills dealing with immigration were passed between 1989 and 1995. Two bills were related to the International Organization for Migration (48-PE-89 and 362-PE-90). The first approved some modifications to the constitution of the ICM. The second bill approved an agreement between the Argentine government and the International Organization for Migration to cooperate on immigration issues. Although this agreement had no direct impact on the immigration policies of the Argentine State, it included activities to make the government more sensitive to the needs of immigrants.

A bill introduced during this period proposed the removal of an impediment established in the 1981 law that barred persons with a physical and/or psychological disability from applying for a visa in Argentina. Six different proposals dealing with the removal of this impediment were initiated during the period (744-PE-93, 4449-D-93, 71-PE-93, 5114-D-93, 654-D-95, and 3128-D-95). This highly discriminatory prohibition violated international agreements subscribed to by the Argentine government.

Table 6.9. Bills Introduced in the House: 1989–1995

ID No.	Year	Approved	Party	Description	Permissive?
Comprehensive Laws					
5611-D	1994		UCR	Proposes comprehensive immigration law	+
3341-D	1995		PJ	Proposes comprehensive immigration law	+
3300-D	1995		PJ	Proposes comprehensive immigration law	+
People with Disabilities; Penalties					
4449-D	1993		PJ	Revokes prohibition of applying for residency for people with disabilities	+
71-PE	1993	L. 24393	PEN	Revokes prohibition of applying for residency for people with disabilities; updates penalties	0
5114-D	1993		UCR	Revokes prohibition of applying for residency for people with disabilities; benefits Mercosur	+
2134-D	1994		PJ	Updates penalties for immigration offenses	–
0654-D	1995		UCR	Revokes prohibition of applying for residency for people with disabilities	+
3128-D	1995		PJ	Revokes prohibition of applying for residency for people with disabilities; updates penalties	0
Deportation Provisions					
0006-D	1993	Y	PJ	States that foreigners who break labor, taxation, or social security laws should be expelled	–
0616-D	1993		PJ	States that foreigners sentenced to prison be expelled from the country	–
1523-D	1994	Y	PJ	States that foreigners sentenced to prison be expelled from the country	–
5827-D	1994		PJ	States that foreigners sentenced to prison be expelled from the country	–
4554-D	1993		Other	Revokes Decree 2771/93 with norms for deportation of foreigners	+

Table 6.9. Bills Introduced in the House: 1989–1995 (*cont.*)

ID No.	Year	Approved	Party	Description	Permissive?
Changes to Other Immigration Legislation					
3150-D	1992	Y	PJ	Facilitates the admission of foreigners to educational institutions	+
2133-D	1993		UCR	Charges a fee to people who cross the border on a regular basis (not as immigrants)	–
2959-D	1993	L. 24493	PJ	Reserves jobs for Argentines and documented immigrants	–
1785-D	1995		UCR	Charges a fee to people who cross the border on a regular basis (not as immigrants)	–
5912-D	1995		Other	Provides amnesty for bordering migrants	+
Other					
41-PE	1990		PEN	Allows Immigration Agency to delegate tasks to regional offices and police	0
6305-D	1990	L. 24008	Other	Allows Immigration Agency to delegate tasks to regional offices and police	0
4213-D	1992		Other	Creates financial division in Immigration Agency	0
6014-D	1992		PJ	Creates a federal committee for migration	0
0831-D	1995		PJ	Creates a federal committee for migration	0
362-PE	1990	L. 24001	PEN	Approves agreement with International Organization for Migration	0

Table 6.10. Bills Introduced in the Senate: 1989–1995

ID No.	Year	Approved	Party	Description	Permissive?
People with Disabilities; Penalties					
744-S	1993		PEN	Revokes prohibition of applying for residency for people with disabilities; updates penalties	0
27-CD	1994	L. 24393	D	Revokes prohibition of applying for residency for people with disabilities; updates penalties	0
Deportation Provisions					
63-CD	1993		D	States that foreigners who break labor, taxation, or social security laws should be expelled from the country (6-D-93)	–
77-CD	1994		D	States that foreigners sentenced to prison should be expelled from the country (1523-D-94)	–
Changes to Other Immigration Legislation					
66-CD	1993		D	Facilitates the admission of foreigners in educational institutions (3150-D-92)	+
92-CD	1993	L. 24493	D	Reserves jobs on ships for Argentines; work limitations for transitory immigrants	–
Other					
48-PE	1989	L. 23816	D	Approves creation of Intergovernmental Committee for Migration	0
362-PE	1990	L. 24001	PEN	Approves agreement with International Organization for Migration	0
43-CD	1991	L. 24008	D	Allows Immigration Agency to delegate tasks to regional offices and police (6305-D-90)	0

Also, a fourteen-year-old girl from Uruguay with Down syndrome, Carla Bernasconi, had been unsuccessfully trying to get her residency for seven years (*Página 12* 02/04/1994). In February 1994 the media publicized the unfairness of Carla's situation, prompting President Menem to award permanent residency to Carla shortly after. In November Congress passed Law 24393, which eliminated the prohibition.

The Executive also updated penalty amounts for immigration offenses (744-S-93, 71-PE-93, and 27-CD-94). Proposals to update the amounts of the fines were also made by two representatives from the PJ (2134-D-94 and 3128-D-95). The Executive made a strategic move in addressing both issues in the same bill. In the message that accompanied the bill, Menem emphasized the importance of removing the obstacles for the regularization of the immigration status of people with disabilities but said little about the amount for fines.

More restrictive in its tone, and prompted by the deteriorating economic situation, was a bill (92-CD-93 and 2959-D-93) initiated by three representatives of the PJ and intended to preserve jobs for Argentines and those authorized to work in Argentina by the Immigration Agency. Passed in May 1995, this bill became known as the National Labor Law and was intended to "discourage the practice of hiring clandestine labor" (2959-D-93). According to the text accompanying the bill, "The crisis of the labor market made this bill necessary for guaranteeing the fair competition between businesses." The bill declared that all remunerated work in the country should be done by Argentines or persons authorized by the Immigration Agency to work (Law 24493, article 1). In reality, the effect of this legislation was minimal because the labor and immigration legislation already stated the same rules.

The House passed three other immigration bills, all introduced by PJ legislators, that did not obtain later approval in the Senate. Two of these bills expanded the broad deportation provisions established in Law 22439 of 1981 (6-D-93 and 1523-D-94). Law 22439 awarded extensive power to the Executive to deport immigrants who were sentenced to five years in prison or were engaged in activities affecting social peace, national security, or public order, or who were simply undocumented. At the end of 1993, the Executive passed Decree 2771/93, which authorized it to deport those immigrants who committed crimes or illegally occupied dwellings.

The two bills under analysis were in perfect harmony with this decree and added other cases in which foreigners could be deported (6-D-93 and 1523-D-94).

Paul Gilroy (1991) states that respect for the law is a basic requirement for belonging in a national community. In tune with this idea, one bill explained that those who intend to integrate into Argentine society "should assimilate to our lifestyle and social, cultural, and moral values" (1523-D-94). Laws, according to this PJ representative, protect the highest principles of "Argentinity" and social life, and they should be respected by foreigners and nationals alike (1523-D-94). Moreover, "those foreigners who are not willing to adapt to our society by complying with the law and respecting its values, should not stay" (1523-D-94). The statements by this legislator parallel the discourses of Executive officials in 1993 and 1994 regarding immigration.

The third bill approved by the House but not the Senate authorized certain transitory immigrants who were in prison to attend educational institutions (3150-D-92). According to article 102 of Law 22439, only temporary or permanent residents could attend educational institutions in Argentina. This bill showed a high degree of regard for the rights of immigrants and cited a number of international conventions to justify its provisions, including the 1969 American Convention on Human Rights (also known as the Pact of San José, Costa Rica) and the 1966 International Covenant on Economic, Social and Cultural Rights, which, according to the Argentine Constitution, should take precedence over all other laws, including the Constitution itself. It also mentioned that the provisions of Law 22439 of 1981 contradicted the principles of process of integration in the Southern Common Market with Argentina's bordering countries.

OTHER BILLS INTRODUCED, 1989–1995

Overall, the bills approved by one or both chambers of the Argentine Congress in the period 1989 to 1995 were considerably restrictive and in tune with the policies approved by the Executive in 1993 and 1994. Further, the discourses on immigration by some legislators paralleled those of the Executive's officials during this time. Some bills that were not passed, however, would have made immigration policies more permissive. A number of these proposals were initiated in the House of Representatives, namely, bills proposing the annulment of Decree 2771/93 (4554-D-93), the enactment of an amnesty for immigrants (5912-D-95), and the "federalizing" of the immigration decision-making process through the creation of a federal committee of migration (6014-D-92 and 831-D-95). Finally, three bills proposing comprehensive immigration policies are the object of the next section.

Perhaps the bill that most openly conflicted with the Executive's policies was the one submitted by a representative from a smaller leftist party to revoke Decree 2771/93 (4554-D-93). This decree had authorized the Executive to deport immigrants who were caught committing any crime or illegally occupying dwellings. According to this bill, the Executive's decree was unconstitutional and contradicted criminal law (4554-D-93). It critiqued that the decree did not target employers, some of whom made immigrants work and live in conditions comparable to those in the Middle Ages (4554-D-93). Overall, this bill built a strong case against the deportation policies of the Argentine Executive, providing persuasive justifications for their annulment.

Another bill, put forward by a representative from a smaller center-left party, proposed an amnesty for undocumented immigrants (5912-D-95). This bill sought to improve the situation of the immigrants from neighboring countries who were exploited in the context of a deep regional socioeconomic crisis (5912-D-95). The duty of the state, this bill stated, was to look for ways to remedy the marginalization facing immigrants. This bill was likely a response to the scapegoating of immigrants after 1993 in Argentina, which was initiated by Argentine state officials, unions, and part of the media. "In moments of instability and job loss," the bill explained, "the state should not encourage prejudices and discrimination" (5912-D-95). The bill concluded by urging Congress to pass and put an end to exclusionary and discriminatory practices against immigrants.

Finally, a House bill initiated by a PJ representative proposed the creation of a federal immigration council, composed by the federal government, the provinces, and the City of Buenos Aires, which would take charge of plans to promote immigration (6014-D-92 and 831-D-95). According to the 1981 law, the federal government should promote immigration in areas of the country that were not densely populated, but this was not happening. The creation of the federal council would ensure that the will of the provinces was heard and respected. Only immigration policies conceived in this way, the bill stated, would benefit all the provinces and the country as a whole.

Although the bill did not propose specific immigration policies, its author believed that the country needed an ambitious immigration policy. He also celebrated the Executive's plan to attract immigrants from Central and Eastern Europe and thought that the Executive should bring in more than one hundred thousand immigrants a year (6014-D-92). When first introduced in 1992, this bill was consistent with the immigration policies of the Executive and intended to regularize the immigration status of neighboring immigrants and to encourage the immigration of Central and Eastern Europeans (6014-D-92). When resubmitted for approval in 1995, however, this bill was far more liberal than the immigration policies of the Argentine Executive (832-D-95).

COMPREHENSIVE IMMIGRATION BILLS

One novelty during this period was that, for the first time since the re-establishment of democracy, some of the bills introduced proposed comprehensive immigration reform. The creation of the population committees at the beginning of the 1990s probably facilitated these proposals. Three bills of this kind were initiated in the House in 1994 and 1995, and although they were not passed, they represented a positive step toward the passage of new legislation. With some variation, these bills proposed immigration rules that were to some extent more liberal than those in place.

One bill was authored by a UCR representative, Marcelo B. Miguel Muñoz (5611-D-94), and the others by two PJ representatives, Horacio A. Macedo (3341-D-95) and Francisco P. Toto (3300-D-95). Table 6.11 shows how these bills compare with the 1981 law. Out of the bills analyzed here, the only one that clearly stated that the Argentine government should encourage immigration to Argentina is Macedo's (article 7). Unlike the 1981 law, which encouraged the immigration of "those foreigners whose cultural characteristics permit their integration into the Argentine society" (Law 22439, article 2), Macedo's bill was open to all kinds of immigrants and encouraged immigration according to the social needs of the country.

Regarding the categories under which immigrants could be admitted in the country, the bills under analysis did not innovate much. They mirrored either the general provisions of the 1981 law, which classified immigrants as permanent, temporary, or transitory (Macedo, article 27 and ff.) or the requirements for applying for each type of immigration category established in Decree 1023/94 (Muñoz, article 13 and ff.; Toto, article 22 and ff.).[2] In one aspect, however, the bills differed. As shown in Table 6.11, Macedo's bill was unique in giving a central role to the regional integration process of the Southern Common Market, stating that Mercosur citizens could obtain a work visa at the border if they wanted to stay and work in Argentina (article 32).

One important feature of immigration policies is the bundle of rights awarded to immigrants, which has a major impact on their lives. Macedo's bill protected the civil rights of all immigrants and not just certain categories (article 68). Moreover, it protected their rights to education and to preservation of cultural identity in the process of integration (articles 11 and 8). The other two bills mostly repeated the provisions of Law 22439. The bills by Muñoz (article 44) and Toto (article 50) established that only permanent residents would enjoy civil rights in Argentina but extended labor rights to permanent or temporary residents (Muñoz, article 47; Toto, article 53).

Unlike citizens, immigrants in most countries can be deported. Toto's bill, however, awarded protections against deportation, stating that courts should intervene in deportation processes (article 45). In addition, and unlike the 1981 law, all three bills established that the Executive could give immigrants the option of regularizing their immigration status before deporting them (Muñoz, article 31; Macedo, article 99; Toto, article 37). However, these bills all proposed to harden the deportation provisions of 1981 in that they reduced the number of prison years for which an immigrant could be deported (Muñoz, article 32; Macedo, article 106; Toto, article 39).

Finally, all three bills showed a concern for preserving the constitutional division of powers while encouraging inter-power coordination, providing ways for making the immigration decision-making process more participatory and less centralized within the Executive. For this purpose, the bills all proposed the creation of boards, composed of representatives from different executive agencies as well as the congressional population committees, that would have a role in the immigration decision-making

Table 6.11. Comparison of the Provisions of Law 22439 (1981) with the Bills by Muñoz, Macedo, and Toto

	Law 22439	*Muñoz*	*Macedo*	*Toto*
Encourages Immigration?	Immigrants whose cultural characteristics permit integration into society Article 2	No	According to the social needs of the country Article 7	No
Types of Residency	Permanent, Temporary, and Transitory (does not specify requirements) Article 12	Permanent, Temporary, and Nonresident (specifies requirements) Article 13 and ff.	Permanent, Temporary, and Transitory (does not specify requirements) Article 27 and ff.	Permanent, Temporary, and Nonresident (specifies requirements) Article 22 and ff.
Mercosur Citizens			Natives of Mercosur can apply for Transitory Residency and work Article 32	
Rights for Immigrants?	Only permanent residents enjoy civil rights Article 15	Only permanent residents enjoy all civil rights Article 44	All residents enjoy civil rights Article 68	Only permanent residents enjoy all civil rights Article 50
Deportation Provisions	Undocumented are deported Article 37	Undocumented have options before deportation Article 31	Undocumented have options before deportation Article 99	Undocumented have options before deportation Article 37
	If sentenced to 5 years in prison or for activities that affect social peace Article 95	If sentenced to 6 months in prison Article 32	If sentenced to 2 years in prison or for activities that affect social peace Article 106	If sentenced to 6 months in prison Article 39
Who Decides Deportation?	Ministry of Interior Article 37	Immigration Agency or Ministry of Interior Article 38	Immigration Agency or Ministry of Interior Article 102	Intervention of Courts Article 45
Decision of Immigration Policies	Centralized on the Executive/ Ministry of Interior Article 2	Immigration Agency, advised by National Immigration Board Articles 3 and 11	Executive, advised by National Immigration Board Articles 2 and 15	Immigration Agency and Federal Population Board Articles 2 and 3

process. In the bills by Muñoz (article 12) and Macedo (article 15), these boards had advisory, nonbinding roles. In the Toto bill, the board had a binding role and shared decision-making powers with the Ministry of the Interior.

These bills show Congress taking charge of immigration policy matters. Even though these bills did not become law, Congress nonetheless took its first steps in the direction of enacting comprehensive immigration policies. Additionally, these bills called for immigration policies more liberal than those put in place by the Executive. For one thing, all three removed discriminatory references to "cultural compatibility" and extended civil and other rights to immigrants. For another, all three aimed to make immigration decisions less centralized within the Executive. Overall, between 1989 and 1995, Congress was significantly active in producing and approving bills dealing with immigration issues. Although most of the legislation passed during this period was more restrictive than the immigration rules then in place, Congress considered an important number of proposals that would have made immigration policies more liberal (30 percent).

BILLS INTRODUCED, 1995–1999

During the period 1995 to 1999, the total number of congressional proposals regarding immigration issues decreased from the period 1989 to 1995. More specifically, whereas Congress initiated 108 bills and other decisions in the period 1989 to 1995, it initiated 75 in the period 1995 to 1999 (see Tables 6.3 and 6.4). However, considering that the constitutional reform of 1994 reduced presidential terms to four years, the proportional number of proposals regarding immigration issues slightly increased. Moreover, the number of bills introduced during both periods was comparable (34 versus 30) (Tables 6.3 and 6.4). As in the previous period, the productivity of the Senate and the House in generating immigration bills differed. The House was more productive than the Senate, generating all but one of the 24 bills it considered. The Senate, on the other hand, showed a 400 percent increase in productivity when compared with the previous period, generating 4 of the 6 bills it considered.

The bills initiated between 1995 and 1999 covered a wide range of topics (see Tables 6.12 and 6.13). Most of them proposed changes to existing

Table 6.12. Bills Introduced in the House: 1995–1999

ID No.	Year	Approved	Party	Description	Permissive?
Comprehensive Laws					
2979-D	1996		PJ	Proposes comprehensive immigration law	?
Amnesty for Latin American Immigrants					
8089-D	1998		Other	Proposes amnesty for immigrants from Latin America	+
People with Disabilities					
3894-D	1997		PJ	Revokes prohibition of applying for residency for people with disabilities	+
Deportation Provisions					
6629-D	1996		UCR	Requires court order for deportation	+
1577-D	1997		PJ	Lowers level of prison sentence for deportation	–
1724-D	1997		Other	Requires court order for deportation	+
0087-PE	1998		PE	Proposes deportation provisions, prison sentence for those who help undocumented immigrants	–
Smaller Changes to Immigration Legislation					
6490-D	1996		PJ	Proposes several changes to immigration law	0
4728-D	1997		PJ	Proposes creation of immigration courts	+
5096-D	1997		Other	Proposes amnesty for Latin American immigrants	+
1212-D	1998		Other	Proposes amnesty for Latin American immigrants	+
7952-D	1998		PJ	Proposes several changes to immigration law (reproduces 6490-D-96)	0

Table 6.12. Bills Introduced in the House: 1995–1999 (cont.)

ID No.	Year Approved	Party	Description	Permissive?
Other				
2311-D	1996	Other	Proposes approval of UN International Convention on the Protection of the Rights of All Migrant Workers and Members of Their Families (1990)	+
3382-3	1996	Other	Changes regulations for nationalization	+
6174-D	1996	Other	Allows foreigners with 10 years of residence to vote in elections	0
2778-D	1997	UCR	Changes regulations for naturalization	+
3806-D	1997	PJ	Establishes day to celebrate Ukrainian immigrants	0
3809-D	1997	Other	Creates rules to protect temporary migrants	+
0079-D	1998	Other	Proposes approval of UN International Convention on the Protection of the Rights of All Migrant Workers and Members of Their Families (1990)	0
1826-D	1998	Other	Allows foreigners with 10 years of residence to vote in elections	+
1979-D	1998	Other	Approves immigration agreement with Bolivia	–
2819-D	1998	Other	Changes regulations for naturalization	+
6250-D	1998	UCR	Declares city of Comodoro Rivadavia as capital of immigrant groups	0
6297-D	1998 L. 25116	PJ	Declares September as month of immigrant groups	0

Table 6.13. Bills Introduced in the Senate: 1995–1999

ID No.	Year	Approved	Party	Description	Permissive?
Changes to Immigration Legislation					
1369-S	1998		PJ	Modifies sanctions for immigration violations	–
0008-S	1998	L 25098	PE	Approves immigration agreement with Bolivia	
0009-S	1998	L 25099	PE	Approves immigration agreement with Peru	
2328-S	1998		UCR	Proposes amnesty for undocumented immigrants	–
Other					
1290-S	1997		PJ	Establishes day to celebrate Ukrainian immigrants	0
1325-S	1997		UCR	Establishes day to celebrate Ukrainian immigrants	0

immigration legislation in areas such as the admission of persons with disabilities, the deportation of immigrants, and amnesties for immigrants from Latin America. Some dealt with the right of immigrants with ten years of residence to vote. The remaining bills addressed topics ranging from the creation of immigration courts to the approval of international conventions.

BILLS PASSED, 1995–1999

Only three bills generated during this period became law: two approving immigration treaties with Bolivia and Peru and one designating September as the month to commemorate immigrants. The Executive requested approval by Congress of the two treaties previously signed with Bolivia and Peru. According to Article 75.22 of the Constitution, Congress must approve treaties with foreign powers (Honorable Senado de la Nación Argentina n.d.). The messages accompanying the Executive's requests were almost identical and stated that the purpose of the treaties was to provide an adequate framework for immigrant workers from Bolivia and Peru. These treaties provided ninety-day visas, after the expiration of which immigrants had to comply with the immigration rules in place requiring a job offer to be eligible for a work visa. The third bill proposed commemorating immigrant communities in the month of September of every year. It described the process of colonization of the city of Comodoro Rivadavia, Chubut, and mentioned all the immigrant communities that contributed to the settlement of this area of the country, including those from Europe, South Africa, and Latin America.

OTHER BILLS INTRODUCED, 1995–1999

The bills proposed during this period covered a broad range of issues. One proposed to award people with disabilities the same immigration category as their guardians (3894-D-97). A couple of bills proposed changes to deportation provisions. The first of these, initiated by the Executive, proposed several smaller changes to the 1981 law, including increasing penalties for those who helped or hired undocumented immigrants and reducing the prison sentence that made immigrants eligible for deportation from five to two years. A similar bill proposed by a representative from the PJ echoed the latter proposal regarding immigrants' eligibility for deportation. Conversely, two bills initiated by UCR representatives and a smaller party mandated the participation of courts in the deportation process.

One bill initiated by a representative from a third party proposed a broad amnesty for Latin American immigrants. This bill justified the proposed measure in light of the Argentine Constitution and documents produced by the Argentine Catholic Church and Pope John Paul II. Another bill, also initiated by a third-party representative, proposed extending voting rights in national elections to immigrants who had resided in the country for ten years. The remaining bills addressed topics ranging from the creation of immigration courts to the approval of international conventions.

COMPREHENSIVE IMMIGRATION BILLS

The only comprehensive immigration bill initiated during this period was the bill by Representative Muñoz, originally introduced in the previous period and described above.

INFORMATION REQUESTS

For the period 1989 to 1995, information requests demanding changes on the part of the Executive were dominant, comprising 74 percent of the requests considered, while for the period 1995 to 1999, this ratio changed dramatically, with requests aimed at oversight representing 61 percent of the total.

Number, Topics, and Initiation of the Information Requests

The number of information requests related to immigration issues more than tripled from the Alfonsín administration to the first Menem administration. This increase is partly explained as an increase in congressional activity regarding immigration after the creation of the population committees. Also, as democratic principles settled after the reestablishment of democracy, legislators may have made more use of information requests to put a check on Executive power. For the period 1989 to 1995, the House approved eleven information requests, the Senate ten, and together both chambers considered another twenty-six that were unapproved (see Tables 6.14 and 6.15). For the period 1995 to 1999, both chambers approved seven information requests and considered another ten that were unapproved (see Tables 6.16 and 6.17).

Precisely because information requests play an important role in oversight of the Executive, they are often initiated by opposition parties. During the Peronist Menem administration of 1989 to 1995, 77 percent of the information requests were initiated by the UCR or by smaller parties. During Menem's administration of 1995 to 1999, this number was 82 percent. The UCR retained an important supervisory role during the periods under consideration, but third parties also became increasingly important. In the House, Frepaso originated more than half of the information requests considered in Congress. In the Senate, two provincial parties were particularly active in initiating information requests between 1989 and 1995: Movimiento Popular Neuquino, a center-left party from the southern province of Neuquén, and Partido Autonomista, a center-right party from the northeastern province of Corrientes. Both provinces share borders with sources of immigration to Argentina: Neuquén with Chile and Corrientes with Uruguay and Brazil. Perhaps because of this fact, small parties in these provinces share a strong interest in immigration issues.

Content of the Information Requests, 1989–1995

The topics covered by the information requests included a broad range of issues (see Tables 6.14–17). For the period 1989 to 1995, these topics included general matters of immigration policy, Central and Eastern European immigration, neighboring immigration, the Immigration Agency, and alleged illegal activities. For the period 1995 to 1999, they involved general matters of immigration policy, neighboring migration, and the Immigration Agency.

Executive's Response to the Information Requests

As mentioned earlier, information requests can be an effective way of supervising the Executive, but legislatures lack a means to force a response on the part of the Executive. A semistructured interview conducted with twenty-six members of Congress showed that 55 percent of them thought that the Executive did not consistently respond to information requests. Corroborating this, for both periods the Executive responded to only 57 percent of the information requests (see Tables 6.14–6.17). Further, 37 percent of the members of Congress complained that the Executive took too long to respond and explained that the timing of responses was a crucial factor in providing a reliable check on Executive power. Argentine legislators also had complaints about the quality of the responses by the Executive (27 percent). One representative explained that the responses from the Executive were often too abstract to be helpful.[3] Another explained that the depth of the responses by the Executive was not satisfactory.[4] Still another expressed the opinion that the responses were many times only a formality, incapable of producing real change in Executive behavior.[5]

Table 6.14. Information Requests House: 1989–1995

ID No.	Year	Approved	Responded	Party	Description	Critical of Executive
General						
4862-D	1990	Y		PJ	Memos elaborated by Interministerial Demography Committee	Oversight
4564-D	1991			Other	Executive immigration policies and plans	Oversight
2432-D	1994	Y	Y	UCR	Procedures used to control the entry of neighboring immigrants to the country; estimates of undocumented immigrants	Critique/change
5793-D	1994	Y	Y	UCR	Inspections conducted by the Immigration Agency/Internal Revenue Agency	Oversight
Central & Eastern European						
4844-D	1991			Other	Menem's offer before the European Parliament to bring 300,000 Central and Eastern European immigrants to Argentina	Critique/change
4854-D	1991			UCR	Existence of studies relating to the plan to bring Central and Eastern Europeans	Critique/change
4983-D	1991			UCR	Menem's offer before the European Parliament to bring 300,000 Central and Eastern European immigrants to Argentina	Critique/change
5108-D	1991			UCR	Menem's offer before the European Parliament to bring 300,000 Central and Eastern European immigrants to Argentina	Critique/change
1303-D	1992	Y		UCR	Menem's offer before the European Parliament to bring 300,000 Central and Eastern European immigrants to Argentina	Critique/change
3420-D	1992	Y	Y	UCR	Menem's offer before the European Parliament to bring 300,000 Central and Eastern European immigrants to Argentina	Critique/change
5401-D	1992			UCR	Menem's offer before the European Parliament to bring 300,000 Central and Eastern European immigrants to Argentina	Critique/change
5453-D	1992			UCR	Menem's offer before the European Parliament to bring 300,000 Central and Eastern European immigrants to Argentina	Critique/change

Table 6.14. Information Requests House: 1989–1995 (cont.)

ID No.	Year	Approved	Responded	Party	Description	Critical of Executive
Bordering Migration						
4962-D	1993			UCR	Procedures used to control the entry of neighboring immigrants to the country; estimates of undocumented immigrants	Critique/change
1082-D	1994			PJ	Procedures used to control the entry of neighboring immigrants to the country; estimates of undocumented immigrants in the NE province of Misiones	Critique/change
2792-D	1995	Y	Y	PS	Instructions given to border control officers to control the amount of money that tourists have for their stay in Argentina; violation of Constitution	Critique/change
Administration of Immigration Agency						
6298-D	1990	Y		Other	Expenses relating to the Immigration Agency offices in Cordoba	Critique/change
2226-D	1992			UCR	An employee from the Immigration Agency who was transferred	Critique/change
2999-D	1993	Y		PJ	Administration of resources in the Immigration Agency	Oversight
175-D	1995	Y	Y	UCR	A paid phone information service provided by the Immigration Agency	Critique/change
691-D	1995	Y	Y	UCR	A paid phone information service provided by the Immigration Agency	Critique/change
4838-D	1995			UCR	A public bid to contract a private service for immigration control	Oversight
Illegal Activities						
708-D	1992			UCR	The Immigration Agency's director; declaration regarding the existence of an illegal network in this agency that charges immigrants to grant them their papers	Critique/change
5794-D	1994	Y	Y	UCR	Reasons why the population secretary has seized control over the Immigration Agency, impeding the latter from self-administration	Critique/change

Table 6.15. Information Requests Senate: 1989–1995

ID No.	Year	Approved	Responded	Party	Description	Critical of Executive
General						
0234-S	1990	Y		PJ	Implementation of the immigration legislation	Oversight
1083-S	1991			UCR	Inviting ministers of economy and the interior to inform about fees paid at international bridges	Critique/change
71-S	1992	Y		UCR	Regulations for issuing visas and passports	Critique/change
1587-S	1992	Y		Other	How the entry of immigrants to the country is controlled (neighboring and Asian)	Critique/change
1966-S	1993	Y	Y	Other	Extent to which 1991 census data has been processed	Oversight
Central & Eastern European						
1383-S	1992	Y	Y	Other	The plan to bring Central and Eastern Europeans	Critique/change
Bordering Migration						
749-S	1993	Y		Other	Entry of Brazilian citizens to the country	Critique/change
1408-S	1993	Y	Y	PJ	Employment of Brazilian workers in an electrical plant	Critique/change
1692-S	1993	Y		UCR	How the amnesty passed by Decree 1033/92 is being implemented	Critique/change
1967-S	1993			Other	Partial outcome of amnesty decree of 1992	Oversight
341-S	1995		Y	Other	Immigration policy the Executive is implementing	Oversight
745-S	1995			Other	Control measures at the borders	Critique/change
1951-S	1995	Y		Other	Official estimates regarding the existence of 800,000 illegal immigrants	Critique/change
1979-S	1995	Y	Y	Other	Data about neighboring immigrants residing in the country	Critique/change
Illegal Activities						
193-S	1992			Other	Visas issued at the Argentine Consulate in China	Critique/change

Table 6.16. Information Requests House: 1995–1999

ID No.	Year	Approved	Responded	Party	Description	Critical of Executive
General						
4818-D	1996	Y		PJ	Information about the existence of data on the entry of foreign citizens	Oversight
4820-D	1996	Y	Y	Other	Information on the number of citizenships granted in courts	Oversight
2403-D	1997			PJ	Information about citizenship awarded to citizens from Southeast Asia	Oversight
2867-D	1997			Other	Information about citizenship awarded to citizens of Syria	Oversight
4000-D	1997			UCR	Information about the existence of a project to detain undocumented immigrants	Critique/change
7930-D	1998			Other	Information about a plan to transfer immigration archives	Oversight
7964-D	1998			Other	Invitation for minister of the interior, secretary of security, and Immigration Agency director to a hearing at the House	Oversight
8044-D	1998			UCR	Request to submit immigration agreements with Peru and Paraguay for congressional consideration	Critique/change
8045-D	1998			UCR	Information about crimes committed by foreigners	Critique/change
6615-D	1998	Y	Y	PJ	Information about immigrants from former Soviet Union republics	Oversight
Bordering Migration						
3826-D	1996			Other	Procedures used to control the entry of immigrants from Bolivia	Critique/change
Administration Immigration Agency						
4464-D	1997	Y	Y	Other	Information about the role of the inspections director of the Immigration Agency	Oversight
5034-D	1997	Y	Y	Other	Information about administrative procedures at the Immigration Agency	Oversight

Table 6.17. Information Requests Senate: 1995–1999

ID No.	Year	Approved	Responded	Party	Description	Critical of Executive
General						
1384-S	1996			UCR	Information about a bid to computerize immigration control	Critique/change
0386-S	1997	Y	Y	UCR	Information about a U.S. government report that portrays Argentina as a bridge state for human trafficking	Oversight
2297-S	1998			UCR	Information about a plan for the settlement of Mercosur residents	Critique/change
2305-S	1998	Y		UCR	Information about the number of undocumented immigrants present in Argentina	Critique/change

FACTORS SHAPING CONGRESSIONAL ACTIVITY DURING THE MENEM ADMINISTRATION

The creation of the legislative committees put immigration issues on the legislative agenda and created an opportunity for the passage of new policies. However, this process was slow and no bills to enact comprehensive immigration policies were considered until the mid-1990s. When bills were proposed, they were as restrictive as the policies of the Executive. The comprehensive immigration reform bills introduced were generally liberal, which may explain why they did not obtain sufficient support. It is true that immigration from neighboring countries was never encouraged by the Argentine State; nonetheless, I believe Argentina's self-image as a country of immigrants worked against the enactment of restrictive comprehensive immigration policies by Congress.

Between 1983 and 1989, 70 percent of the proposals considered in the Argentine legislature were aimed at making immigration rules more liberal. In addition, the bills approved were considerably more liberal than Executive policies. Furthermore, when the Executive enacted restrictive immigration policies, Congress expressed its distress in several documents. Between 1989 and 1995, the immigration policies of the Argentine Congress mirrored those of the Executive. Most measures proposed, as well as the discourses relating to immigration, were unfriendly to immigrants. Furthermore, as the information requests showed, Congress wanted more restrictive immigration rules for both European and neighboring immigrants. This does not mean, however, that Congress was cohesive in this respect. Some dissenting voices emerged in the mid-1990s and criticized the policies and practices of the Argentine State regarding neighboring immigrants, sometimes proposing comprehensive immigration reform.

Information requests are important instruments for making the Argentine Executive more accountable if one considers the range of topics covered and the depth of the questions posed. However, the Executive's responses to these requests either took too long or never arrived. Moreover, the content of these responses was also considered inadequate by the legislators interviewed. The creation of rules to enforce the Executive's compliance with information requests could potentially enhance the supervisory role of these important congressional documents.

SEVEN

Immigration and Immigration Policies in the 2000s

In the late 1990s, the Argentine Congress made only minor changes to immigration policies established by law. In 2002 Mercosur presidents announced that they would allow for the free movement of people within the countries of the bloc. A year later, Congress passed liberal and comprehensive immigration legislation despite the severe economic crisis. This new immigration legislation was a stark departure from previous policies, awarding a significant number of immigrant rights and prioritizing the immigration of citizens from Southern Cone countries. Why was the Argentine Congress unable to agree on new immigration law for twenty years? What factors influenced the passage of this new immigration law? How has immigration in Argentina diversified in recent years? Does this mean that the preference for European immigration is no longer part of Argentine immigration policies? What has changed under the Macri administration? These questions are explored throughout this chapter.

ARGENTINA'S FOREIGN-BORN POPULATION IN 2001

The census of 2001 recorded 1,527,320 foreign-born people living in Argentina, 60 percent of whom were citizens of bordering countries, namely Brazil, Uruguay, Paraguay, Bolivia, and Chile (Cerrutti 2009) (see Table 7.1).

Table 7.1. Foreign-Born Population in Argentina: 2001

Country of Origin	Percentage of the Foreign-Born Population
Paraguay	21
Bolivia	15
Chile	14
Italy	14
Spain	9
Uruguay	8
Peru	6
Brazil	2
Poland	1
Germany	1
Former Yugoslavia	0
Other	9

Source: 2001 census data from Cerrutti 2009

The rest of the foreign-born population was primarily from Italy (14 percent) and Spain (9 percent). Between 1991 and 2001, the proportion of immigrants from Italy and Spain combined decreased, from almost 34 percent to 23 percent (Cerrutti 2009, 10 ff.). This finding makes sense, considering that immigration from European countries virtually ended in the aftermath of World War II. In 2001 Latin American immigration in Argentina was mostly from Paraguay, followed by Bolivia, Chile, Uruguay, Peru, and Brazil (see Table 7.1).

NEW IMMIGRATION POLICIES: DECEMBER 2003

Congress passed a new immigration law in 2003 (Law 25871) to replace the one enacted during the last military dictatorship. This law produced a historical change in the immigration policies of Argentina, particularly in the recognition of the human right to migrate (article 4) (Gómez and Piana 2014; Novick 2012). Also, and departing from a long tradition of prioritizing European immigration, it grants citizens of Mercosur countries,[1] Bolivia, and Chile priority over other immigrants to live and work in Argentina.

In addition, the 2003 law grants an important bundle of rights to immigrants, including those awarded in the Constitution's Bill of Rights and in international agreements subscribed to by the Argentine government, such as access to social services, public goods, health, education, justice, work, and social security (article 6). Independent of immigration status, it awards immigrants the right to education (article 7), health and welfare services (article 8), family reunification (article 10), and participation in local elections (article 11). The law also establishes that government will facilitate the integration of immigrants through a variety of means (article 14) and the regularization of their immigration status (article 15). Finally, this law restricts deportation and awards the right to appeal deportation decisions before a court (articles 61 and ff.). The extensive rights afforded to immigrants by this legislation put Argentina's immigration policies among the most progressive in the world (Hines 2010).

Following the passage of Law 25871, two decrees allowed for the regularization of immigrants who were already residing in the country, first from countries outside Mercosur (Decree 836/2004) and then those within it (Decree 1169/2004) (Novick 2012). The first legalized about 12,000 people, most of whom were Chinese and Korean, followed by Colombians and Dominicans (Novick 2012). The second, known as Patria Grande (Big Fatherland), affected close to 424,000 persons, most of whom were Paraguayan, Bolivian, or Peruvian (2012). Unlike the amnesties that became common during democratic governments after 1949, these decrees allowed immigrants to become permanent residents. Thus, like Law 25871, they were considerably more liberal than previous policies.

The 2003 law establishes the different cases in which immigrants can obtain a permanent, temporary, or transitory residence. The only foreigners who can apply for permanent residence are relatives of Argentine citizens (article 22). Several other foreigners can apply for temporary residence, including those who come to work for an employer, retired people, investors, scientists and skilled workers, athletes, representatives of different religions, and students and nationals of Mercosur countries, Chile, or Bolivia (article 23). Finally, tourists, people in transit, and seasonal workers can apply for transitory residence (article 24). There are two major novelties when compared with Decree 1023/94. First, immigrants are not required to have a job contract to be eligible for a visa. Second, nationals of Mercosur countries can apply for temporary visas.

WHY WAS CONGRESS UNABLE TO AGREE ON A NEW IMMIGRATION POLICY BETWEEN THE YEARS 1983 AND 2003?

Democracy in Argentina was reestablished in December 1983. However, the Argentine Congress was unable to pass a new immigration law until 2003. What are the factors explaining this delay? I asked this question of twenty-seven Argentine congresspersons, and their answers shed light on the issue (see Appendix III). Some legislators thought that economic and other crises relegated migration issues. For instance, a representative from a third party explained, "Legislators gave priority to other kinds of legislation that were considered more urgent at the time." A PJ representative stated, "The problems of our country were so complex during the 1990s that immigration was not considered." Or, as a PJ senator noted, "Political issues of a different nature made Congress postpone the discussion of immigration bills." As these comments show, multiple economic and political crises diverted the attention of legislators toward more urgent matters.

Other legislators highlighted the difficulties in achieving consensus on immigration issues. In this sense, a representative of the PJ explained, immigration "has always been a multifaceted issue that generates intense debates within Congress. Argentina walked a thin line between policies guaranteeing the rights of immigrants and xenophobia. It was necessary for legislators to distance themselves from these positions to approve objective and reasonable legislation." Similarly, a PJ senator noted, "There hasn't been consensus about what is the right immigration policy for Argentina, and positions oscillated between restricted and open." A UCR representative stated, "There's no agreement about what type of immigration policy to follow, and positions vary between an open policy compatible with democratic principles and one that promotes certain immigrant groups over others." As these comments show, Argentine legislators had to make important, sometimes difficult decisions about the openness of the Argentine nation to immigrants and could not agree on its degree.

WHAT FACTORS EXPLAIN ARGENTINA'S
2004 PROGRESSIVE IMMIGRATION POLICIES?

Several explanations can account for this break with traditional Argentine immigration policies. This book and other scholarship argue that economic factors and the number of immigrants who are present in a country can shape immigration policies (Petras 1980; Timmer and Williamson 1996). In turn, public officials may draw on ideas about the perceived appropriateness of certain groups of immigrants for membership in the imagined community to restrict immigration policies toward them (Albarracín 2004). Also, regional integration agreements such as the EU and Mercosur can override other factors and influence immigration policies (Cornelius, Martin, and Hollifield 1994; Jurje and Lavenex 2014). Further, a division of labor between the branches of government can influence immigration decisions because, while the Executive may respond promptly to crises by restricting immigration policies, the legislative branch may be more likely to react to long-term goals and a diversity of views (Albarracín 2004). This chapter considers these and other factors in the shaping of immigration policies during the 2000s.

The Role of Mercosur

Neoliberal institutionalism argues that supranational organizations and international regimes help overcome dilemmas of common interest and facilitate collaboration and coordination between countries (Meyers 2000). Several authors (DeLaet 2000; FitzGerald and Cook-Martín 2014; Hollifield 1992b; Hollifield, Martin, and Orrenius 2014; Krasner 1983; Zolberg 1991) examine the applicability of neoliberal institutionalism to immigration. They usually conclude that international regimes generally have had little impact on immigration policies. Normally, receiving countries do not need to cooperate internationally due to the high political costs of immigration, the difficulty of distributing its benefits, and the almost unlimited supply of labor (Hollifield 1992b). This is reversed, however, in cases where special integration treaties among countries, such as the EU and Mercosur, exist. Still, even within the EU, international cooperation on migration issues faces many obstacles (Jurje and Lavenex 2014).

In 1991 Argentina, Brazil, Uruguay, and Paraguay signed the Treaty of Asunción to create the Southern Common Market (Mercosur n.d.). Several additional countries later joined Mercosur, including Bolivia and Venezuela as full members and Chile, Ecuador, Peru, Colombia, Guyana, and Suriname as associate members. The treaty states that the common market involves the free movement of goods, services, and factors of production between the member countries (Ceriani Cernadas 2013). The EU was established in the aftermath of World War II, with the idea that increased interdependence could deter conflict. Whereas the EU emerged as a major driver of globalization, Mercosur—especially with the rise of the left-of-center government—did so as a potential counterglobalization formation (Munck and Hyland 2014).

The inclusion of immigration issues on Mercosur's agenda happened in an incremental way (Culpi and Pereira 2016). The Treaty of Asunción made no explicit references to migration other than the above-mentioned statement about the free movement of factors of production. Further, until 1997 Mercosur lacked a committee working on the issue of immigration (2016). As the former director of legal affairs at the Immigration Agency explained, "Mercosur started as an economic bloc, but the parties involved realized early on that immigration couldn't be excluded from the group's agenda."[2] Further, as a former director of the Immigration Agency stated, "Even in the European Union it took decades for migration issues to become a central part of the agenda. . . . In the case of Mercosur, the lack of interest on the part of Brazil slowed down progress in this respect."[3] Thus, even though Mercosur didn't explicitly include migration issues, these issues eventually became important to the bloc's development.

In December 2002 Mercosur countries signed the Residence Agreement, establishing the free movement of people from the region and within the region without eliminating border controls (Ceriani Cernadas 2013). Article 1 of this treaty stated that the nationals of a party state who wish to reside in the territory of another party state may obtain legal residence in the latter by accrediting their nationality. With this, Mercosur follows the EU, regarded in Latin America as a role model in regional integration (Munck and Hyland 2014). Decisions within Mercosur, however, need ratification by the member countries. The Residence Agreement went into effect only in 2009 when all parties had ratified it. Why did Argentina, then, take the lead at the end of 2003 and pass immigration legislation?

Several of the key players in immigration policy making believed the progress of Mercosur influenced the passage of the new immigration legislation, even though Argentina was not yet bound by the Residence Agreement. For instance, Senator Antonio Cafiero, the president of the Senate's Committee on Population and Human Development, expressed that the international pressures to make immigration policies more liberal and in tune with the progress of Mercosur toward the free residence of people within the bloc pressured legislators. In a similar vein, Representative Rubén Giustiniani, original author of the new immigration bill and president of the Population and Human Resources Committee of the Chamber of Deputies, thought that the relevance given to the integration with the countries of the Southern Cone in recent years contributed to the passage of the new immigration law.[4]

Further, the weight of Mercosur also became clear during its parliamentary debate. For instance, UCR Senator Mario Losada stated, "It's alarming to have waited this long to pass legislation with these characteristics. We are talking about integration, about the brotherhood of our Latin American countries" (Honorable Senado de la Nación Argentina 2003). In a similar vein, Senator Cafiero expanded, "In December 2002, the presidents of Argentina, Bolivia, Brazil, Chile, Paraguay, and Uruguay resolved through an agreement the free movement of the nationals of these countries in each other's territories. In a moment in which xenophobia is introduced in the culture of the rich, northern countries, we, countries of the south, lead with the example of how humans should be treated." As these statements show, the progress of Mercosur, but also human rights considerations, was behind the passage of the 2003 legislation.

Legislators' Beliefs

Legislators' policy preferences are likely to shape their support for policy (Albarracín 2004). Soon after the presidents of Mercosur countries signed the free-movement agreement, almost 90 percent of the legislators who had been surveyed expressed support. Moreover, several legislators from the PJ gave strong reasons for this support. One legislator stated, "We need to achieve the objectives stated in the Asunción treaty: economic, cultural, and social integration of the member countries." Another PJ legislator said, "Argentina needs to debate a new immigration policy that considers the new challenges and demands posed by the regional integration process." Still another legislator from the same party went further and stated that freedom is always positive and that the best immigration policy was the complete freedom of movement within Mercosur. Finally, another congressperson said, "We need to push the economic integration of the region: first Mercosur, then Latin America, and later the rest of the world." As these statements show, members of the Argentine Congress, especially those from the PJ, had a significant interest in strengthening Mercosur and adapting the immigration policies of the Argentine State to fit Mercosur needs. These comments are consistent with the 2003 law.

Further, 40 percent of respondents thought that immigration policies should be liberal and provide equal treatment to all citizens, regardless of their origin. In this case, Argentine legislators advocated for permissive immigration policies for all people and not just those from Mercosur countries. In addition, only 4 percent of the legislators surveyed believed Argentina should select immigrants according to their national origin. Perhaps more importantly, only 8 percent of them believed immigration policies should respond to the constitutional mandate of prioritizing immigration from European countries. Does this mean that the preference for European immigration effectively no longer exists in Argentina?

LEGISLATORS' BELIEFS REGARDING THE IMPACT OF DIFFERENT IMMIGRANT GROUPS ON ARGENTINA

Since its consolidation as a modern nation, Argentina has shown a recurrent preference for European immigration, one that is also visible in the media until the 1990s. Had these ideas changed by 2003? What did legislators think about the impact of different groups of immigrants on Argentine society? In the survey administered to the members of the Argentine Congress (see Appendix III), I asked legislators to rank the impact of different groups of immigrants on Argentina from 1 to 5 (1 standing for "not beneficial at all" and 5 for "absolutely beneficial") (see Table 7.2). The

Table 7.2. Argentine Legislators' Beliefs about the Impact of Immigrants from Different Countries on Argentina

Immigrant Groups	Legislators' Beliefs about the Impact of Immigrant Group*
Europe before WWII	4.35
Arab Countries	3.74
Uruguay	3.48
Brazil	3.67
Paraguay	3.26
Bolivia	3.22
Chile	3.39
Central & Eastern Europe	3.14

*Score ranges from 1 (not beneficial at all) to 5 (absolutely beneficial).

question was posed in broad terms, without explaining what was meant by *impact*, to allow respondents to evaluate a different range of issues (economic, social, racial, cultural, and so on) in their responses. The immigrant groups listed were Europeans before WWII, Arabs, neighboring immigrants (Uruguayan, Brazilian, Paraguayan, Bolivian, Chilean), and recent arrivals from Central and Eastern Europe. Not surprisingly, the impact attributed to European immigrants who arrived before WWII was the most beneficial (4.35). This finding is consistent with the entrenched belief in the Argentine society that immigration from Europe contributed to the construction of a great country. The impact attributed to immigrants from Arab countries was the second most beneficial one (3.74). Immigration from Arab countries to Argentina was also significant during Argentina's golden era, settling mostly in the northwest.

The beliefs about the impact of neighboring immigration were, however, less optimistic. The average impact attributed to immigrants from countries bordering Argentina ranked third (3.40), making it 20 percent less beneficial than that of European immigration before WWII. This finding is consistent with the scapegoating of bordering immigration in the preceding periods, when the support for this immigration by the Argentine population dropped to 21 percent (Nueva Mayoría 2001). Narratives about how Western Europeans in the nineteenth and early twentieth centuries contributed to the spectacular growth of Argentina likely shaped

legislators' preferences. Immigrants from neighboring countries participated from the start in the agricultural economies of the different Argentine regions and provided part of the labor force for the industrialization
initiated in the 1930s. However, these contributions by neighboring immigrants seemed to be ignored.

Some legislators and policy makers discussed the scapegoating of immigrants after the 1990s. Representative Giustiniani stated, "Many times,
immigrants have been blamed for the ills afflicting Argentina, like unemployment or crime, even though statistics proved this attribution of blame
wrong."[5] Professor Gabriel Chausovsky agreed, saying that the 1981 law "allowed the government to take advantage the weak position of immigrant
communities and use them as scapegoats for the ills affecting the country."[6]
As these statements show, the scapegoating of immigrants during the 1990s
may have influenced legislators' views regarding this immigration.

Further, legislators assessed the impact of immigrants from different
countries in different ways. Of the bordering countries, Uruguay, one of
the whitest countries in the region, ranked second highest, just after Brazil
(see Table 7.2).[7] Many immigrants from neighboring countries are of indigenous origin, and, in the words of Organización Internacional para las
Migraciones attorney Luis Bogado Poisson, "The Buenos Aires ruling elite
has always seen itself as European and reacted against brown Latin America."[8] Argentines consider themselves to be Western European in both descent and culture. This may be a reason why discrimination is widespread.
In 2001 72 percent of Argentines thought that discrimination against
other races, cultures, or nationalities in Argentina is "significant" or "quite
significant" (Gallup Argentina 2001). However, minority groups in Argentina are small. The indigenous population was decimated, as was the
population of former African slaves and their descendants. Thus, the 2.5
percent of the population that comes from bordering countries is more
visible as "different."

The sizable Jewish community in Argentina has certainly suffered discrimination in the past. Opinion polls show that Argentines would be more
tolerant of racial diversity than cultural diversity. For instance, 29 percent of
respondents to one survey thought it was better for the country if people
looked alike, while 69 percent judged diversity to be better for the country
(Catterberg 2000). However, when asked about cultural diversity in a differ-

ent survey, Argentines' opinions changed. Only 34 percent of the respondents thought that having people from different cultures in the country was good or very good, while 62 percent were either indifferent or thought it was bad or very bad for the country (Gallup Argentina 2001). This cultural intolerance may also explain the lower beneficial impact attributed to immigration from Central and Eastern Europe, as analyzed below.

Legislators' Beliefs about the Impact of Recent Immigrants from Central and Eastern Europe on Argentina

Interestingly, Argentine legislators believed the impact of Central and Eastern European immigrants on Argentine society was less beneficial (3.14) than that of neighboring immigrants (see Table 7.2). Does this totally disconfirm the possibility that Argentine legislators have racial preferences? At first the answer seems to be affirmative. In the beginning of the 1990s, both the press and public officials were highly optimistic about a plan to attract Central and Eastern European immigrants to Argentina. Throughout the 1990s, this view changed. Not all Central and Eastern European immigrants were, however, negatively viewed in the press. The group that became stigmatized was Romanian, racialized as "gypsy." This stigmatization of Romanian immigrants in the press may have shaped the negative image that Argentine legislators had about immigrants from Central and Eastern Europe.

The plan for Central and Eastern European immigrants went on without major problems during the 1990s. Some 8,944 immigrants benefited from the program (Cancillería Argentina 2002). Seventy-one percent of these immigrants came from Ukraine. Although unemployment among recent arrivals was high (26 percent), the government recorded no unemployed within the group that arrived between 1994 and 1998. According to a government survey of prospective Ukrainian immigrants, educational attainment was quite high. Of the participants in the survey, 66 percent had tertiary education and 32 percent had completed a college degree. All had completed primary schooling. These immigrants also had a positive view of the experience of other Ukrainians who had migrated to Argentina. Overall, the immigration experience of these Europeans did not justify the negative attitude of Argentine legislators toward them.

In contrast, Romanian immigration became visible and problematized at the end of the 1990s in Argentina. I presume that most of them arrived after 1998. Some of these immigrants made a living playing music in the streets and panhandling. In 2001 30 percent of the people begging in the streets in Buenos Aires city were thought to be Romanian (*La Nación* 11/03/2001). "They are identifiable even if women don't wear those wide skirts we were told about when we were kids. We still know they are gypsies," a reporter confidently stated, "because their children play the accordion and they all look like they come from a different century, from a different world" (*La Nación* 12/18/1999). As these stories show, immigrants from Romania, although white, were stigmatized. Another journalist wrote that it was a novelty to see a blond child with blue eyes begging in the streets of Argentina (*La Nación* 11/01/2001).

Additionally, Romanians were said to lie about their health, family, and other conditions to make people feel sorry for them. According to a 2000 article, "fake blind people," "mutes that speak," and "children walking away from their wheelchairs" populated the Buenos Aires downtown (*La Nación* 02/02/2000). According to this article, Romanian immigrants were faking all kinds of illnesses to succeed in their begging. The story also speculated that certain organizations were behind this "industry of begging." The association between Romanians and pretense was so significant that on several occasions Romanians were referred to as "false Romanians," or "false Romanian kids" (*La Nación,* March 3, April 21, and August 18, 2001, February 23, 2002, and April 13, 2004). Due to the alleged problems related to immigrants from Romania, the Argentine government stopped awarding visas to them (*La Nación* 02/02/2002).

Legislators' Beliefs on the Impact of Immigration by Political Party

I found important differences in legislators' views on immigration between the members of the PJ and UCR (see Table 7.3). The members of these two parties considered the impact of European immigration before WWII to be beneficial (4.20 and 4.44, respectively). However, they disagreed on the impact of other groups of migrants on Argentina. More specifically, UCR members appeared to be optimistic only about European

Table 7.3. Argentine Legislators' Beliefs about the Impact of Immigrants from Different Countries on Argentina by Political Party

Immigrant Groups	Legislators' Beliefs about the Impact of Immigrant Group*	
	PJ	UCR
Europe before WWII	4.20	4.44
Arab Countries	3.80	3.33
Uruguay	3.90	2.78
Brazil	3.78	3.38
Paraguay	3.70	2.56
Bolivia	3.50	2.67
Chile	3.70	2.78
Central & Eastern Europe	3.56	2.44

*Score ranges from 1 (not beneficial at all) to 5 (absolutely beneficial).

immigration before World War II. Their opinion of Arab immigration (3.33) was considerably lower than that of their PJ counterparts (3.80). Even more contrasting were the views on neighboring migration and recent immigration from Central and Eastern Europe. Whereas PJ legislators assigned the former an average beneficial score of 3.71, UCR legislators did not (2.83). In turn, while PJ congressmembers attributed a beneficial impact to recent immigration from Central and Eastern Europe (3.56), their UCR counterparts once again did not (2.44).

This finding likely requires further research. It may be that the UCR is a middle-class party and most of its constituents are descendants of European settlers. In contrast, the PJ is a working-class party and immigrants from the Southern Cone are more likely to join it. Whatever the reason, the UCR believed that immigration from Western Europe was clearly the most beneficial. In comparison with their PJ peers, they also held the view that Arab, neighboring, and Central and Eastern European migration were less beneficial for Argentina. An attitude, however, does not automatically translate into a policy choice. In this sense, Argentine legislators did not show a strong inclination to pass immigration policies that encourage European immigration. For instance, only 8 percent of the members of Congress surveyed expressed their agreement with this type of policy.

Work in the Population Committees

The committees on population issues were created in the early 1990s. Consistent with the work by Barbara Hines (2010), my data show that the tireless work of these committees with immigrant rights organizations, especially in the House, was instrumental in the passage of Law 25871. In the opinion of Representative Giustiniani, "Years of work at the population committee of the Chamber of Deputies, which ended with unanimous support on the committee for a bill we introduced in 2000, and the work of different civic organizations, grouped under La Mesa ["table"; a coalition] of Organizations for the Defense of Immigrant Rights . . . provided the context within which the new law became possible."[9] According to other opinions, the work of Representative Giustiniani himself was essential. Former Immigration Agency director Jorge Gurrieri said, "Regarding long-term factors [that facilitated the passage of the new legislation], I believe the five-year job by Giustiniani was essential."[10]

The former president of the National Institute against Discrimination, Xenophobia, and Racism outlined the role of La Mesa, saying, "There were people who fought for the change for many years. . . . Civic organizations composed of Argentines and immigrants alike, immigrant communities, and researchers were part of this fight."[11] Original members of this coalition were the Argentine Commission for Refugees, Centro de Estudios Legales y Sociales, Asamblea Permanente por los Derechos Humanos, Movimiento Ecuménico por los Derechos Humanos, Servicio Paz y Justicia, Fundación de la Comisión Católica para las Migraciones, Centro de Estudios Migratorios de América Latina, and Departamento de Migraciones de la Confederación de Trabajadores Argentinos. La Mesa outlined the problems of the prior law in the light of human rights standards, presented a bill to the representatives serving on the Population and Human Resources Committee, and testified at public hearings (Hines 2010).

Role of the Executive

It is impossible to talk about this period of Argentine history without referencing the progressive characteristics of the Kircher administration (2002–2007), including the renegotiation of Argentina's external debt, export-oriented policies, pension reform, salary increases, and an emphasis on Latin American integration (Levitsky and Murillo 2008). To be sure, some accounts of the almost unique role of this administration in the passage of this law have been exaggerated (Recalde 2012). Nonetheless, my data show that the progressive policies of the Kirchner administration provided the right context for the enactment of the 2003 law. Enrique Oteiza, for instance, thought that "The rejection by certain sectors of society of the previous [immigration] model was considered by the new administration."[12] Chausovsky stated, "The advent of the progressive-spirited executive ... facilitated the way for the passage of the new law."[13] Giustiniani, in turn, said, "The change in the human rights and regional integration policies of the new government generated the right conditions for the passage of the new immigration law."[14] As these accounts show, the new administration may have provided the right context for the new immigration policies. Even though Giustiniani introduced the bill that became law in 2000, three years before Kirchner became president, data show that the progressive nature of his government was influential.

Emigration

Only twenty years after the reestablishment of democracy in Argentina did Congress agree on a new immigration law. Immigrants and Argentines alike left the country after the 2001 economic and political collapse. In December 2001, as Argentina faced a major economic and political crisis, widespread demonstrations forced the resignation of President Fernando de la Rúa of the UCR (Goddard 2006). Net international migration to Argentina in the period 1995 to 2000 was negative, with a loss of 82,235 people (Solimano 2003, 32). "The images of long lines of Argentines waiting at the door of European consulates to obtain their visas and the Buenos Aires international airport full of youngsters fleeing to Europe and the United States"[15] likely influenced the passage of liberal immigration policies.

Moreover, after Argentines and immigrants left the country in significant numbers, unemployment rates did not go down, reaching 14.5 percent at the end of 2003. Therefore, the xenophobic discourses of the 1990s that accused immigrants of taking jobs from Argentines were discredited.

Senator Cafiero's comments are illustrative in this respect: "With the hike of unemployment rates in 1994, discourses called for a restriction of immigration from neighboring countries to lower unemployment rates. However, things changed when statistics questioned these discourses as the flight of immigrants after 2001 did not lower unemployment rates in significant numbers."[16] Thus, the negligible impact of the exodus of immigrants on unemployment rates may have influenced the passage of Law 25871.

THE DIVERSIFICATION IN IMMIGRATION IN ARGENTINA AND ITS RECEPTION

In 2010 a little more than 40 million people lived in Argentina, up from 36 million in 2001. Out of these, 4.5 percent were born in other countries, compared to 4 percent in 2001, when emigration in Argentina became significant. The composition of the immigrant population also changed in the first decade of the 2000s, with immigrants from the Americas rising from 68 percent of that population to 81 percent (see Table 7.4). This change probably corresponded to the death of many immigrants from Europe who had come to Argentina prior to World War II.

The origin of immigrants from within the Americas also changed. Whereas in 2001, more than 88 percent of immigrants from the Americas came from the countries bordering Argentina, in 2010 this number was 84 percent. The original members of Mercosur were Argentina, Brazil, Uruguay, and Paraguay, but later Venezuela, Bolivia, Chile, Colombia, Peru, and Ecuador were added to the common market. Immigrants from these countries therefore benefited from the provisions of Law 25871, which made it easy for a person from Mercosur countries to reside in Argentina. Thus, this provision contributed to the diversification of immigration in Argentina, increasing immigration from countries in the Americas besides those bordering Argentina.

Unfortunately, the data from national censuses published in Argentina do not break down the immigrant population by every country of origin. However, the Immigration Agency compiles and publishes information about those who apply for residency in Argentina. According to these data, close to 650,000 residencies were awarded between 2011 and

Table 7.4. Foreign-Born Population in Argentina: 2001 and 2010

Country/Region of Origin	2001	2010
Americas	1,041,117 (68%)	1,471,399 (81%)
Bordering Countries	923,215 (60%)	1,245,054 (69%)
Europe	432,349 (28%)	299,394 (17%)
Asia	29,672 (2%)	31,001 (2%)
Africa	1,883 (1%)	2,738 (1%)
Oceania	747 (1%)	1,425 (0%)

Source: Instituto Nacional de Estadistica y Censos: 2001 and 2010 censuses

2015. Most of these went to Paraguayans, Peruvians, and Bolivians (see Table 7.5). One novelty, however, was that 8 percent of the temporary residencies and 4 percent of the permanent ones were awarded to immigrants from Colombia, surpassing the numbers for two traditional sources of immigrants, Chile and Uruguay. As the next sections show, public discourses about immigration to Argentina blamed immigrants from Colombia for increasing drug trafficking in Argentina.

Whereas immigration from Asian countries increased only slightly, immigration from Africa increased by 45 percent (see Table 7.4). People of African descent were practically invisible in Argentina before the 2000s. "Although there is a popular belief that Argentina never had a significant African presence, historians of Argentina know better, realizing that Buenos Aires was a major center for slave importation and that, throughout the nineteenth century, Africans and their Afro-Argentine descendants were significant percentages of the population of Buenos Aires and other Argentine regions" (Cottrol 2007, 140). In some parts of Buenos Aires during the 1800s, Afro-Argentinians made up 30 percent of the population (Frigerio 2000). The cultural influence of African cultures in Argentina is significant and most noticeable in the national music and dance, the tango (Cottrol 2007).

In 1954, however, the black population of Argentina was estimated at five thousand. Different theories account for this sharp decrease, including intermarriage, the impact of yellow fever, and participation by Afro-Argentines in different wars, to mention just a few (Andrews 1980). Other people of African descent in Argentina included a small Cabo Verdean immigrant population that arrived at the end of the nineteenth century

Table 7.5. Temporary and Permanent Residencies Awarded 2011–2015

Country of Origin	Temporary Residency (Percentage)	Permanent Residency (Percentage)
Paraguay	40	44
Peru	24	26
Bolivia	14	14
Colombia	8	4
Chile	2	2
Uruguay	2	2
Venezuela	2	1
Ecuador	1	1
Dominican Republic	1	1
United States	1	1
Spain	1	1
China	1	1
Senegal	1	n/a
Other	2	2

Source: Dirección Nacional de Migraciones, Argentina

(Maffia 2008) and Afro-Uruguayans who have migrated since colonial times (Frigerio 2000). During the 2000s, groups of immigrants came to Argentina from Senegal, Nigeria, Congo, and Ghana (Maffia 2008). Most immigrants from African countries work as street vendors (Traore 2006).

IMMIGRATION DURING THE MACRI ADMINISTRATION

What was the reaction of the population to the diversification of immigration in Argentina? A story published in 2016, which reported on a study of public attitudes toward immigration in Argentina, compared Argentine attitudes toward immigration to the views of then American President Elect Trump. This story explained, "We have heard Trump describing Mexican immigrants as people with problems, who bring drugs, crime, and are rapists. . . . These prejudices coming out of his mouth are not far from those by some Argentines" (Clarín 11/11/2016). One of the studies cited in this story showed that 60 percent of Argentines believed the country should restrict immigration. Prejudices were not limited to immigrants from Latin American and African countries. Argentines also feared that receiving refugees from Syria could create a terrorist threat (*Clarín* 11/11/2016).

A 2017 study by an international firm indicated that only 12 percent of Argentines thought that immigration had a positive impact on Argentina and 54 percent thought that Argentina had too many immigrants (Ipsos 2017). According to the same study, people in only four countries had more negative views on immigration than Argentines: Russia, Turkey, Serbia, and Hungary. Moreover, 55 percent of Argentines thought immigrants were placing pressure on public services, and other Argentines feared losing their jobs. Whereas in Europe the fear of immigration is usually associated with terrorism, in Latin American countries this fear is associated with perceived insecurity due to crime and fear of losing jobs (*La Nación* 09/19/2017).

Public attitudes on immigration mirrored public discourses by Argentine politicians. One such case is Mauricio Macri, former mayor of the City of Buenos Aires and president of Argentina as of this writing. Macri was elected president in 2015. After three presidential terms by Néstor Kirchner and Cristina Fernández de Kirchner, who instituted a model of extensive government regulations and social programs, Macri, a center-right candidate, won the presidential election with a coalition known as Cambiemos (Fraga 2017). This election echoed electoral defeats of the left in Venezuela, Bolivia, and Ecuador. Macri had formed an alliance with a number of center and center-right parties, mainly based on opposition to the Kirchners and aimed at the creation of a "normal country" (Vommaro 2016, 4). What Macri meant by "normal" is unclear, but his agenda includes improving relations with advanced countries and increasing foreign investment, among other issues.

Before becoming president, Macri was the mayor of Buenos Aires for eight years. In this position he voiced his opposition to the open immigration policies of the Kirchner administrations. In 2010, for instance, he made a call to change the permissive, "out of control" immigration policies (*La Nación* 12/10/2010). Macri's statements referred to a group of squatters from a Buenos Aires shantytown, known as Villa 20, who took over a park (the Parque Indoamericano). Although there is no proof that most of these occupiers were from other countries—Argentines, Paraguayans, and

Bolivians live in Villa 20—government officials were quick to blame immigrants for this "invasion" (*La Nación* 12/15/2010). In reaction to this scapegoating, the Bolivian government issued a statement accusing Macri of xenophobia. Moreover, the brutal response of both the federal and city governments left two dead and five injured (*La Nación* 08/19/2014).

Despite these incidents, the immigration policies of the Kirchner administrations remained fairly liberal. It was not until Macri became president that immigration policies took a restrictive turn. To begin, between 2015 and 2017, deportation increased by 3,150 percent.[17] Also, in January 2017, making use of exceptional powers awarded by the Argentine Constitution, Macri passed an executive order (DNU 70/17) amending Law 25871 and rolling back immigrants' rights and protections. This decree triggered comparisons of the Argentine president to President Trump in the *New York Times*.[18] Usually used to pass economic measures in times of severe crises (Cervio and Dettano 2016), DNUs are reserved for situations of "necessity and urgency," allowing the Executive to pass legislation without previous approval by Congress. This decree was unsuccessfully challenged in the courts and later approved by Congress. What were the reasons behind this policy change?

This book argues that in times of economic crisis, public officials may draw on ideas about the appropriateness of certain groups of immigrants for membership in the imagined community to restrict immigration policies toward them (Petras 1980; Albarracín 2004). Because immigration policies have strong symbolic meanings, countries confronted with sluggish economic performance can strengthen the unity of the nation by scapegoating outsiders and blaming them for failing policies (Andreas 1999; 2000). The Macri administration faced an economic downturn in 2016, when growth rates became negative and inflation climbed to 30 percent (Focus Economics 2017). One newspaper editorial exposed this scapegoating tactic: during "an election year, the policies passed were destined to make some noise. They are unlikely to be effective. They are just a move by the government to blame immigrants for the problems facing Argentina and get a few more votes" (*Página 12* 01/31/2017).

Decree 70/17 had several goals, including the creation of several new reasons for residency denial, the establishment of expedited removal proceedings, and modification of the Argentine citizenship law. Some provisions were clearly incongruent with the Argentine Constitution. A case in point is that among the several causes for denial of residency, whereas Law 25871 established that a person sentenced for a crime was not eligible for residency in Argentina, the new norm stated that a person indicted or who "participated" in a crime was not eligible for residency. In other words, the mere accusation or suspicion of having participated in a crime could prevent a person from immigrating to Argentina. The Constitution establishes the presumption of innocence in its Bill of Rights, applicable to all inhabitants and not just Argentines. Decree 70/17, which applied sanctions to people accused of crimes, is in clear violation of this presumption.

Decree 70/17 also affected rules for deportation. Whereas during the military dictatorship only people sentenced to five years of prison were deportable (Law 22439), Decree 70/17 added a long list of crimes punishable with a lower prison sentence. In addition, immigrants who had been sentenced or indicted, or who merely participated in certain crimes, became deportable. As an expert in immigration rights explained, those "picketing on a street, selling on the streets without a permit," resisting arrest, or squatting were now at risk of deportation.[19] It is worth remembering that many African immigrants are street vendors (Maffia 2008), and Latin American immigrants were accused of squatting in 2010. As in the Trump administration, deporting people for minor crimes seems a disproportionate response.

Decree 70/17 also established an expedited removal process (Proceso Sumarísmo), which also mirrored President Trump's January executive order to expand the use of the expedited removals previously used for people apprehended within two weeks of their arrival in the United States and within one hundred miles of the border (American Immigration Council 2017), now applicable to immigrants who have been in the country for less than two years (U. S. Citizenship, Immigration, and Naturalization Services n.d). One novelty of Law 25871 was to establish judicial review for deportation proceedings together with reasonable deadlines for appeals and judicial review of deportation decisions. Decree 70/17 limited the cases in which deportation decisions were subject to review and shortened the deadlines to a degree that made it almost impossible for immigrants to fight their cases. According to the decree, these deportation proceedings took too long and therefore impeded compliance with international norms and limited the right of the government to select and deport immigrants.

The text of Decree 70/17 justified these extreme measures in a long list of reasons. Several pointed to statistics about the proportion of immigrants in jails, though these numbers were challenged in the media. For instance, the decree stated that 21.35 percent of inmates in prisons and 30 percent of persons involved in drug trafficking were immigrants. However, these numbers reflect only those held in federal prisons. If all detention centers in Argentina are considered, these numbers change. Some two million immigrants lived in Argentina in 2013, according to estimates by the United Nations (*La Nación* 01/31/2017). Out of these, 4,300 are inmates in detention centers, representing 6 percent of that population. As for those accused of drug trafficking, only 1,400 are foreigners, representing 17 percent of the total (*La Nación* 01/31/2017). Thus, Decree 70/17 highly exaggerated the extent to which immigrants contribute to crime.

Paralleling recent scapegoating of immigrants in the United States, led by President Trump and part of the media (Bobo 2017), discourses in Argentina also demonized immigrants. Senator Miguel Pichetto (PJ) called on Argentines to restrict immigration on several occasions. In early November 2016, he spoke of "Peruvians who traffic drugs, and Colombians who commit crimes" (*Página 12* 11/06/2016). He also accused immigrants from African countries of facilitating drug trafficking by Latin American immigrants when controlling the streets (*La Nación* 01/15/2017). According to Pichetto, Argentina works to "alleviate poverty in Bolivia and crime in Peru" (*Clarín* 11/11/2016). Several immigrant rights organizations and foreign governments filed complaints against this high-profile senator, who is, ironically, from the Kirchnerist Victory Front faction and is also the minority leader in the Senate. As in other cases, journalists put Pichetto's statements in international perspective, drawing comparisons with Donald Trump and French politician Marine Le Pen (*Página 12* 11/06/2016).

Macri began his scapegoating of immigrants during his term as mayor of Buenos Aires. In 2017, while proposing to create a criminal code to more severely punish youth under eighteen, Macri stated "because of a lack of action"—probably a reference to the Kirchner administrations— "we can't allow criminals to choose Argentina as a place to commit crimes" (*Página 12* 11/18/2017). In a statement to the press after the passage of Decree 70/17, which motivated complaints by a civic organization before the National Institute against Discrimination, the Macri administration's minister of security, Patricia Bullrich, stated, "Paraguayans and Peruvians come here and end up killing each other for the control of drug trafficking" (*Página 12* 01/31/2017). As these statements show, the association between immigration, crime, and drug trafficking affected residents from Latin America.

Unlike the mid-1990s, when immigrants who were scapegoated for problems affecting Argentines remained somewhat silent, in 2017 immigrants mobilized. In March 2017 several immigrant rights organizations and immigrant communities from different countries, including Armenia, Bolivia, Brazil, Colombia, Cuba, Paraguay, Peru, Senegal, Spain, and Uruguay, participated in a Day without Immigrants to protest Decree 70/17 (*Página 12* 04/30/2017). Coincidentally, a month earlier, immigrants in the United States had organized a similar action.[20] As in the United States, protesters withheld labor in the afternoon and left workplaces to march from the Congressional Palace to the Presidential Palace (*Página 12* 03/30/2017). A leader from the Paraguayan community explained, "In Argentina, discrimination, labor precariousness, and exclusion have existed for years but have increased in the Cambiemos administration both at a discursive and concrete level" (*Página 12* 03/30/2017). As this comment shows, immigrants in Argentina felt their situation worsened during the Macri administration.

FACTORS SHAPING IMMIGRATION POLICIES IN THE 2000s

Recent changes in Argentine immigration policies that favor immigrants from Mercosur countries seemed to reverse the historic norms favoring European immigration. Several explanations can account for this break with traditional Argentine immigration policies. Certainly, the liberalization of mobility policies between Mercosur member and associate countries played a role, but important domestic factors did so as well. For instance, it took a Congress dominated by legislators who believed in the advantages of allowing immigrants from Mercosur countries to reside in Argentina to turn this decision into law much earlier than in the other member countries. Further, this Congress was dominated by Peronist legislators who were more likely to consider immigration from other Latin American countries as beneficial.

The creation of the congressional committees on population in the early 1990s, which allowed for the elaboration of several immigration bills, facilitated the repeal and replacement of Law 22439 from the last military dictatorship. Moreover, the work done by the author of that bill, Representative Giustiniani, with the diverse La Mesa coalition predated the 2002 Mercosur decision (Brumat and Torres 2015). In turn, the progressive policies of the Kirchner administration provided a favorable context for a progressive policy change. Finally, after the economic collapse of 2001, Argentina became a country of emigration, which probably made the liberal immigration polices enacted more likely to be accepted.

The preference for European immigration, however, seems to have remained in place. Argentine legislators believed the impact of European immigration was considerably more beneficial to Argentine society than the impact of Southern Cone immigration. Further, the scapegoating of immigrants during the 2010s by public officials, the rollback of immigrant rights during the Macri administration, and the recent public opinion polls discussed above show that the reception of immigrants from Latin America and Africa has been uneven. Time will tell if the current administration will continue to challenge the liberal immigration policies enacted by the Argentine Congress in the early 2000s.

EIGHT

Conclusion

This book seeks to understand the factors shaping immigration policy in Argentina. It shows that right after independence, Argentina designed a national project to select European immigrants that remained in place, with some exceptions, for the next 150 years. Although Argentina became open to immigrants from Latin American countries after 2003, Argentines blame these immigrants for crime, drug violence, and increasing the number of people living in shantytowns. Further, the Macri administration, perhaps emulating U. S. President Trump's immigration policies, rolled back some of the rights awarded to immigrants in 2003 through an executive order from 2017.

To understand the factors shaping immigration policy decisions, it is important to consider the different spheres of interaction involved in the admission of immigrants into a country. According to Aristide Zolberg (1999, 81), from the capitalist perspective, immigrants of any kind are first and foremost workers and only secondly a political and cultural presence. Immigrants are also subjects of nation-states and as such can be affected by the relationships between the sending and receiving countries. These multiple aspects of immigration shed light on the complex interests at stake when a state makes decisions about the selection and admission of foreign citizens.

Because immigrants are first and foremost workers, economic approaches shed light on immigration policies. More specifically, they describe the role of immigrant workers in a capitalist society and correctly predict the short-term correlation between economic cycles and immigration policies: in times of economic expansion immigration policies tend to be more liberal, and in times of economic crisis immigration policies tend to be more restrictive. Aside from the sporadic amnesties, the Argentine economy tended to shape immigration policies after the 1930s, but ethnic or cultural considerations moderated the effect of economic factors. This book argues that, although economic factors are important in explaining immigration policies and often determine how many immigrants a country is willing to accept, notions of ethnic and/or cultural eligibility of certain immigrant groups for membership in the imagined community dictate who is admitted.

Importantly, the centralization of the decision-making processes— whether it is the Executive or the Legislative that enacts the policies— determines the weight of the factors affecting immigration policies. For instance, the Argentine Executive responded quickly to changes in economic conditions or sudden international pressures such as wars, was more concerned with legitimacy, and seemed to remain loyal to ethnic or cultural preferences. In contrast, the Argentine Congress, at least in recent times, appeared to be more receptive to long-term considerations such as regional integration.

THE ERA OF MASS MIGRATION

Due to the sparse population and desired effect of immigration on the local population, the liberal elites encouraged European immigration to achieve their dream of turning Argentina into an agricultural exporter. Juan Bautista Alberdi and Domingo Faustino Sarmiento, influential thinkers during the forging of the nation, also had other reasons to prefer European immigration. These thinkers thought European immigration could replace or improve the unfit, racially mixed, local population. Unlike the United States, however, Argentina did not ban certain classes of immigrants from becoming citizens or from entering the country until later (FitzGerald and Cook-Martín 2014). However, according to the interpretation of the Constitution by the Argentine Supreme Court, the government has the obligation to encourage European immigration (Corte Suprema de Justicia de la Nación 1932). Between 1870 and 1914,

5.9 million migrants arrived in Argentina and more than half of them settled permanently in the country, a figure topped only by the United States
during this period (Rock 1987). The government helped this effort by establishing immigration offices in Europe, subsidizing travel, and promis-
ing land to immigrants.

ECONOMIC HARDSHIP OPENED AN OPPORTUNITY
FOR SELECTING IMMIGRANTS

On several occasions, economic hardship influenced the desired number
of immigrants and provided an opportunity to redefine who would be
admitted into the national community. This happened in the 1900s, 1930s,
1980s, 1990s, and 2010s. After an intense economic crisis and deep economic and social transformations that led to strikes and civil unrest, and
paralleling the United States, the Argentine Congress passed the first restrictive immigration law in 1902. Instead of understanding the demands
of the labor movement, the government blamed immigration. As a result,
as in the United States (Calavita 1994, 57), the Argentine government
passed a law facilitating the deportation of anarchist and socialist immigrants, a measure which, without significantly limiting immigration, gave
the impression that the government was doing something about civil unrest while avoiding drastic decisions that would cripple industry. Although immigration reached its peak ten years later, not just any European immigrant would be accepted in the Argentine community. The
state could exclude those who because of their ideologies were likely to
become troublemakers.

The Great Depression put an end to the era of mass migration and
liberal immigration policies. Several changes were noticeable during
this period, including the arrival of refugees fleeing from Nazism, Fascism, and the Spanish Civil War. Within this context, the Executive enacted several immigration restrictions. In 1932 it required a job contract
to apply for a visa in Argentina. Later bureaucratic restrictions mainly
affected Jewish and Spanish refugees trying to flee their countries. Although racism and anti-communist sentiments were likely behind these
restrictions, the government did not overtly use ethnic criteria in the selection of immigrants.

The Avellaneda Law defined an immigrant as a person who came to Argentina on a ship originating in Europe (Devoto 2003). Despite this, migrants from neighboring countries managed to settle in Argentina; whereas migrants from the Southern Cone represented almost 9 percent of the foreign population in 1914, this number climbed to 18 percent in 1960. The entire administrative apparatus of the Argentine State was devoted to attracting European immigrants, but immigration from neighboring countries was only superficially controlled. Not unlike the United States during the Bracero program, for several decades migrants from neighboring countries were recruited at the border and their papers were superficially controlled (Villar 1984). Like Mexican immigrants in the United States, Southern Cone immigrants were not considered ideal citizens in Argentina, but they had the advantage of constituting a less demanding labor force and, at first, not settling permanently in the country (Albarracín 2004).

The immigration policies of Alfonsín's government provide another example of economic hardship opening an opportunity for selecting immigrants according to their origin. As the economic conditions worsened during the 1980s, Argentine immigration rules became stricter. While economic factors help to understand the approval of the immigration restrictions of 1985 and 1987, they cannot account for the special immigration regime for European citizens passed in 1988 by the Immigration Agency. Justified by constitutional provisions and historical reasons, the Argentine government prioritized European immigrants over other groups of immigrants, continuing with the tradition of promoting a white, European Argentina. It is worth mentioning that countries around the world had abandoned ethnic preferences by the 1960s (FitzGerald and Cook-Martín 2014).

Economic reasons alone are also insufficient to account for the immigration policy changes of the 1990s. As the economy deteriorated, immigrants from the Southern Cone were constructed as undesirable Others after 1993. While overlooking possible weaknesses in its own economic model, the Executive blamed immigrants for the ills of Argentine society. When immigration restrictions were passed in 1993 and 1994, these measures seemed to be justified in the name of the common interest of the Argentine nation. At the end of 1994, the Immigration Agency excluded immigrants from Central and Eastern Europe from immigration restrictions.

Once again, during an economic crisis, the boundaries of the imagined community were redrawn to exclude immigrants from Latin America. As in 1987, and as we see below, second- and third-line bureaucrats had the power to prioritize immigrants from Europe (Calavita 2010).

The economic crises that followed the Kirchner administrations also influenced another qualified action on the part of the Executive. In January 2017, the Executive approved important deportation provisions (Decree 70), thereby modifying Law 25871 by executive order. Using a decree of necessity and urgency, a last-resort mechanism that allows the Executive to enact legislation in extreme situations, the Executive justified these drastic measures as responding to increasing crime rates. As public official discourses preceding this measure show, the deportation provisions enacted by Decree 70 focused on immigrants from Latin American countries. Further, some have spoken of the Trump effect in Argentina, referring to U. S. President Trump's executive orders increasing border security and changing priorities for deportation to include persons who have committed minor crimes (Barbero 2016).

CASES IN WHICH ETHNIC PREFERENCES PREVAILED INDEPENDENT OF THE ECONOMIC SITUATION

At other times, ideas about Europeans as appropriate potential members of the imagined community influenced immigration policies regardless of the economic situation. This happened in the 1940s and 1950s, and during the military dictatorships that held power between 1955 and 1983. Until the 1930s, the immigration policies of the Argentine State were relatively independent of the economic situation and strongly encouraged European immigration. It is true that agricultural labor was essential to incorporate Argentina into the world markets as an agricultural exporter. But there were also strong cultural reasons to encourage European immigration. In turn, the immigration of citizens from Latin American countries was ignored.

The emphasis of the Perón administration (1946–1955) on industrialization generated a need for growing numbers of workers. Despite this need, different ethnic preferences were put in place. For one thing, this administration made the last serious effort to attract European immigrants and signed treaties with Italy and Spain for this purpose. In addition, in response to the growing migration from Southern Cone countries, for the first time in Argentine history the government regularized immigration from these countries through amnesties. Not unlike Greece, Italy, Portugal, Spain, and the United States, after the 1940s, democratic governments in Argentina passed periodic amnesties to regularize the status of immigrants from bordering countries. Although the migration of Southern Cone citizens was facilitated through amnesty decrees during the Peronist governments, it was not encouraged like the immigration from Italy and Spain. Other ethnic preferences were also reflected in the Peronist immigration policies. As in the earlier period, the immigration of Jewish refugees from Nazi Europe was discouraged by various means. In addition, the country received refugees who had formerly collaborated with the Nazis in Europe. None of these ethnic preferences was related to the economic situation.

The immigration policies of the several military governments that followed the fall of Perón in 1955 had several features in common. All showed a preference for European immigration and a strong concern with strict regulation of immigration from neighboring countries. In their own words, military governments encouraged the immigration of persons "whose cultural characteristics permit their integration into Argentine society" (Law 22439 of 1981). Moreover, they combined permissive policies for European immigrants, including those trying to flee Africa after decolonization, with strict requirements and broad deportation provisions for bordering immigrants. Further, ideological preferences complemented, and in some cases overrode, ethnic ones. The military regimes' geopolitical interests made them join the war against communism, and their immigration policies reflected this concern and allowed for the immigration of noncommunist persons from South Korean, Vietnam, Laos, and Kampuchea.

CASES IN WHICH INTERNATIONAL FACTORS WERE INFLUENTIAL

Different international factors can shape immigration policy decisions. I argue that the weight of international factors is better understood if one classifies them as short and long term. Acute crises, such as World War II and the Spanish Civil War, triggered the enactment of further immigration restrictions in Argentina by the Executive. The fear of the arrival of refugees from Nazi Europe and Spain justified these restrictions. In 1938 the government restricted the immigration of foreigners who were not coming to work in agriculture. In 1941 the government created a special war counsel to (arbitrarily) decide on the admission of individual foreign citizens.

The Cold War influenced the immigration policies of the different military governments. This was particularly true after the 1960s. As Fidel Castro consolidated his power, the United States worried about the export of communism to the rest of Latin America. Latin American right-wing military regimes mirrored this concern. Despite the limited impact of the first guerrilla groups that appeared during the 1960s, the Argentine government enacted different rules to prevent the rise of communism. Some of these repressed crimes against national security, prohibited the entry of people professing a communist ideology, and subjected immigrants from communist countries to strict controls. In addition, they approved important provisions applicable to those engaging in activities that could threaten public order. Punishments for these behaviors included deportation, prison, and loss of Argentine citizenship.

Increased cooperation and regional integration of nations' markets, on the other hand, can influence the decisions made by a more representative institution such as Congress. There is evidence that Argentina is on its way to solving immigration dilemmas in a cooperative manner with other states. In the early 1990s, the Southern Common Market justified amnesty for neighboring immigrants. Later, a year after member presidents announced they would allow the free movement of people in 2002, the Argentine Congress passed new immigration rules that would allow all citizens of Mercosur countries and associates to apply for a work visa in Argentina. These new immigration rules signified a radical change in the immigration policies of Argentina, which had prioritized the immigration of European citizens for over a century.

CONGRESS AND THE EXECUTIVE BRANCH
IN IMMIGRATION POLICY MAKING

The literature on democratization does not fully account for the centralization of the immigration decision-making process in Argentina for many years. For one thing, this literature does not explain the emergence of a centralizing Executive during the Alfonsín administration. In addition, it falls short in accounting for cases in which delegation patterns arise because of congressional inaction. Economic and institutional crises likely played a role in this congressional inability. In addition, Congress had difficulty in defining a long-term project of the nation in the absence of Executive guidance.

Congress's prospects of approving comprehensive immigration policies increased progressively. First, the creation in the early 1990s of the legislative committees dealing with immigration put immigration issues on the agenda and created an opportunity for the passage of new policies. However, this process was slow and no bills to enact comprehensive immigration policies were introduced until the mid-1990s. When bills were first introduced, Congress was leaning toward restrictive immigration measures, but Argentina's self-image as a country of immigration seems to have worked against the enactment of restrictive immigration policies. In addition, democracy is not learned overnight and Congress needed time to assume its responsibilities.

The Argentine Congress approved new immigration legislation in December 2003. Prioritizing the immigration of citizens from Southern Common Market countries, this new legislation changed Argentina's long-standing preference for European immigration. The progress of Mercosur seemed to be an important priority in the eyes of Argentine legislators and a factor that would help the long-term development of Argentina. However, the provision that the federal government should encourage European immigration is still part of the 165-year-old Argentine Constitution.

OTHER FACTORS REQUIRING FURTHER RESEARCH:
THE ROLE OF INTEREST GROUPS

Interest groups seemed to influence immigration policies on at least two occasions in the 1990s and 2000s. In the 1990s, a sense of crisis was created through the action of public officials and union leaders that led to the enactment of immigration restrictions. In the 2000s, a diverse coalition of immigrant rights groups and research institutions known as La Mesa played a role in the passage of Law 25871. The pluralist or interest group view of immigration policy making is that a variety of groups and individuals compete, bargain, and mutually adjust incrementally, pursuing policy goals that they believe are in their self-interest (Fitzgerald 1996).

However, the picture emerging from this research is a messier one. Unions had direct access to the government in the 1990s, probably due to the historically symbiotic relationship between the Peronist governments and the unions. President Menem enacted neoliberal economic reforms at the onset of the decade. The Federal Confederation of Workers split between those who uncritically accepted Menem's economic reforms and those who believed in a more independent role of unions (Albarracín 2004). In 1993, in the midst of an economic downturn, state officials, reacting to demands from some unions caused by the hiring of immigrants on temporary visas, blamed immigrants for most social ills during a successful campaign to disguise the failure of the economic plan. "Supporting" unions was instrumental to coopt them into accepting the additional planned neoliberal reforms, which included the liberalization of the labor market (Albarracín 2004).

In turn, Representative Rubén Giustiniani, the author of the bill that became Law 25871, worked very closely with immigrant rights organizations, including the International Organization for Migration, academics, and others in La Mesa, to the point that it became difficult to draw a line between government and interest groups. Unlike predictions from the interest group approach, this collaboration went well beyond participation in hearings in Congress and entailed meetings held for years, which led the literature to term this collaboration "extra-parliamentary" (Brumat and Torres 2015). In turn, members of La Mesa generated an immigration bill, which influenced the Giustiniani bill. Therefore, the picture that emerges from this research requires a relational understanding of the multiple connections between state and society that make them almost indistinguishable from one another (Jessop 1990).

Legislation Included

The legislation analyzed in this book is listed below. For full texts, please consult www.infoleg.gob.ar or www.boletinoficial.gob.ar.

Table A.1. Immigration Policy Legislation and Regulations (1853–2017)

Year	Norm	Main Provisions
1853 (includes reforms up to 1994)	Constitution	Preamble invites all good-willed citizens of the world to immigrate to Argentina. Establishes that foreigners have all the same civil rights as citizens (Article 20) Establishes that the federal government will foment European immigration (Article 25)
1869	Law 346	Foreigners with two years of residence can acquire Argentine citizenship (Article 2). Persons born in the former provinces of Río de la Plata may acquire Argentine citizenship (Article 1.5).
1876	Law 817 (Avellaneda Law)	Defines *immigrant* as a foreigner below seventy years of age who could prove his aptitude to develop an industry, art, or occupation (Article 12) Creates offices in Europe to promote immigration to Argentina (Article 4) Immigrants are benefited with subsidized passages, temporary lodging, and transport inland from port of arrival. In addition, the government helps them in finding a job or occupation (Article 14). Creates agricultural colonies and establishes the rules for their functioning (Article 61 and ff.)

Table A.1. Immigration Policy Legislation and Regulations (1853–2017) (*cont.*)

Year	Norm	Main Provisions
1902	Law 4144 (Residence Law)	Allows the Executive to deport those immigrants who had committed crimes abroad (Article 1) or those who behave in ways that threaten national security or public order (Article 2) The government can reject immigrants in the situations described above (Article 3).
1910	Law 7209 (Social Defense Law)	Prohibits the entry into the country of criminals, anarchists, or others who profess the use of violence against the government or those who were previously expelled from the country (Article 1)
1932	Decree of November 26	Prohibits the entry of immigrants who do not have a job in Argentina
1938	Decree 8972/38	Prohibits the entry of immigrants who do not come to work in the agricultural colonies
1941	Decree 100,908/41	Creates a special immigration counsel for the war period to decide on the admission of foreigners
1949	Decree 15972/49	Amnesty that allows all foreigners to apply for residency by furnishing proof of identity and date of entry into the country
1951	Decree 13721/51	Amnesty that allows "braceros" to apply for residency
1954	Law 14345	Approves the constitution of the Intergovernmental Committee for European Migration
1960	Decree 11619/60	Provides special treatment for Belgian citizens residing in Congo
1961	Decree 5466/61	Facilitates the immigration of Europeans formerly residing in African countries
1963	Decree 4805/63	Establishes basic rules for admission and deportation of immigrants. Consulates can award only temporary residencies for a period of six months. Defines who is considered an "illegal immigrant" and authorizes the Executive to deport these persons. Establishes penalties for violations of the immigration rules.
1963	Decree 788/63	Represses a long list of crimes against "national security" (treason, espionage, sabotage, professing leftist ideologies, among others). Foreigners receive the same penalties as Argentines, ranging from a year in prison to life sentence.
	Decree 4124/63	Prohibits the Communist Party from developing activities in Argentina. Bans communists from government and academic positions. Prohibits the entry of communist foreigners to the country. Punishes naturalized foreigners who participate in communist activities with the loss of citizenship.

Table A.1. Immigration Policy Legislation and Regulations (1853–2017) (*cont.*)

Year	Norm	Main Provisions
	Decree 2457/63	Rules on the admission of foreign citizens of countries under communist regimes. It awards to these foreigners a visa for a maximum of three months. At the same time, it subjects them to several controls once they arrive in the country, such as periodically reporting to the federal police and carrying a special ID.
1964	Decree 49/64	Establishes an amnesty for migrants from neighboring countries, which allows them to apply for permanent residency by furnishing proof of identity, lack of criminal record, and date of entry into the country
1965	Decree 4418/65	Establishes the persons who can apply for permanent residency (immigrants, refugees, former residents, and relatives of Argentines) and nonpermanent residency (temporary residents, tourists, seasonal workers, persons in transit, awardees of political asylum, daily border crossings) Establishes a list of persons who cannot apply for residency (those with illnesses, who have no occupation or means of subsistence, who are involved in prostitution or addicted to drugs, and who are condemned for crimes that deserve prison sentences) Establishes deportation provisions and increases the penalties imposed on those who give work or lodging to undocumented workers
1967	Law 17294	Prohibits the work of undocumented workers and persons not authorized to work by Immigration Agency. Obliges employers and hotels to control immigration papers. Employers can fire migrants who do not regularize their immigration status.
1969	Law 18235	Enables the Executive to deport a person who has been sentenced to prison or engages in activities that affect social peace, national security, or public order
1974	Decree 87/74	Establishes a generous amnesty for migrants from neighboring countries, allowing them to apply for permanent residency by furnishing proof of identity and date of entry into the country
1977	Decree 3938/77	Provides that the government will encourage immigration that is healthy and culturally compatible with the native population (i.e., European). The government will also promote immigration to the country abroad and create jobs for immigrants. The federal government will also determine land for settlement. With respect to immigrants from the region, the decree mandates that the federal government organize a regime that carefully selects and channels immigrants. Deportation provisions are still in effect from the previous government (Law 18235).

Table A.1. Immigration Policy Legislation and Regulations (1853–2017) (*cont.*)

Year	Norm	Main Provisions
1979	Resolution 64/79	Closes 15 border crossings with Chile
1981	Law 22439	Expresses a preference for European immigration and allows the Executive to create norms and procedures to encourage the immigration of foreigners "whose cultural characteristics permit integration into the Argentine society." A special fund is created to finance the settlement of these immigrants in regions of the country to be determined by Executive decision. The Executive is also in charge of creating the rules for selecting other immigrants, who will be admitted in three categories: permanent, temporary, and transitory residents.
1984	Decree 780/84	Allows all foreigners to apply for residency by furnishing proof of identity and date of entry into the country
1985	Resolution 2340/85	Establishes that the only persons who can apply for a work visa are relatives of Argentines or permanent residents, skilled workers, artists, and sports persons of documented solvency, religious workers, and immigrants with investment capital. There is no distinction between Europeans and Latin Americans. (Issued by the National Directorate of Migration.)
1987	Decree 1434/87	Repeats the provisions from Resolution 2340/85
1988	Resolution 700/88	Exempts Europeans from the application of Article 15 of Decree 1434/87. Europeans can apply for residence by merely furnishing proof of origin. (Issued by the National Directorate of Migration.)
	Law 23564	Updates amounts of penalties for immigration offenses
1990	Law 23768	Removes strict regulations for immigrants coming from Communist countries
1992	Decree 1033/92	Approves an amnesty for immigrants from neighboring countries that allows them to apply for residency by furnishing proof of identity and date of entry into the country
1993	Decree 2771/93	Gives extensive deportation powers to the Executive to deport immigrants caught in the commission of a crime or engaged in illegal occupation of dwellings. It also mandates increased inspections in the places where immigrants live. [Although it was directed to immigrants from the region, I consider it applicable to all foreigners.]
1994	Decree 1023/94	Requires a written job contract in order to be eligible for a work visa. It also allows the following foreigners to apply for residency: relatives of Argentines or permanent residents, artists and athletes of documented solvency, religious workers, and immigrants with investment capital.

Table A.1. Immigration Policy Legislation and Regulations (1853–2017) (*cont.*)

Year	Norm	Main Provisions
	Resolution 4632/94	Formalizes the plan of 1992 and enables citizens from Central and Eastern Europe to apply for permanent residency in the country. (Passed by the Ministry of the Interior.)
	Law 24393	Removes physical or mental disabilities as grounds for inadmissability
1998	Decree 1117/98	Prohibits immigrants from changing their visa type once they enter the country
2004	Law 25871	Protects rights of immigrants, establishes liberal immigration rules for citizens from Mercosur countries, and promotes the regularization of immigrants
	Decree 836/04	Creates the National Program of Immigration Regularization for non-Mercosur citizens
	Decree 1169/04	Allows for the regularization of immigrants from non-Mercosur countries
2005	Decree 578/05	Extends the National Program of Immigration Regularization to Mercosur
2013	Resolution 1 and 2	Special regularization plan for Senegalese and Dominicans
2017	Decree 70/17	Rolls back protections from deportation and allows for the deportation of people accused of certain crimes

Table A.2. Immigration Agreements with Countries Outside South America

Country	Year	Provisions
Switzerland	1937	Facilitates immigration for agricultural colonies
Denmark	1937	Favors immigration to Argentina
Low Countries	1938	Favors immigration to Argentina
Italy	1947	Facilitates immigration of agricultural and other kinds of manual and intellectual workers
Spain	1948	Promotes the immigration of skilled workers
Spain	1960	Facilitates immigration to Argentina
Japan	1961	Promotes immigration of skilled workers and technological investments in Argentina
France	1964	Seeks the establishment of agricultural colonies in Argentina with French citizens formerly residing in North Africa

Table A.3. Immigration Agreements with South American Countries

Country	Year	Provisions
Paraguay	1958	Facilitates the hiring of seasonal workers
Bolivia	1964 and 1978	Facilitates the hiring of seasonal workers
Chile	1971	Establishes the rules applicable to seasonal workers
Bolivia	1999	Nationals of both countries can obtain a temporary visa for six months. After this, they either comply with the requirements of Decree 1023/94 or register as self-employed before the Taxation Agency.
Peru	1999	Nationals of both countries can obtain a temporary visa for six months. After this, they either comply with the requirements of Decree 1023/94 or register as self-employed before the Taxation Agency.

Table A.4. Other Laws and Regulations

Year	Norm	Provisions
2006	Law 26122	Regulates DNUs (decrees of necessity and urgency)

Print Media Data

The articles were collected from the newspapers *La Nación* and *Clarín* for the years 1983 to 1987, and from *La Nación* and *Página 12* for the years 1992 to 1994. The idea was to have a sample of the center (*La Nación*) and center-left (*Clarín* and *Página 12*) print media in Argentina.

Stories were selected by the author by hand and through searches for the keywords *immigration, immigrant/s, illegal,* and *undocumented,* as well as words related to the main countries of origin for Latin American immigrants in Argentina (Bolivia, Brazil, Chile, Paraguay, Peru, Uruguay). All articles that discussed issues related to immigrants or immigration were coded for six-month periods in the years 1983 and 1984 (October–March), 1987 (March–August), 1992 (January–June), 1993 (July–December), and 1994 (January–June). Opinion pieces were collected and included in present analysis. The terms and themes referring to different groups of European and non-European immigrants were coded separately.

TERMS USED TO REFER TO IMMIGRANTS

The terms used to refer to immigrants were coded as negative or positive. The instances that showed respect and consideration for immigrants as human beings were coded positive, while those that described them as somehow undesirable were coded as negative. Many terms, such as *immigrants, migrants,* and *immigration,* were evaluated as neutral and were not included. Additionally, the instances that disrespected immigrants, treated them as things, or tended to exaggerate the growth in immigrant population were counted as negative.

PROBLEMS AND BENEFITS ASSOCIATED
WITH IMMIGRATION

A reference to a beneficial effect of immigration was coded as positive. Instances that described economic, health, or social problems associated with immigration were coded as negative.

Questionnaire for Congresspersons and Interviews with Key Players

QUESTIONNAIRE FOR MEMBERS OF CONGRESS

A survey was conducted by the author, during 2003 and 2004, with approximately 8 percent of the members of the Argentine Congress (N = 26). The surveys were responded to via e-mail. The sample is approximately representative of the composition of the Argentine Congress. Of those surveyed, 70 percent were male and 30 percent were female. Forty-eight percent of respondents belonged to the Peronist Partido Justicialista, 30 percent to the Unión Cívica Radical, and 15 percent to third parties. Nineteen of those surveyed belonged to the House of Representatives and eight to the Senate. The text of the survey administered follows:

I prefer that my identity is not revealed____

Gender:

Political Party:

Beginning of Mandate:

End of Mandate:

Congressional Committees in which the legislator participates:

1. Do you agree with the immigration policies of the Argentine Executive that require a job contract in order to be eligible for a work visa?

1___   2 ___   3 ___   4 ___   5 ___
Completely agree   Completely disagree

2. Why?

3. It has been argued that the current immigration legislation gives discretional powers to the Executive to decide on the admission of foreign citizens. Do you agree with this assessment?

1___   2 ___   3 ___   4 ___   5 ___
Completely agree   Completely disagree

4. Why do you believe Congress has been unable to agree on a new immigration policy since the reestablishment of democracy?

5. To what extent do you believe the following groups of immigrants have been beneficial to the country?

a. European (up to WWII):
1___   2 ___   3 ___   4 ___   5 ___
Not beneficial at all   Absolutely beneficial

b. From Arab Countries:
1___   2 ___   3 ___   4 ___   5 ___
Not beneficial at all   Absolutely beneficial

c. Paraguayan:
1___   2 ___   3 ___   4 ___   5 ___
Not beneficial at all   Absolutely beneficial

d. Bolivian:
1___   2 ___   3 ___   4 ___   5 ___
Not beneficial at all   Absolutely beneficial

e. Uruguayan:
1___   2 ___   3 ___   4 ___   5 ___
Not beneficial at all   Absolutely beneficial

f. Brazilian:

1___   2___   3___   4___   5___

Not beneficial at all   Absolutely beneficial

g. Chilean:

1___   2___   3___   4___   5___

Not beneficial at all   Absolutely beneficial

h. Recent immigrants from Central and Eastern Europe:

1___   2___   3___   4___   5___

Not beneficial at all   Absolutely beneficial

6. Would you vote affirmatively for the free movement of people within Mercosur?

Yes___   No___

7. Why?

8. Argentina needs an immigration policy with the following characteristics (mark all that apply):

a) Selective, which responds to the country's needs for
   professional and skilled workers ___
b) Selective, with attention to the national origin of immigrants ___
c) Selective, which establishes quotas with regard to
   profession/occupation ___
d) Generous, which considers regional integration agreements ___
e) Generous, which gives equal treatment to all nations ___
f) That gives preferential treatment to Europeans, according to
   the Argentine Constitution ___
g) That establishes special rules for seasonal workers that do
   not settle permanently in Argentina ___
h) Other:
i) Other:

9. In your experience, are congressional requests to the Executive satisfactorily responded to by the latter?

You can add as many comments and questions as you wish:

INTERVIEWS WITH KEY PUBLIC OFFICIALS

The semistructured interviews with key actors of immigration policy making were conducted between 2001 and 2004. Questions usually centered around the reasons for each immigration policy change and the reasons why Congress took twenty years to enact new comprehensive immigration legislation. Persons interviewed included:

Alfonso, Adriana, former director of legal affairs for the Immigration Agency. Interview with the author July 14, 2002.

Aruj, Roberto, researcher. Interview with the author July 10, 2002.

Bogado Poisson, Luis, adviser to the International Organization for Migration. Interview with the author May 27, 2004.

Cafiero, Antonio, former senator and president of the Committee on Population and Human Development of the Argentine Senate. Interview with the author July 11, 2004.

Chausovsky, Gabriel, director of the graduate degree in immigration law (curso de especialización en derecho de extranjería), Universidad del Litoral. Interview with the author May 16, 2003.

Father Fabio, head of the Pastoral Commission for Migration, Buenos Aires Archdiocese. Interview with the author July 28, 2001.

Gasparri, Mario, adviser to the mega union Workers Confederation (Confederación General del Trabajo). Interview with the author December 19, 2002.

Giustiniani, Rubén, former representative and president of the Committee on Population and Human Resources of the Chamber of Deputies (2000–2003). Interview with the author May 26, 2004.

Gris, Ildo, head of the Catholic Committee for Migration (Comisión Católica para las Migraciones). Interview with the author July 26, 2001.

Gurrieri, Jorge, former director of the Immigration Agency (1993–1995). Interviews with the author July 15, 2002, and May 12, 2004.

Huayre, Gustavo, member of the Consulting Council of the Peruvian Consulate in Argentina. Interview with the author May 10, 2004.

Iglesias, Evaristo, former director of the Immigration Agency (1983–1987). Interview with the author March 22, 2003.

Lépore, Silvia, former adviser to the director of the Immigration Agency (1983–1987). Interview with the author May 24, 2003.

Mármora, Lelio, former director of the International Organization for Migration's office in Argentina (1995–2002). Interview with the author July 21, 2001.

Oteiza, Enrique, former president of the National Institute against Discrimination, Xenophobia, and Racism. Interview with the author June 14, 2004.

Rocca, Gustavo, commandant of Gendarmería Nacional, in charge of the Border Department (1998–present). Interviews with the author June 26, 2004, and July 16, 2004.

Rodriguez Onetto, Sergio, former director of the Immigration Agency (1987–1989). Interview with the author June 2, 2003.

Santillo, Mario, director of the Latin American Center for Migration Studies (CEMLA; Centro de Estudios Migratorios Latinoamericanos). Interview with the author July 12, 2001.

Vecino, Juan Manuel, adviser to the National Institute against Discrimination, Xenophobia, and Racism (1999–2001). Interview with the author July 15, 2001.

House and Senate Bills
and Other Decisions

The different decisions and bills considered by the House and Senate were identified using search engines at http://www.senado.gov.ar/parlamentario /parlamentaria/.

The keywords used for searches were *inmigrantes, inmigración, migrantes,* and *migración.*

The full text of the resolutions, declarations, and bills from Congress and bills initiated by the Executive were found in *Trámite Palamentario* (Buenos Aires, Cámara de Diputados de la Nación).

Occasionally, the *Diario de Sessiones de la Cámara de Diputados* and *Diario de Sesiones de la Cámara de Senadores Congreso de la Nación* (Buenos Aires, Congreso de la Nación) were consulted to see the debates of the bills.

NOTES

ONE. Introduction

1. Since the seventeenth century, the world has been increasingly divided spatially into nation-states where, since the nineteenth century, these separate populations have been constructed legally and ideologically by the legal categories of nationality and citizenship (Bovenkerk, Miles, and Verbunt 1990).

2. Despite a general tendency to see political processes as a neutral, some pluralists recognize the importance of political structures as explanations for political results. For instance, see Charles Edward Lindblom, *The Intelligence of Democracy: Decision Making through Mutual Adjustment* (New York: Free Press, 1965).

3. The expansive tendency of immigration policy can be reversed because of economic reasons or the tendency of migration to generate more migration through networks.

4. The argument of the author does not really relate to how immigration policy is shaped. However, his disquisitions about the use of discursive practices against immigrants are of interest for this study. Mehan (1997) believes that since the end of the Cold War, the search for enemies in the United States has turned inward. The state, in an alliance with other powerful groups in society, encourages the treatment of the immigrant, the poor, and the unfortunate as the enemy (250).

TWO. Argentine Immigration Policies in Comparative Perspective, 1853–2017

1. See "Vivir en Perpetuo Sitio," *El Derecho,* 183–1070.

2. It has been shown, however, that Romantic, organicist authors such as Herder did not create xenophobic conceptions of national identity. His ideas accepted that foreign influences could be positively channeled through assimilation into the community.

3. Gauchos are men, sometimes of mixed racial origin, who live in rural areas and work with cattle. *Cholo* is a pejorative word used to refer to a person of indigenous origin.

4. I use *mestizaje,* as does L. Martínez-Echazábal, "*Mestizaje* and the Discourse of National-Cultural Identity in Latin America, 1845–1959" (*Latin American Perspectives* 100, no. 25 [1998]: 21–42), to refer to a process that does not necessarily mean "miscegenation." *Mestizaje* can encompass intermarriage but it more importantly includes cultural fertilization between different groups.

5. I say *partly* because his work does not build on a strong concern with historical objectivity and his political positions, highly biased against *Federales,* are clear throughout his early work.

6. This view comes with the Rousseauian idea that men are naturally good and therefore can be "civilized" under another regime. See Banton 1998, 23 and ff.

7. Caudillos were personalistic political or military leaders in the provinces who fought against the centralization of power by Buenos Aires.

8. Attacking the caudillos Juan Manuel de Rosas and Facundo Quiroga constituted part of Sarmiento's political agenda. Additionally, he was probably positioning himself for the national presidency, which he occupied between 1868 and 1874.

9. Authors debate the extent to which the government made broad use of subsidized transportation. For instance, Donald Castro (1995, 83 and ff.) shows that Congress outvoted the necessary funds for the passages, which were only established in the late 1880s and for a short period of time.

10. The land promised to immigrants was not always available. As agricultural exports expanded and land prices rose, immigrants could not acquire land.

11. A constitutional provision of 1860 stated that any person who had been residing in the country for two years could become a citizen. Decree 3213/84 established that the two-year residence in the country could be proved by a certificate issued by the immigration office: in other words, a *lawful* residence. Further, the courts played a role in restricting constitutional rights to migrants who had lawfully entered the country.

12. The government approved universal male suffrage in 1912.

13. This number includes land and cattle-breeding operations owners, renters, administrators, and laborers.

14. In the Buenos Aires region, where land had been mostly devoted to cattle breeding and raising, landowners needed big parcels to make their enterprises profitable. As the nineteenth century progressed, Argentina's pastoral economy became more complex and labor intensive. Cattle breeding and the beef export industry required large numbers of laborers to erect fences and to plant alfalfa. Ranchers then welcomed immigrants but were still unwilling to share their land with them.

15. The average family of five people lived in a single room. Additionally, 73 percent of the inmates in the Buenos Aires beggars' asylum were foreigners (see Rock 1987, 94 and ff.). As in the case of labor unrest, the Argentine elites and intellectuals tried to account for beggary and poverty in terms of the racial characteris-

tics of the immigrant population. In this regard, see Eugenia Scarzanella, *Ni gringos* (Quilmes, Argentina: Universidad de Quilmes, 1999), 24 and ff.

16. Skilled workers entered reformist socialist unions, and the unskilled proletariat joined the anarchist ones. The anarchist unions, more engaged in direct action, soon became highly visible through the organization of strikes.

17. By 1958, when the law was finally amended, only 383 people had been deported.

18. In 1910 a band of vigilantes attacked socialist and anarchist unions, killing several people. Also, the 1919 strikes were repressed with the help of the armed forces. The use of the military was probably not a smart choice, as it increased the belief of the armed forces that they were the guardians of internal security and that democratic governments' weakness justified their intervention in domestic politics.

19. Indeed, the field of criminology was developed after the 1880s in Argentina to explain immigrants' rising crime. For more information, see Rosa del Olmo, "Argentina and the Development of Criminology," *Social Justice* 26, no. 2 (Summer 1999) or Scarzanella, *Ni gringos*, 200.

20. Sergio Rodriguez Onetto, interview with the author, June 2, 2003.

21. For instance, the British government intervened actively to investigate the "Massacre of the Pampas," when some sixty-one foreigners (Spanish, Italian, French, and British) were killed by a band of armed men. For more details, see John Lynch, *Massacre in the Pampas, 1872: Britain and Argentina in the Age of Migration* (Norman: University of Oklahoma Press, 1998). Another example was the threat to send troops to Uruguay in 1882, when the police tortured several Italian immigrants. For more details see Bertoni 2001, 25 and ff. Finally, in 1888, Argentina almost faced an international conflict with Italy over the administration of the Italian schools in Buenos Aires.

22. In the 1880s, for instance, Argentina almost went to war with Chile.

23. Jews were barred from professions, and the Nuremberg laws prohibited intermarriage between "non-Aryan" and "Aryan" Germans. Later, Jewish property was confiscated and the community's newspapers closed.

24. A total of 360,000 to 370,000 Jews left the borders of the expanded Reich between 1933 and 1939, representing one-third of the Jews who lived in the area.

25. In this regard, see Senkman 1991 on Argentina and on the United States R. Breitman and A. M. Kraut, *American Refugee Policy* (Bloomington: Indiana University Press, 1987).

26. The Italian government provided transportation to the port of departure, and the Argentine government financed transportation to Argentina.

27. No official data are available about the foreigners who regularized their immigration status through this amnesty. It is also supposed to have benefited Jewish immigrants and Nazi and anti-communist refugees.

28. I consider Guido's presidency to be military because he assumed power after the military deposed President Frondizi in 1962, with assistance from the

factions within the military that prevented agreement on a military figure to head the government.

29. As this chapter shows, democratic governments passed different amnesties to allow for the regularization of undocumented immigrants.

30. Three of these groups were Peronist: Montoneros, Fuerzas Armadas Peronistas, and Fuerzas Armadas Revolucionarias. The other group, the Ejercito Revolucionario del Pueblo, was of Trotskyite extraction.

31. Sol Amaya, "La Lupa sobre Los Inmigrantes: Qué Impacto Real Tienen en Argentina?," *La Nación*, November 28, 2016, http://www.lanacion.com.ar/1957161 -la-lupa-sobre-los-inmigrantes-que-impacto-real-tienen-sobre-la-argentina (June 26, 2017).

THREE. Immigration Policies after the Reestablishment
of Democracy, 1983–1989

1. It was the first time that the Peronist party lost a fair election to the Radicals. Between 1955 and 1973, when the Peronist party was prohibited from competing in elections, two "democratic" presidents were elected: Arturo Frondizi in 1958 and Arturo Illia in 1963.

2. Interior Undersecretary Raúl Galván, interview with the author, *Clarín*, January 31, 1984.

3. Author's estimate based on data provided by Dirección Nacional de Migraciones, Radicaciones Temporarias y Definitivas 1970–1980.

4. Mario Gasparri, interview with the author, December 19, 2002.

5. Due to the large number of newspaper articles analyzed, only the newspaper and date are referenced in the text. For an explanation of the methods, see Appendix II.

6. According to Article 77 of the Argentine Constitution, the president can introduce certain bills for consideration by Congress.

7. Silvia Lépore, interview with the author, May 24, 2003.

FOUR. Immigration Policies during Menem's
Administration, 1989–1995

1. Jorge Gurrieri, interview with the author, July 15, 2002.

2. Due to the large number of newspaper articles analyzed, only the newspaper and date are referenced in the text.

3. Adriana Alfonso, interview with the author, July 14, 2002.

4. Jorge Gurrieri, interview with the author, July 15, 2002.

5. Ibid.

6. Father Ildo Gris, interview with the author, July 13, 2001.

7. The data on inspections and deportation are very difficult to obtain. For one thing, the Immigration Agency is reluctant to release it. In addition, the records are poor. For instance, Gendarmería Nacional, in control of 130 border crossings in Argentina, only keeps records since 1997. I was informed of this by Commandant Rocca, then in charge of the Border Department of Gendarmería Nacional, during an interview conducted on June 23, 2004.

8. Lelio Mármora, interview with the author, July 21, 2001.

9. Data obtained from the report by the Population Secretary in reply to an information request by the Chamber of Deputies identified as 5793-D-95.

10. See note 9.

FIVE. Gridlock or Delegative Democracy?

1. This executive action also contains provisions for border security, interior enforcements, removals, Deferred Action for Childhood Arrivals (DACA), parole, provisional unlawful presence waivers, highly skilled foreign workers, immigrant integration and naturalization, immigrant visa system, labor protection, and crime victims.

2. At the time this book was being finalized, the rescission of DACA by President Trump from September 2017 was also blocked in the courts.

3. In 1989, for instance, the Executive initiated two bills for congressional approval (Laws 23696 and 23697) to obtain more power in matters of economic policy.

4. Jorge Gurrieri, interview with the author, May 5, 2004.

5. Since more than two-thirds of the legislators who responded to the questionnaire chose to remain anonymous, I decided not to identify any of the legislators participating by name.

6. Questionnaire response, by a PJ senator in Buenos Aires, August 7, 2003.

7. Questionnaire response, by a UCR representative in Buenos Aires, August 20, 2003.

8. Gustavo Huayre, interview with the author, May 10, 2004.

9. Questionnaire response, by a UCR senator in Buenos Aires, August 6, 2003.

10. Questionnaire response, by a representative from a provincial party in Buenos Aires, June 6, 2003.

11. Gabriel Chausovsky, interview with the author, May 16, 2003.

12. Jorge Gurrieri, interview with the author, May 5, 2004.

13. The questionnaire for Argentine legislators did not include a question regarding the role of Congress in immigration policies. The comments analyzed in this section arose from different open-ended questions. Also, for this reason, only roughly more than one-third of the legislators commented on the role of Congress.

14. Questionnaire response, by a representative from Frente Grande in Buenos Aires, June 6, 2003.

15. Questionnaire response, by a UCR representative in Buenos Aires, August 26, 2003.

16. Questionnaire response, by a UCR senator in Buenos Aires, September 6, 2003.

17. Questionnaire response, by a UCR representative in Buenos Aires, September 16, 2003.

18. Questionnaire response, by a UCR representative in Buenos Aires, October 2, 2003.

19. Questionnaire response, by a UCR senator in Buenos Aires, September 6, 2003.

20. The presidential term in Argentina was six years. The constitutional reform of 1994 reduced the term to four years and allowed for reelection to one consecutive term.

21. The data include all proposals considered by Congress except for bills.

22. These parties were Movimiento Popular Neuquino, a regional party from Neuquén, and Democracia Cristiana, a social-democratic front that was important in Buenos Aires and provided the basis for the later creation of Frepaso (Frente País Solidario).

23. The bills proposed by the Executive have *PE* (Poder Ejecutivo) in their ID numbers.

24. One of the bills proposed by the Executive, 48-PE, was approved by the Senate in a later period.

25. Law 23564, see Appendix I.

26. Law 23768, see Appendix I.

27. Law 24393, see Appendix I.

SIX. Delegative Democracy Revisited

1. The total for the second presidential period may be smaller because presidential terms were cut from six to four years.

2. On the provisions of Decree 1023/94, see Appendix I.

3. Questionnaire response, by a UCR representative, October 2, 2003.

4. Questionnaire response, by a representative from a provincial party, October 2, 2003.

5. Questionnaire response, by a UCR representative, May 5, 2003.

SEVEN. Immigration and Immigration Policies in the 2000s

1. Mercosur includes Argentina, Brazil, Uruguay, Paraguay, and, since 2012, Venezuela (although the status of Venezuela is unclear at the time of publication).

Associate states include Bolivia, Chile, Colombia, Peru, Ecuador, Guyana, and Surinam. Venezuela was added as a full member but was suspended and Bolivia was in the process of becoming a full member as of March 2018.

2. Adriana Alfonso, interview with the author, July 14, 2002.

3. Sergio Rodriguez Onetto, interview with the author, June 2, 2003.

4. Rubén Giustiniani, interview with the author, May 26, 2004.

5. Ibid.

6. Gabriel Chausovsky, interview with the author, May 16, 2003.

7. Different explanations may account for the more beneficial assessment of the impact of Brazilian immigration. First, immigrants from Brazil migrate to Argentina in low numbers. Second, the Brazilians who vacation in Argentina are mainly white. Finally, there is a mixture of rivalry and admiration at play with Brazil.

8. Luis Bogado Poisson, interview with the author, May 17, 2004.

9. Rubén Giustiniani, interview with the author, May 26, 2004.

10. Jorge Gurrieri, interview with the author, December 5, 2004.

11. Enrique Oteiza, interview with the author, June 14, 2004.

12. Ibid.

13. Gabriel Chausovsky, interview with the author, May 16, 2003.

14. Rubén Giustiniani, interview with the author, May 26, 2004.

15. Luis Bogado Poisson, interview with the author, May 17, 2004.

16. Senator Antonio Cafiero, interview with the author, July 11, 2004.

17. Federico Fahsbender, "La Justicia avaló el decreto de Macri para echar extranjeros: Las deportaciones aumentaron 3150% en dos años," Infobae.com, October 25, 2017, https://www.infobae.com/sociedad/policiales/2017/10/25/la -justicia-avalo-el-decreto-de-macri-para-echar-extranjeros-las-deportaciones -aumentaron-3150-en-dos-anos/.

18. Simon Romero and Daniel Politi, "Argentina's Trump-Like Immigration Order Rattles South America," *New York Times,* February 4, 2017, https://www.ny times.com/2017/02/04/world/americas/argentinas-trump-like-immigration -order-rattles-south-america.html.

19. Fahsbender, "La Justicia."

20. Holly Yan and David Williams, "Nationwide 'Day Without Immigrants' Shuts Down Businesses," CNN.com, February 16, 2017, https://www.cnn.com /2017/02/16/us/day-without-immigrants-vignettes/.

REFERENCES

Adamovsky, Ezequiel. 2015. "El Criollismo en las Luchas por la Definición del Origen y el Color del Ethnos Argentino, 1945–1955." *Estudios Interdisciplinarios de América Latina y el Caribe* 26(1): 31–63.

Adelman, Jeremy. 1999. *Republic of Capital: Buenos Aires and the Legal Transformation of the Atlantic World.* Palo Alto, CA: Stanford University Press.

Akmir, Abdelwahed. 1991. "La Inserción de los Inmigrantes Árabes en Argentina (1880–1980): Implicaciones Sociales." *Anaquel de Estudios Arabes* 2: 237.

Albarracín, Julia. 2004. "Selecting Immigration in Modern Argentina: Economic, Cultural, International and Institutional Factors." Ph.D. diss., University of Florida.

———. 2005. "Inmigración en la Argentina Moderna: Un Matrimonio en la Salud y en la Enfermedad con Europeos?" In *Migraciones Contemporáneas y Diversidad Cultural en Argentina*, edited by Eduardo Domenech, 19–40. Cordoba, Argentina: Centro de Estudios Avanzados, Universidad Nacional de Córdoba.

Alberdi, Juan Bautista. 1966. *Bases y Puntos de Partida para la Organización Política de la República Argentina.* Buenos Aires: Eudeba. Original edition 1852. Reprint 1966.

American Immigration Council. 2017. "A Primer on Expedited Removal." Washington, DC: American Immigration Council. https://www.americanimmigration council.org/research/primer-expedited-removal.

Andermann, Jens. 2016. "It's the Ideology, Stupid! In Macri's Argentina: A Reportage." *Journal of Latin American Cultural Studies* 25(1): 7–17.

Anderson, Benedict. 1991. *Imagined Communities: Reflections on the Origin and Spread of Nationalism.* New York: Verso Books.

Andreas, Peter. 1999. "Borderless Economy, Barricaded Border." *NACLA Report on the Americas* 33(3): 14–21.

———. 2000. *Border Games: Policing the US–Mexico Divide.* Ithaca, NY: Cornell University Press.

Andrews, George R. 1980. *The Afro-Argentines of Buenos Aires, 1800–1900.* Madison: University of Wisconsin Press.

Avni, Haim. 1991. *Argentina and the Jews: A History of Jewish Immigration.* Tuscaloosa: University of Alabama Press.

Avni, Haim, and Sibila Seibert. 1983. "La Agricultura Judía en la Argentina: ¿Éxito o Fracaso?" *Desarrollo Económico* 22(88): 535–48.

Baer, James A. 2015. *Anarchist Immigrants in Spain and Argentina.* Champaign: University of Illinois Press.

Baily, Samuel L. 1987. Review of *Adventurers and Proletarians: The Story of Migrants in Latin America,* by Magnus Mörner and Harold Sims. *Journal of American Ethnic History* 7(1): 103–5.

Banton, Michael. 1998. *Racial Theories.* Cambridge: Cambridge University Press.

Barbero, María V. 2016. "Struggles over Rights and Representations in the Migrant Metropolis: Reverberations of the Trump Effect in the Global South." *Metropolitics,* December 7. https://www.metropolitiques.eu.

Barfield, Thomas. 2010. *Afghanistan: A Cultural and Political History.* Princeton, NJ: Princeton University Press.

Barker, Martin. 1981. *The New Racism: Conservatives and the Ideology of the Tribe.* Toronto: Junction Books.

Bauder, Harald. 2008. "Neoliberalism and the Economic Utility of Immigration: Media Perspectives of Germany's Immigration Law." *Antipode* 40(1): 55–78.

Bauer, Otto. 1996. "The Nation." In *Mapping the Nation,* edited by Gopal Balakrishnan, 39–77. New York: New Left Review & Verso.

Beard, Charles Austin, and Mary Ritter Beard. 1944. *Beard's Basic History of the United States.* New York: Doubleday.

Behdad, Ali. 1997. "Nationalism and Immigration to the United States." *Diaspora: A Journal of Transnational Studies* 6(2): 155–78.

———. 2005. *A Forgetful Nation: On Immigration and Cultural Identity in the United States.* Durham, NC: Duke University Press.

Bertoncello, Rodolfo, and Alfredo E. Lattes. 1997. "Dinámica Demográfica, Migración Limítrofe y Actividad Económica en Buenos Aires." *Estudios Migratorios Latinoamericanos* 12(35): 5–30.

Bertoni, Lilia Ana. 2001. *Patriotas, Cosmopolitas y Nacionalistas: La Construcción de la Nacionalidad Argentina a Fines del Siglo XIX.* Buenos Aires: Fondo de Cultura Económica.

Beyer, Audun, and Jörg Matthes. 2015. "Public Perceptions of the Media Coverage of Irregular Immigration: Comparative Insights from France, the United States, and Norway." *American Behavioral Scientist* 59(7): 839–57.

Bialogorski, Mirta. 2004. "La Presencia Coreana en la Argentina: La Construcción Simbólica de una Experiencia Inmigratoria." Ph.D. diss., Universidad de Buenos Aires.

Bjerg, Maria. 1995. "Sabiendo el Camino o Navegando en las Dudas: Las Redes Sociales y las Redes Interpersonales en la Inmigración Danesa en la Argentina, 1848–1930." In *Inmigración y Redes Sociales en la Argentina Moderna,* edited by Maria Bjerg and Hernán Otero, 107–32. Tandil, Argentina: Universidad Nacional del Centro.

Bletz, May E. 2010. *Immigration and Acculturation in Brazil and Argentina: 1890– 1929.* New York: Springer.

Blinder, Scott. 2015. "Imagined Immigration: The Impact of Different Meanings of 'Immigrants' in Public Opinion and Policy Debates in Britain." *Political Studies* 63(1): 80–100.

Bobo, Lawrence D. 2017. "Racism in Trump's America: Reflections on Culture, Sociology, and the 2016 US Presidential Election." *British Journal of Sociology* 68(S1): 85–104.

Boswell, Christina. 2007. "Theorizing Migration Policy: Is There a Third Way?" *International Migration Review* 41(1): 75–100.

Bovenkerk, Frank, Robert Miles, and Gilles Verbunt. 1990. "Racism, Migration and the State in Western Europe: A Case for Comparative Analysis." *International Sociology* 5(4): 475–90.

Boyd, Monica, and Michael Vickers. 2000. "100 Years of Immigration in Canada." *Canadian Social Trends* 58(2): 2–12.

Branton, Regina, and Johanna Dunaway. 2008. "English- and Spanish-Language Media Coverage of Immigration: A Comparative Analysis." *Social Science Quarterly* 89(4): 1006–22.

Breuilly, John. 1994. *Nationalism and the State.* Chicago: University of Chicago Press.

———. 1996. "Approaches to Nationalism." In *Mapping the Nation*, edited by Gopal Balakrishnan, 146–74. New York: New Left Review & Verso.

Briggs, Vernon M. 1994. *Mass Immigration and the National Interest.* Armonk, NY: M. E. Sharpe.

Brodsky, Adriana M. 2016. *Sephardi, Jewish, Argentine: Community and National Identity, 1880–1960.* Bloomington: Indiana University Press.

Brubaker, Rogers. 1992. *Citizenship and Nationhood in France and Germany.* Cambridge, MA: Harvard University Press.

———. 1995. "Comments on 'Modes of Immigration in Liberal Democracies.'" *International Migration Review* 29(4): 903–8.

Brumat, Leiza, and Rayen Amancay Torres. 2015. "La Ley de Migraciones 25 871: Un Caso de Democracia Participativa en Argentina." *Estudios Políticos* 46: 55–77. https://www.researchgate.net/publication/271841557_La_Ley_de_Migraciones _25_871_un_caso_de_democracia_participativa_en_Argentina.

Bunk, Brian D. 2002. "'Your Comrades Will Not Forget': Revolutionary Memory and the Breakdown of the Spanish Second Republic, 1934–1936." *History and Memory* 14(1–2): 65–92.

Calavita, Kitty. 1980. "A Sociological Analysis of US Immigration Policy." Ph.D. diss., University of Delaware.

———. 1994. "US Immigration and Policy Responses: The Limits of Legislation." In *Controlling Immigration: A Global Perspective*, edited by Wayne A. Cornelius, Philip L. Martin, and James F. Hollifield, 55–82. Stanford, CA: Stanford University Press.

―――. 1998. "Gaps and Contradictions in US Immigration Policy: An Analysis of Recent Reform Efforts." In *The Immigration Reader: America in a Multidisciplinary Perspective*, edited by David Jacobson, 92–112. Malden, MA: Blackwell.

―――. 2010. *Inside the State: The Bracero Program, Immigration, and the INS*. New Orleans: Quid Pro Books.

Cancillería Argentina. 2002. "Política de Tratamiento Especial para Europa Central y Oriental." Unpublished memo: Argentine Foreign Affairs Ministry.

Canedo, Alfredo. 1974. *Aspectos del Pensamiento Político de Leopoldo Lugones*. Buenos Aires: Marcos.

Castells, Manuel. 1975. "Immigrant Workers and Class Struggles in Advanced Capitalism: The Western European Experience." *Politics and Society* 5(1): 33–66.

Castles, Stephen. 2004a. "The Factors That Make and Unmake Migration Policies." *International Migration Review* 38(3): 852–84.

―――. 2004b. "Why Migration Policies Fail." *Ethnic and Racial Studies* 27(2): 205–27.

Castles, Stephen, and Godula Kosack. 1973. *Immigrant Workers and Class Structure in Western Europe*. London: Oxford University Press.

Castro, Donald. 1995. "We Are a Separate Race! The Images of the Jew in the Argentine Popular Theatre, 1890–1935." Paper presented at the annual meeting of the Latin American Studies Association, Washington, DC.

Catterberg, Edgardo. 2000. "Tolerancia Étnica en Argentina." http://www.argentina-rree.com/home_nueva.htm.

Cavarozzi, Marcelo. 1997. *Autoritarismo y Democracia (1955–1996): La Transición del Estado al Mercado en Argentina*. Buenos Aires: Editorial Ariel.

CELS (Centro de Estudios Legales y Sociales). 2002. *Informe Anual Sobre La Situación de los Derechos Humanos en Argentina*. Buenos Aires: CELS.

Ceriani Cernadas, Pablo. 2013. "Apuntes Críticos sobre Derechos Humanos, Migraciones y Libre Circulación de Personas en el MERCOSUR." *Libro de Derechos Humanos: Reflexiones desde el Sur*, 83–118. Buenos Aires: Ed. Infojus.

Cerrutti, Marcela. 2009. *Diagnóstico de las Poblaciones de Inmigrantes en Argentina*. Buenos Aires: Dirección Nacional de Población, Ministerio del Interior and Organización Internacional para las Migraciones.

Cervio, Ana Lucía, and Andrea Dettano. 2016. "7 Necesidades y Urgencias Sociales en Argentina: Una Retrospectiva Analítica desde sus Definiciones 'Ejecutivas.'" In *Los Cuerpos Expuestos: Emergencias y Catástrofes*, edited by Diego Benegas Loyo and Dinorah Otero, 61–70. Buenos Aires: Tombó Ediciones.

Chambliss, William J. 1979. "On Lawmaking." *British Journal of Law and Society* 6(2): 149–71.

Clarín. 1945–present. [Newspaper]. Buenos Aires, Argentina. https://www.clarin.com/

Comisión de Estudios sobre Inmigración. 1986. *Sistema Migratorio Argentino: Exposición Cronológica de la Política de Inmigración en Argentina*. Buenos Aires: Comisión de Estudios sobre Inmigración.

Cook, Fay Lomax, Tom R. Tyler, Edward G. Goetz, Margaret T. Gordon, David Protess, Donna R. Leff, and Harvey L. Molotch. 1983. "Media and Agenda Setting: Effects on the Public, Interest Group Leaders, Policy Makers, and Policy." *Public Opinion Quarterly* 47(1): 16–35.

Cook-Martín, David, and David FitzGerald. 2010. "Liberalism and the Limits of Inclusion: Race and Immigration Law in the Americas, 1850–2000." *Journal of Interdisciplinary History* 41(1): 7–25.

Cornelius, Wayne A., Philip L. Martin, and James F. Hollifield. 1994. "Introduction: The Ambivalent Quest for Immigration Control." In *Controlling Immigration: A Global Perspective*, edited by Wayne A. Cornelius, Philip L. Martin and James F. Hollifield, 3–41. Stanford, CA: Stanford University Press.

Cornelius, Wayne A., and Idean Salehyan. 2007. "Does Border Enforcement Deter Unauthorized Immigration? The Case of Mexican Migration to the United States of America." *Regulation and Governance* 1(2): 139–53.

Corte Suprema de Justicia de la Nación. 1932. "Los Deportados del Chaco de la Armada Nacional contra Estado Nacional." *Fallos* 164: 344.

Cottrol, Robert J. 2007. "Beyond Invisibility: Afro-Argentines in Their Nation's Culture and Memory." *Latin American Research* Review 42(1): 139–56.

Culpi, Ludmila, and Alexsandro Eugenio Pereira. 2016. "The Argentine Role in the Promotion of Migration Policy in Mercosur (1991–2014)." *Fédéralisme Régionalisme* 16: 1–7.

Dalle, Pablo. 2014. "Sociologando: Aproximación al Origen Étnico y Movilidad Social Intergeneracional en Argentina." *Boletin Cinetífico Sapiens Research* 4(1): 32–39.

Da Orden, María Liliana. 2010. *Una Familia y un Océano de por Medio: La Emigración Gallega a la Argentina: Una Historia a través de la Memoria Epistolar.* Barcelona: Anthropos.

de Búrca, Gráinne, Robert O. Keohane, and Charles Sabel. 2012. "New Modes of Pluralist Global Governance." *NYU Journal of International Law and Politics* 45: 723.

de Eichbaum, Marta E. Jurkowicz. 1999. *Cuando las Mujeres Hacen Memoria: Testimonios de Historia Oral de la Inmigración Judía en la Argentina.* Buenos Aires: Grupo Editor Latinoamericano.

DeLaet, Debra L. 2000. *US Immigration Policy in an Age of Rights.* Westport, CT: Greenwood.

DeLaney, Jeane. 1997. "National Identity, Nationhood, and Immigration in Argentina: 1810–1930." *Stanford Electronic Humanities Review* 5: 30.

De la Torre, Adela, and Julia Mendoza. 2007. "Immigration Policy and Immigration Flows: A Comparative Analysis of Immigration Law in the US and Argentina." *Modern American* 3: 46.

De Marco, Graciela. 1986. "Extranjeros en la Argentina: Cuantía y Continuidad de los Flujos Inmigratorios Limítrofes, 1970–1985." *Estudios Migratorios Latinoamericanos* 1(3): 323–55.

Demo, Anne Teresa. 2004. "Policy and Media in Immigration Studies." *Rhetoric and Public Affairs* 7(2): 215–29.

Devoto, Fernando J. 2001. "El Revés de la Trama: Políticas Migratorias y Prácticas Administrativas en la Argentina (1919–1949)." *Estudios Migratorios Latinoamericanos* 41(162): 281–304.

———. 2002. *Nacionalismo, Fascismo y Tradicionalismo en la Argentina Moderna: Una Historia.* Buenos Aires: Siglo Veintiuno Editora Iberoamericana.

———. 2003. *Historia de la Inmigración en la Argentina.* Buenos Aires: Editorial Sudamericana.

Devoto, Fernando, and Roberto Benencia. 2003. *Historia de la Inmigración en la Argentina.* Buenos Aires: Sudamericana.

Dirección Nacional de Migraciones, Ministerio del Interior, Argentina. 2010. Patria Grande: Programa Nacional de Regularización Documentaria Migratoria. http://www.migraciones.gov.ar/pdf_varios/estadisticas/Patria_Grande.pdf

Dirección Nacional de Población, Ministerio del Interior, Argentina. 2010. "Encuesta a Inmigrantes en Argentina 2008–2009." *Serie de Documentos de la Dirección Nacional de Población* 4 (May): 11–75.

Domenech, Eduardo. 2005. "Políticas Migratorias y Estrategias de Integración en Argentina: Nuevas Respuestas a Viejos Interrogantes." Paper presented at the 25th Conferencia Internacional de Población, Tours, France. http://iussp2005.princeton.edu/download.aspx.

Douglass, William A. 2006. *Global Vasconia: Essays on the Basque Diaspora.* Reno, NV: Center for Basque Studies.

Dudley, Steven. 2014. "Criminal Evolution and Violence in Latin America and the Caribbean." InSight Crime, June 26. https://www.insightcrime.org/news/analysis/evolution-crime-violence-latin-america-caribbean/.

Epstein, Lee, and Jeffrey A Segal. 2000. "Measuring Issue Salience." *American Journal of Political Science* 44(1): 66–83.

Erjavec, Karmen. 2001. "Media Representation of the Discrimination against the Roma in Eastern Europe: The Case of Slovenia." *Discourse and Society* 12(6): 699–727.

Escudé, Carlos. 1992. *Realismo Periférico: Fundamentos para la Nueva Política Exterior.* Buenos Aires: Planeta.

Facchini, Giovanni, Anna Maria Mayda, and Prachi Mishra. 2011. "Do Interest Groups Affect US Immigration Policy?" *Journal of International Economics* 85(1): 114–28.

Figallo, Beatriz J. 2016. "Con la República y contra la República: La Argentina y Fla Guerra Civil Española." *Temas de Historia Argentina y Americana* 24: 41–82.

FitzGerald, David S., and David Cook-Martín. 2014. *Culling the Masses: The Democratic Origins of Racist Immigration Policy in the Americas.* Cambridge, MA: Harvard University Press.

Fitzgerald, Keith. 1996. *The Face of the Nation: Immigration, the State, and the National Identity.* Stanford, CA: Stanford University Press.

Focus Economics. 2017. "Argentina Economic Outlook." https://www.focus-economics.com/countries/argentina.

Foner, Nancy, Rubén G. Rumbaut, and Steven J. Gold. 2000. "Immigration and Immigration Research in the United States." In *Immigration Research for a New Century: Multidisciplinary Perspectives*, edited by Nancy Foner, Rubén G. Rumbaut, and Steven J. Gold, 2–21. New York: Russell Sage Foundation.

Foucault, Michel. 1972. *The Archaeology of Knowledge*. Translated by A. M. Sheridan Smith. London: Tavistock.

Fox, Cybelle. 2015. "What Counts as Racist Immigration Policy?" *Ethnic and Racial Studies* 38(8): 1286–91.

Fraga, Rosendo. 2017. "Argentina 2011–2016: De Cristina a Macri." *Nueva Revista de Cultura, Política y Arte*. https://www.nuevarevista.net/la-revista/.

Freeman, Gary P. 1995. "Modes of Immigration Politics in Liberal Democratic States." *International Migration Review* 29(4): 881–902.

———. 2006. "National Models, Policy Types, and the Politics of Immigration in Liberal Democracies." *West European Politics* 29(2): 227–47.

Freeman, Gary P., and James Jupp. 1992. "Comparing Immigration Policy in Australia and the United States." In *Nations of Immigrants: Australia, the United States and International Migration*, edited by Gary P. Freeman and James Jupp, 1–20. Melbourne: Oxford University Press.

Freytes, Carlos, and Sara Niedzwiecki. 2016. "A Turning Point in Argentine Politics: Demands for Change and Territorial Cleavages in the 2015 Presidential Election." *Regional and Federal Studies* 26(3): 381–94.

Frigerio, Alejandro. 2000. "Blacks in Argentina: Contested Representations of Culture and Ethnicity." Paper presented at the annual meeting of the Latin American Studies Association, Miami.

Gaddis, John Lewis. 2005. *Strategies of Containment: A Critical Appraisal of American National Security Policy during the Cold War*. Oxford: Oxford University Press.

Gallup Argentina. 2001. "Estudio de Opinión Pública sobre Discriminación." http://www.gallup.com.ar.

Gellner, Ernest. 1996. "The Coming of Nationalism and Its Interpretations: The Myth of Nation and Class." In *Mapping the Nation*, edited by Gopal Balakrishnan, 98–145. New York: New Left Review & Verso.

Germani, Gino. 1966. "Mass Immigration and Modernization in Argentina." *Studies in Comparative International Development* 2(11): 165–82.

———. 1994. "Mass Migration and Modernization in Argentina." In *Race and Ethnicity in Latin America*, edited by Jorge I. Domínguez, 37–54. New York: Garland.

Gilroy, Paul. 1991. *There Ain't No Black in the Union Jack*. London: Routledge.

Goddard, Victoria. 2006. "'This Is History': Nation and Experience in Times of Crisis—Argentina 2001." *History and Anthropology* 17(3): 267–86.

Gómez, Abigail Gabriela, and Ricardo Sebastián Piana. 2014. "El Migrante en Argentina y el Acceso a sus Derechos: Un Breve Recorrido por las Normas, las

Políticas y sus Historias." *Revista de la Facultad de Derecho* 36: 101–26. http://revista.fder.edu.uy/index.php/rfd/article/view/247.

Goñi, Uki. 2002. *The Real Odessa: Smuggling the Nazis to Perón's Argentina*. Buenos Aires: Granta.

Gorz, Andre. 1970. "Immigrant Labour." *New Left Review* 61: 28–31.

Gotsbachner, Emo. 2001. "Xenophobic Normality: The Discriminatory Impact of Habitualized Discourse Dynamics." *Discourse and Society* 12(6): 729–59.

Grimson, Alejandro. 1999. *Retratos de la Diferencia y la Igualdad: Los Bolivianos en Buenos Aires*. Buenos Aires: Eudeba.

Ha, Shang E., and Seung-Jin Jang. 2015. "Immigration, Threat Perception, and National Identity: Evidence from South Korea." *International Journal of Intercultural Relations* 44: 53–62.

Haggard, Stephan, and Robert R. Kaufman. 1995. *The Political Economy of Democratic Transitions*. Princeton, NJ: Princeton University Press.

Hier, Sean P., and Joshua L. Greenberg. 2002. "Constructing a Discursive Crisis: Risk, Problematization and Illegal Chinese in Canada." *Ethnic and Racial Studies* 25(3): 490–513.

Higham, John. 1955. *Strangers in the Land: Patterns of American Nativism, 1860–1925*. New Brunswick, NJ: Rutgers University Press.

Hines, Barbara. 2010. "The Right to Migrate as a Human Right: The Current Argentine Immigration Law." *Cornell International Law Journal* 43: 471.

Hing, Bill Ong. 2004. *Defining America: Through Immigration Policy*. Philadelphia: Temple University Press.

Hollifield, James F. 1992a. *Immigrants, Markets, and States: The Political Economy of Postwar Europe*. Cambridge, MA: Harvard University Press.

———. 1992b. "Migration and International Relations: Cooperation and Control in the European Community." *International Migration Review* 26(2): 568–95.

———. 2015. "Debunking American Exceptionalism and Rescuing Liberalism." *Ethnic and Racial Studies* 38(8): 1312–18.

Hollifield, James F., Philip L. Martin, and Pia M. Orrenius. 2014. "The Dilemmas of Immigration Control." In *Controlling Immigration: A Global Perspective*, edited by James F. Hollifield, Philip L. Martin, and Pia M. Orrenius, 3–34. Stanford, CA: Stanford University Press.

Honorable Senado de la Nación Argentina. 2003. *Diario De Sesiones*, December 17.

———. n.d. "Constitución Argentina." http://www.senado.gov.ar/bundles/senado parlamentario/pdf/institucional/constitucion_nacional_argentina.pdf.

Iglesias, Evaristo. 1996. *Rindiendo Cuentas*. Buenos Aires: Honorable Congreso de la Nación.

INDEC. 1997. *La Migración Internacional en la Agentina: Sus Características e Impacto*. Buenos Aires: Instituto Nacional de Estadísticas y Censos.

———. 1999. *Características Migratorias de la Población en el IV Censo General de la Nación del Año 1947*. Buenos Aires: Instituto Nacional de Estadísticas y Censos.

———. 2010. "Población Total Nacida en el Extranjero por Lugar de Nacimiento, Según Sexo y Grupos de Edad." https://www.indec.gob.ar.

———. 2016. "Migraciones." https://www.indec.gob.ar.

Ipsos. 2017. "Global Views on Immigration and the Refugee Crisis." https://www.ipsos.com/en/global-views-immigration-and-refugee-crisis.

Jeon, Yun Sil. 2005. "La Comunidad Coreana en Argentina: Aspecos Lingüísticos y Extralingüísticos." *Revista de Occidente* 287: 51–75.

Jessop, Bob. 1990. *State Theory: Putting the Capitalist State in Its Place.* University Park: Pennsylvania State University Press.

———. 2007. *State Power.* New York: Polity.

Jones, Mark P. 2002. "Explaining the High Level of Party Discipline in the Argentine Congress." In *Legislative Politics in Latin America*, edited by Scott Morgenstern and Benito Nacif, 147–84. New York: Cambridge University Press.

Joppke, Christian. 1998. *Challenge to the Nation-State: Immigration in Western Europe and the United States.* Oxford: Oxford University Press.

———. 1999. *Immigration and the Nation-State: The United States, Germany, and Great Britain.* Wotton-under-Edge, UK: Clarendon.

Jupp, James. 2002. *From White Australia to Woomera: The Story of Australian Immigration.* New York: Cambridge University Press.

Jurje, Flavia, and Sandra Lavenex. 2014. "Trade Agreements as Venues for Market Power Europe? The Case of Immigration Policy." *JCMS: Journal of Common Market Studies* 52(2): 320–36.

Kagan, Michael. 2015. "A Taxonomy of Discretion: Refining the Legality Debate about Obama's Executive Actions on Immigration." *Washington University Law Review* 92: 1083.

Kandel, William A., Jerome P. Bjelopera, Andorra Bruno, and Alison Siskin. 2015. *The President's Immigration Accountability Executive Action of November 20, 2014: Overview and Issues.* Washington, DC: Congressional Research Service.

Keohane, Robert O. 1985. *After Hegemony: Cooperation and Discord in the World Political Economy.* Princeton, NJ: Princeton University Press.

Klich, Ignacio. 1998. "Arab-Jewish Coexistence in the First Half of 1900s Argentina: Overcoming Self-Imposed Amnesia." In *Arab and Jewish Immigrants in Latin America*, edited by Ignacio Klich and Jeffrey Lessers, 1–37. London: Frank Cass.

———. 2015. "Árabes, Judíos y Árabes Judíos en la Argentina de la Primera Mitad del Novecientos." *Estudios interdisciplinarios de América Latina y el Caribe* 6(2): 109–43. http://www7.tau.ac.il/ojs/index.php/eial/article/view/1196/1224.

Krasner, Stephen D. 1983. *International Regimes.* Ithaca, NY: Cornell University Press.

Laitin, David D. 1986. *Hegemony and Culture: Politics and Change among the Yoruba.* Chicago: University of Chicago Press.

Laqueur, Walter. 2004. *Generation Exodus: The Fate of Young Jewish Refugees from Nazi Germany.* New York: I. B. Tauris.

Lattes, Alfredo E. 1973. "Las Migraciones en la Argentina entre Mediados del Siglo XIX y 1960." *Desarrollo Económico* 12(48): 849–65.

Leal, David L., Nestor P. Rodríguez, and Gary P. Freeman. 2016. "Introduction: The New Era of Restriction." In *Migration in an Era of Restriction and Recession*, edited by David L. Leal, Nestor P. Rodríguez, and Gary P. Freeman, 1–23. Cham, Switzerland: Springer International.

Lee, Erika. 1999. "Immigrants and Immigration Law: A State of the Field Assessment." *Journal of American Ethnic History* 18(4): 85–114.

Levitsky, Steven, and Maria Victoria Murillo. 2008. "Argentina: From Kirchner to Kirchner." *Journal of Democracy* 19(2): 16–30.

———. 2009. "Variation in Institutional Strength." *Annual Review of Political Science* 12: 115–33.

Linz, Juan J. 1990. "The Perils of Presidentialism." *Journal of Democracy* 1(1): 51–69.

Linz, Juan J., and Alfred Stepan. 1996. *Problems of Democratic Transition and Consolidation: Southern Europe, South America, and Post-Communist Europe.* Baltimore, MD: Johns Hopkins University Press.

Llanos, Mariana. 2001. "Understanding Presidential Power in Argentina: A Study of the Policy of Privatisation in the 1990s." *Journal of Latin American Studies* 33(1): 67–99.

Maffia, Marta. 2008. *Cape Verdeans in Argentina, Transnational Archipelago: Perspectives on Cape Verdean Migration and Diaspora.* Amsterdam: Amsterdam University Press.

Maguid, Alicia. 1995. "Migrantes Limítrofes en la Argentina: Su Inserción Laboral e Impacto en el Mercado de Trabajo." *Estudios del Trabajo* 10: 47–76.

Mansilla, Lucio. 1907. *Un País sin Ciudadanos.* Paris: Garnier.

March, James G., and Johan P. Olsen. 1983. "The New Institutionalism: Organizational Factors in Political Life." *American Political Science Review* 78(3): 734–49.

Marín-Guzmán, Roberto. 1997. *La Emigración Libanesa en los Siglos XIX y XX: Análisis de sus Causas Económicas-Sociales.* San José, Costa Rica: Alma Mater.

Mármora, Lelio. 1988. "La Fundamentación de las Políticas Migratorias Internacionales en América Latina." *Estudios Migratorios Latinoamericanos* 3(10): 375–96.

Marshall-Goldschvartz, Adriana Julieta. 1973. *The Import of Labour: The Case of the Netherlands.* Rotterdam: Rotterdam University Press.

Martel, Julián. 1891. *La Bolsa.* Buenos Aires: Imprenta de la Nación.

Martin, Philip L. 2017. "President Trump and US Migration after 100 Days." *Migration Letters* 14(2): 319–28.

Marx, Karl. 1976 [1867]. *Capital.* Vol. 1. Harmondsworth, UK: Penguin.

McSherry, J. Patrice. 2002. "Tracking the Origins of a State Terror Network: Operation Condor." *Latin American Perspectives* 29(1): 38–60.

Mehan, Hugh. 1997. "The Discourse of the Illegal Immigration Debate: A Case Study in the Politics of Representation." *Discourse Society* 8(2): 249–70.

Mercosur. n.d. "En Pocas Palabras." http://www.mercosur.int/innovaportal/v/3862/2/innova.front/en-pocas-palabras.

Meyers, Eytan. 2000. "Theories of International Immigration Policy—A Comparative Analysis." *International Migration Review* 34(4): 1245–82.

Migdal, Joel S. 1988. *Strong Societies and Weak States: State–Society Relations and State Capabilities in the Third World*. Princeton, NJ: Princeton University Press.

———. 1997. "Studying the State." In *Comparative Politics: Rationality, Culture, and Structure*, edited by Mark I. Lichbach and Alan Zuckerman, 208–35. New York: Cambridge University Press.

———. 2001. *State in Society: Studying How States and Societies Transform and Constitute One Another*. New York: Cambridge University Press.

Mitchell, Timothy. 1991. "The Limits of the State: Beyond Statist Approaches and Their Critics." *American Political Science Review* 85(1): 77–96.

Molinelli, N. Guillermo, M. Valeria Palanza, and Gisela Sin. 1999. *Congreso, Presidencia y Justicia en Argentina*. Buenos Aires: Temas.

Montoya, Silvia, and Marcela Perticará. 1995. "Los Migrantes Limítrofes: ¿Aumentan el Desempleo?" *Novedades Económicas* 17(170): 10–16.

Morgenstern, Scott, John Polga-Hecimovich, and Sarah Shair-Rosenfield. 2013. "Tall, Grande, or Venti: Presidential Powers in the United States and Latin America." *Journal of Politics in Latin America* 5(2): 37–70.

Mörner, Magnus, and Harold Sims. 1985. *Adventurers and Proletarians: The Story of Migrants in Latin America*. Pittsburgh, PA: University of Pittsburgh Press.

Moya, Jose C. 1998. *Cousins and Strangers: Spanish Immigrants in Buenos Aires, 1850–1930*. Berkeley: University of California Press.

Mukherjee, Sahana, Ludwin E. Molina, and Glenn Adams. 2012. "National Identity and Immigration Policy: Concern for Legality or Ethnocentric Exclusion?" *Analyses of Social Issues and Public Policy* 12(1): 21–32.

Munck, Ronaldo, and Mary Hyland. 2014. "Migration, Regional Integration and Social Transformation: A North–South Comparative Approach." *Global Social Policy* 14(1): 32–50.

Museo Social Argentino. 1941. *Primer Congreso de la Población, 26 al 31 de Octubre de 1940*. Buenos Aires: Museo Social Argentino.

Mustapic, Ana María. 2002. "Oscillating Relations: President and Congress in Argentina." In *Legislative Politics in Latin America*, edited by Scott Morgenstern and Benito Nacif, 23–47. New York: Cambridge University Press.

Nación, La. 1870–present. [Newspaper]. Buenos Aires, Argentina. https://www.lanacion.com.ar/.

Nascimbene, Mario C., and Mauricio Isaac Neuman. 2015. "El Nacionalismo Católico, el Fascismo y la Inmigración en la Argentina (1927–1943); Una Aproximación Teórica." *Estudios Interdisciplinarios de América Latina y el Caribe* 4(1): 134–37. http://eial.tau.ac.il/index.php/eial/article/view/1251/1279.

Newton, Ronald C. 1992. *The "Nazi Menace" in Argentina, 1931–1947*. Stanford, CA: Stanford University Press.

Nouwen, Mollie Lewis. 2013. *Oy, My Buenos Aires: Jewish Immigrants and the Creation of Argentine National Identity, 1905–1930*. Albuquerque: University of New Mexico Press.

Novick, Susana. 1992. *Política y Población: Argentina 1870–1989*. Buenos Aires: Centro Editor de América Latina.

———. 1997. "Políticas Migratorias en la Argentina." In *Inmigración y Discriminación: Políticas y Discursos*, edited by Susana Novick, Enrique Oteiza, and Roberto Aruj. Buenos Aires: Grupo Editor Universitario.

———. 2012. "Transformations and Challenges of Argentinean Migratory Policy in Relation to the International Context." *Migraciones Internacionales* 6(3): 205–37.

Nueva Mayoría. 2001. *Inmigrantes de Países Vecinos: Autopercepción*. Buenos Aires: Nueva Mayoría.

O'Donnell, Guillermo A. 1988. *Bureaucratic Authoritarianism: Argentina, 1966–1973, in Comparative Perspective*. Berkeley: University of California Press.

———. 1994. "Delegative Democracy." *Journal of Democracy* 5(1): 55–69.

O'Donnell, Guillermo, and Philippe C. Schmitter. 1986. *Transitions from Authoritarian Rule: Tentative Conclusions about Uncertain Democracies*. Baltimore, MD: Johns Hopkins University Press.

Olivieri, Mabel. 1987. "Un Siglo de Legislación en Materia de Inmigración Italia-Argentina, 1860–1960." *Estudios Migratorios Latinoamericanos* 2(6–7): 225–48.

Organización de los Estados Americanos. 1985. *Migraciones Laborales en América Latina: Diagnostico Demográfico Argentina*. Washington, DC: Organización de Estados Americanos.

Oteiza, Enrique, and Roberto Aruj. 1997. "Inmigración Real, Inmigración Imaginaria y Discriminación en la Argentina." In *Inmigración y Discriminación: Políticas y Discursos*, edited by Enrique Oteiza, Susana Novick, and Roberto Aruj. Buenos Aires: Grupo Editorial Universitario.

Otero, Hernán. 1995. "Redes Sociales Primarias, Movilidad Espacial e Inserción Social de los Inmigrantes en Argentina: Los Franceses de Tandil, 1850–1914." In *Inmigración y Redes Sociales e la Argentina Moderna*, edited by Maria Bjerg and Hernán Otero, 81–105. Tandil, Argentina: Universidad Nacional del Centro.

Página 12. 1987–present. [Newspaper]. Buenos Aires, Argentina. https://www.pagina 12.com.ar/.

Panizza, Francisco. 2000. "Beyond 'Delegative Democracy': 'Old Politics' and 'New Economics' in Latin America." *Journal of Latin American Studies* 32(3): 737–63.

Papademetriou, Demetrios G., and Stephen H. Legomsky. 1997. "American Immigration: History and Overview." In *The Issues of Immigration: Melting Pot or Boiling Point*, edited by Gary E. McCuen, 9–14. Hudson, WI: Gary McCuen.

Pastor, Manuel, Jr., and Carol Wise. 1999. "Stabilization and Its Discontents: Argentina's Economic Restructuring in the 1990s." *World Development* 27(3): 477–503.

Peberdy, Sally. 2009. *Selecting Immigrants: National Identity and South Africa's Immigration Policies, 1910–2008*. Johannesburg: Wits University Press.

Peixoto, João, Joaquin Arango, Corrado Bonifazi, Claudia Finotelli, Catarina Sabino, Salvatore Strozza, and Anna Triandafyllidou. 2012. "Immigrants, Markets and Policies in Southern Europe." In *European Immigrations: Trends, Structures and Policy Implications*, edited by Marek Okólski, 107–47. Amsterdam: Amsterdam University Press.

Pérez Vichich, Nora. 1988. "Las Políticas Migratorias en la Legislación Argentina." *Estudios Migratorios Latinoamericanos* 3(10): 441–63.

Perl, William R. 1995. "Paradise Denied: The State Department, the Caribbean, and the Jews of Europe." *National Interest* 42: 78–84.

Peruzzotti, Enrique. 2001. "The Nature of the New Argentine Democracy: The Delegative Democracy Argument Revisited." *Journal of Latin American Studies* 33(1): 133–55.

Peters, B. Guy. 2011. *Institutional Theory in Political Science: The New Institutionalism*. New York: Bloomsbury.

Petras, Elizabeth. 1980. "The Role of National Boundaries in a Cross-National Labour Market." *International Journal of Urban and Regional Research* 4(2): 157–95.

Petras, Elizabeth M., D. T. Gurak, and F. Caces. 1981. "The Global Labor Market in the Modern World-Economy." In *Global Trends in Migration: Theory and Research on International Population Movements*, edited by Mary M. Kritz, Charles B. Keely, and Silvano M. Tomasi, 44–63. New York: Center for Migration Studies.

Portes, Alejandro, and John Walton. 1981. *Labor, Class, and the International System*. Amsterdam: Elsevier.

Rapoport, Mario. 2000. *Historia Económica, Política y Social de la Argentina*. Buenos Aires: Ediciones Macchi.

Recalde, Aranzazu. 2012. "'Are We Now Equal?' Recent Experiences and Perceptions of South American Migrants in Argentina under MERCOSUR." Ph.D. diss., Universite de Montreal.

Rein, Raanan. 2010. *Argentine Jews or Jewish Argentines? Essays on Ethnicity, Identity, and Diaspora*. Boston: Brill.

Rock, David. 1987. *Argentina, 1516–1987: From Spanish Colonization to Alfonsín*. Berkeley: University of California Press.

Romagnoli, Gino. 1991. "Aspectos Jurídicos e Institucionales de las Migraciones en la República Argentina." Geneva: Organization Internacional para las Migraciones.

Romero, Luis Alberto. 2013. *A History of Argentina in the Twentieth Century: Updated and Revised Edition*. University Park: Pennsylvania State Press.

Rosa, José María. 1963. *Nos los Representantes del Pueblo*. Buenos Aires: Editorial Huemul.

Rudalevige, Andrew. 2012. "The Contemporary Presidency: Executive Orders and Presidential Unilateralism." *Presidential Studies Quarterly* 42(1): 138–60.

Sana, Mariano. 1999. "Migrants, Unemployment and Earnings in the Buenos Aires Metropolitan Area." *International Migration Review* 33(3): 621–39.

Santa Ana, Otto. 1999. "'Like an Animal I Was Treated': Anti-Immigrant Metaphor in US Public Discourse." *Discourse and Society* 10(2): 191–224.

———. 2016. "The Cowboy and the Goddess: Television News Mythmaking about Immigrants." *Discourse and Society* 27(1): 95–117.

Sarmiento, Domingo Faustino. 1959. *Textos Fundamentales*. Buenos Aires: Compañía General Fabril.

———. 1988 [1845]. *Facundo: Civilización o Barbarie*. Buenos Aires: Alianza Editorial.

Sassen, Saskia. 1996a. "Beyond Sovereignty: Immigration Policy Making Today." *Social Justice* 23(3): 9–20.

———. 1996b. *Losing Control? Sovereignty in an Age of Globalization*. New York: Columbia University Press.

———. 2005. "Regulating Immigration in a Global Age: A New Policy Landscape." *Parallax* 11(1): 35–45.

Sassone, Susana. 1987. "Migraciones Ilegales y Amnistías en la Argentina." *Estudios Migratorios Latinoamericanos* 2(6–7): 249–89.

Schmitter, Philippe C. 1994. "Dangers and Dilemmas of Democracy." *Journal of Democracy* 5(2): 57–74.

Schneider, Arnd. 2000. *Futures Lost: Nostalgia and Identity among Italian Immigrants in Argentina*. New York: Peter Lang.

Schwarzstein, Dora. 1997. "La Llegada de los Republicanos Españoles a la Argentina." *Estudios Migratorios Latinoamericanos* 37: 423–47.

Scott, James C. 1998. *Seeing like a State: How Certain Schemes to Improve the Human Condition Have Failed*. New Haven, CT: Yale University Press.

Segal, Uma A. 2010. "United States: The Changing Face of the United States of America." In *Immigration Worldwide: Policies, Practices, and Trends*, edited by Uma A. Segal, Doreen Elliott, and Nazneen S. Mayadas, 29–46. Oxford: Oxford University Press.

Senkman, Leonardo. 1985. "Política Internacional e Inmigración Europea en la Argentina de Post-Guerra (1945–1948): El Caso de los Refugiados." *Estudios Migratorios Latinoamericanos* 1(1): 107–25.

———. 1991. *Argentina, la Segunda Guerra Mundial y los Refugiados Indeseables, 1933–1945*. Buenos Aires: Grupo Editor Latinoamericano.

———. 1992. "Etnicidad e Inmigración durante el Primer Peronismo." *Estudios Interdisciplinarios de América Latina y el Caribe* 3(2): 5–39. https://www7.tau.ac.il/ojs/index.php/eial/article/view/1258/1285.

Shugart, Matthew Soberg, and John M. Carey. 1992. *Presidents and Assemblies: Constitutional Design and Electoral Dynamics.* New York: Cambridge University Press.

Shugart, Matthew S., and Scott Mainwaring. 1997. "Presidentialism and Democracy in Latin America: Rethinking the Terms of the Debate." In *Presidentialism and Democracy in Latin America,* edited by Scott Mainwaring and Matthew S. Shugart, 12–54. New York: Cambridge University Press.

Shumway, Nicolas. 1991. *The Invention of Argentina.* Berkeley: University of California Press.

Silva, Hernán A. 1998. *Significado de la Presencia Española en la Argentina en el Siglo XX.* Bahía Blanca, Argentina: Universidad Nacional del Sur.

Simmons, Alan B., and Kieran Keohane. 1992. "Canadian Immigration Policy: State Strategies and the Quest for Legitimacy." *Canadian Review of Sociology/Revue Canadienne de Sociologie* 29(4): 421–52.

Skocpol, Theda, Peter B. Evans, and Dietrich Rueschemeyer. 1985. *Bringing the State Back In.* New York: Cambridge University Press.

Solberg, Carl. 1970. *Immigration and Nationalism: Argentina and Chile, 1890–1914.* Austin: University of Texas Press.

Solimano, Andrés. 2003. *Development Cycles, Political Regimes, and International Migration: Argentina in the Twentieth Century.* Santiago, Chile: ECLAC, Economic Development Division.

Sorensen, Diana. 1996. *Facundo and the Construction of Argentine Culture.* Austin: University of Texas Press.

Stahringer de Caramuti, Ofelia I., and Miguel Alberto Caramuti. 1975. *La Política Migratoria Argentina.* Buenos Aires: Depalma.

Statham, Paul, and Andrew Geddes. 2006. "Elites and the 'Organised Public': Who Drives British Immigration Politics and in Which Direction?" *West European Politics* 29(2): 248–69.

Steinacher, Gerald. 2011. *Nazis on the Run: How Hitler's Henchmen Fled Justice.* Oxford: Oxford University Press.

Texidó, Ezequiel, Gladys Baer, Nora Pérez Vichich, Ana María Santestevan, and Charles P. Gomes. 2003. "Migraciones Laborales en Sudamérica: El Mercosur Ampliado." *Estudios sobre Migraciones Internacionales* 63.

Tichenor, Daniel J. 2002. *Dividing Lines: The Politics of Immigration Control in America.* Princeton, NJ: Princeton University Press.

Timmer, Ashley S., and Jeffrey G. Williamson. 1996. "Racism, Xenophobia or Markets? The Political Economy of Immigration Policy Prior to the Thirties." National Bureau of Economic Research Working Paper 5867. Cambridge, MA: National Bureau of Economic Research.

Traore, Boubacar. 2006. "Los Inmigrantes Senegaleses en la Argentina: ¿Integración, Supervivencia o Participación?" Paper presented at Primeras Jornadas Afro-argentinos Hoy: Invisibilización, Identidad y Movilización Social, La Plata,

Argentina. https://www.africafundacion.org/IMG/pdf/Traore_Senegaleses
_Argentina.pdf.

U.S. Citizenship, Immigration, and Naturalization Services. n.d. "INA: Act 235-In-
spection by Immigration Officers; Expedited Removal of Inadmissible Arriving Aliens; Referral for Hearing." https://www.uscis.gov/ilink/docView/SLB
/HTML/SLB/0–0-0–1/0–0-0–29/0–0-0–5389.html.

van Dijk, Teun A. 1994. *Prensa, Racismo y Poder*. Mexico, DF: Universidad Iberoamericana.

Villar, Juan M. 1984. "The Argentine Experience in the Field of Illegal Immigration." *International Migration Review* 18(3): 453–73.

Vizcarra, Jael. 2016. "Humanitarian Disappointments: Labor Unrest and the Case
of Laotian Refugees in Dirty War Argentina." *Amerasia Journal* 42(2): 49–70.

Vommaro, Gabriel. 2016. "'Unir a los Argentinos': El Proyecto de 'País Normal' de
la Nueva Centroderecha en Argentina." *Nueva Sociedad* 261: 4–12.

Wallerstein, Immanuel. 1974. *The Modern World-System I: Capitalist Agriculture
and the Origins of the European World-Economy in the Sixteenth Century, with
a New Prologue*. Berkeley: University of California Press.

Walsh, James. 2008. "Navigating Globalization: Immigration Policy in Canada and
Australia, 1945–2007." *Sociological Forum* 23(4): 786–813.

Wasserstein, Bernard. 1999. *Britain and the Jews of Europe, 1939–1945*. London:
Cassell.

Waylen, Georgina. 2014. "Informal Institutions, Institutional Change, and Gender
Equality." *Political Research Quarterly* 67(1): 212–23.

Whitaker, Reginald. 1987. *Double Standard: The Secret History of Canadian Immigration Policy*. Toronto: Lester & Orpen Dennys.

Yang, Zimu. 2016. "2016 IIP Argentina Research Paper." Law School International
Immersion Program Papers, No. 25. Chicago: University of Chicago Law School.

Zolberg, Aristide R. 1991. "Bounded States in a Global Market: The Uses of International Labor Migrations." In *Social Theory for a Changing Society*, edited by
Pierre Bourdieu and James S. Coleman, 301–25. Boulder, CO: Westview Press.

———. 1999. "Matters of the State." In *The Handbook of International Migration:
The American Experience*, edited by Charles Hirschman, Philip Kasinitz, and
Josh DeWind, 71–93. New York: Russell Sage Foundation.

———. 2000. "The Politics of Immigration: An Externalist Perspective." In *Immigra-
tion Research for a New Century: Multidisciplinary Perspectives*, edited by Nancy
Foner, Rubén G. Rumbaut, and Steven J. Gold, 60–68. New York: Russell Sage
Foundation.

———. 2006. *A Nation by Design: Immigration Policy in the Fashioning of America*.
Cambridge, MA: Harvard University Press.

INDEX

247

JULIA ALBARRACÍN

is a professor of political science at Western Illinois University.

She is the author of *At the Core and in the Margins: Incorporation of Mexican Immigrants in Two Rural Midwestern Communities.*

CPSIA information can be obtained
at www.ICGtesting.com
Printed in the USA
LVHW111811180820
663529LV00009B/207